Kessinger Publishing's Rare Reprints
Thousands of Scarce and Hard-to-Find Books!

·   ·   ·
·   ·   ·
·   ·   ·
·   ·   ·
·   ·   ·
·   ·   ·
·   ·   ·
·   ·   ·
·   ·   ·
·   ·   ·
·   ·   ·
·   ·   ·
·   ·   ·
·   ·   ·
·   ·   ·
·   ·   ·
·   ·   ·
·   ·   ·

We kindly invite you to view our extensive catalog list at:
http://www.kessinger.net

INDEX - PART I

THE GREATER SPIRITUAL RESPONSIVENESS OF BODY

AND

AWAKENING THE BRAIN OF SPIRIT

by Brown Landone

THE GATE TO THE PATH - LESSON I

This is the gate that leads to the path that leads to the steps that lead to the portico of the Temple of Transformation.

My very first suggestion in these Lessons may surprise you, for since they are written to help you respond more fully to spirit, I ask you NOT to 'think' too much about details of information given, or how the development is to take place.

You know that thought DOES hinder free expression of spirit.

For years in your own life, many an impulsively joyous desire of spirit, has been restricted in expression, by some thought of whether or not you dared to express it.

So if you ask me, "how many minutes" - or how many times - or often - you should do this or that, - I shall NOT answer!

I will NOT aid in such thoughts, which hinder your development.

Think little of details; but FEEL deeply whatever you DO.

There is rhythmic power in work harmoniously repeated - four or seven times! And when wise, I advise such rhythmic repetition.

But otherwise, the less you 'think' about details, and the more you FEEL, the greater will be your response to spirit!

Another forethought is this: when we later come to the use of spiritual desire, please do NOT center it on picayune things - such as growing a new toe-nail, or a new head of hair!

Most people fail because they desire too little things!

It is right to desire little things, but spirit IS infinite, and IF you too often limit your desire, you will put a 'thought damper' on the greater expression of spirit.

Desire greatly and you attain greatly!

THEN all "those other things, WILL be ADDED unto you."

I am writing these Lessons differently than most courses are written: (1) in real reverence of the subject; and (2) as a friend to lead you to think less and feel more deeply.

First, recognise the difference: Awakening the mind brain

1-3

leads to improvement, but awakening the brain of spirit for greater spiritual responsiveness, leads to transformation.

Second, since the brain of spirit is far down in the body - just above the kidneys - it can be awakened only by those means which do reach down through the body.

Third, any attempt to use DIRECT means of awakening spirit, will hinder full manifestation, just as you injure a rosebud, if you use DIRECT means - try to pull its petals apart!

And fourth, do not try to awaken the brain of spirit by thought - never by affirmation or concentration.

There are two results which you MOST desire!
They are heavenly results, because when they are attained, all other things are added.

The first result you want, is abundant overflowing energy IN your body - energy inspired from the universe - pulsating like a flame of life all THROUGH your body.
This is important, for 99% of your problems would disappear completely, if you had only twice the energy you now have,

The second result you desire is the constant flow of energy OUT INTO free and full activity! Merely possessing abundant overflowing spiritual energy IN your body is not enough.
You want it EVER FLOWING OUT, freely and fully, into ACTION!

To attain the first condition, I teach you to tune-up body to spirit, and awaken the Brain of Spirit, so you WILL inspire (take-in) more divine energy than you have dreamed possible!

To attain the second condition, I teach you to use the Seven Creative Powers of God - to impel all soul power to move out into action to vitalize every cell through which it moves, and transform every condition of your life.

I know you have already tried many means and methods, and that most of them have not come up to your expectations.
BUT you have NOT yet used the UNKNOWN powers!
You do not even know them!
Of course, you know the powers of mind, and love, and life.
But there are other powers unknown to you.
There are the unknown initiating powers - holy light, high electronic energy, mighty silent overtones, and rhythm.
I also call these powers, the operative powers!

Clearly understand, there are two groups of great powers.
One group is the initiative, or operating powers.
The others are conceptive powers - of God and the soul.
The conceptive powers are mind, love, life and spirit.

Most people make the mistake of depending entirely on the conceptive powers, without preparing the body for their use by first using the initiative, or operative powers.

Some claim that only conceptive powers should be used.

This is not sensible. Heat is one of the operative powers, and you know very well that mind, or life, or love can NOT manifest through your body, if it is frozen stiff. Heat IS an essential - so are all other initiative powers.

I am teaching you uses of powers, never taught previously.

First, tune up the body by initiative, or operative powers.

THEN you will never fail to work transforming changes when using the conceptive powers of mind and love and life and spirit.

So please give careful attention to using these mighty operative and initiative powers first. They are powerful.

The light rays you can NOT see, are 1,000 times more powerful than the light rays you can see.

The high unknown electric rays are rejuvenating; although 110 volts will shock you, and a 25,000 volt current can kill!

And there are the mighty unknown powers of silent tone.

The miracle of the UNKNOWN powers is this: Whenever you TUNE-UP a lower destructive power so that it vibrates more like spirit, it then changes its effect, and becomes a constructive power. You can use these to TUNE-UP your body to vibrations of higher unknown powers, so that transformation can take place.

For example, when the low electric current which will kill your body is stepped up a million volts, and its frequency increased, then its deadly current becomes beneficial, because it is more IN-TUNE with the spirit power in your body.

You can not even feel this higher unknown electric power, but when an X-Ray bulb is held against your skin, it glows with a beautiful light; and when a 1,000,000 volt current is passing through your body, it seems to rejuvenate the body.

Another unknown initiating power is the mystic UNHEARD overtones of SILENT sound!

Glorious tones sing IN all things, even in YOUR body.

Our human ears hear only a few tones. Dogs hear many more, and bats and ants hear still more, and higher tones.

You can NOT hear a tone of 25,000 vibrations a second!

But ants hear tones of 50,000; and there are tones of crystal stones that vibrate 500,000 times a second.

There are also tones of atoms and stars.
such tones are absolute SILENCE to our ears.
They vibrate 1,000,000 or more times a second!

The song tones of some STONES are very powerful. When a pebble of laminated crystal is placed near an ant-hill, its song increases activity of ants ten times, and without fatigue!

The unknown tones of atoms and stars have astounding power.

And your body - which IS composed of cells which are composed of atoms - CAN be TUNED-UP to respond to such powers!

These Lessons teach you to tune-up and spiritualize your body, to pulsate in harmony with the spirit of the universe.

To do this, it is necessary to use powers which will reach deep down to awaken the Brain of Spirit to free its powers.

The first start in lifting-up the body to greater responsiveness is effected by use of the initiating, or operative powers. These powers are used to initiate a greater responsiveness of the body, so that it will be prepared for the higher vibration of spirit actually to flow into every cell of the body.

These initiating powers are the higher unknown powers of light, sound, rhythm, cosmic rays, et cetera.

But to lift-up vibration of your body, and prepare it to respond to spirit, you must use powers, the initiating powers which penetrate into the body. Several do not; even X-rays do pass through bone, so they are useless for this purpose.

And you can NOT use the unknown powers of light for such initial awakening, because light never penetrates more then 1/100 of one inch into your skin.

If it tries to go deeper, nature builds up a wall of tan to keep it out, or cooks your skin to blisters.

Light in moderation is beneficial to the outside cells, - that is, to the skin cells.

But it is deadly to the cells of your inner physical Body!

You can not often use the unknown powers of high electric rays, because the machines which produce vibrations of such high frequencies cost several million dollars!

And you can NOT use Mind to awaken the Brain of Spirit, - for thoughts of mind always tend to block expression of spirit.

I do not need to argue this with you, for you know from experience that freedom of spirit has been blocked - perhaps all your life - by thoughts of what you should or should not do!

Yet many teachers have written books and lessons to teach you to use 'only mind' to awaken spirit.

But when you follow such instruction, you ultimately find that you are not attaining that which you wish to attain, - no matter how thrilled you were the first few months of such effort.

And often such methods - if continued for years, lead not only to disturbed body functions, but to unbalancing the mind!

Since your body is not as responsive to spirit as you desire, it is wise - from the practical standpoint - to prepare the body, so that spirit can normally manifest through it more fully.

This is done by means of the operative powers, which INITIATE responsiveness of the body.

But there is ONLY ONE of the initiating powers which you can easily use which has power to effect the initial preparation of the body structure and which also penetrates it, so that its cells will vibrate highly enough to begin to respond to spirit.

Orientals have known this power for centuries. They have tried to teach it to us, but we have understood it only mentally.
And even their own teachers have lost the spiritual understanding of it, and teach only the mental and physical exercises.

The first initiating power to be used, is silent sound - sound that IS silent to your ear, yet ten thousand times more powerful than any sound you can hear!

Silent sound is the harmonizing power of the universe.
We have evidence of this, when its higher overtones are vibrated through matter. It is only the lower tones which rip matters apart and destroy it. The higher overtones - the silent overtones - are so constructive that they actually build up substance, even new tissues of the human body.

It is these higher unheard overtones which I teach you to use to initiate the awakening of the Brain of Spirit, and prepare the body to vibrate harmoniously enough to respond to spirit.

Silent overtones are mystic energies of stars and atoms.
They are the only power you can use to initiate responsiveness of the body - for colors and light can not even penetrate the skin, you can not secure the means of producing the higher electric vibrations; and thought tends to repress the power of spirit.

The four reasons for the use of the higher silent overtones to induce initial awakening of the body, are as follows:

First, mystic silent tones PENETRATE to every body cell;

Second, they HARMONIZE the cells, just as they forever harmonize stars in their courses and the electrons in atoms;

Third, they TUNE-UP the body, so its cells can receive (inspire) the cosmic powers of spirit; and

Fourth, since they reach down to Brain of Spirit itself, they can awaken it, so its powers flow more freely and fully INTO the activities of your body and into action in your life.

THE GREATER SPIRITUAL RESPONSIVENESS OF BODY

AND

AWAKENING THE BRAIN OF SPIRIT

by Brown Landone

<u>TONES</u> of <u>CATHEDRAL</u> <u>BELLS</u> <u>IN</u> <u>YOUR</u> <u>BODY</u> - - - - - - - - - - - LESSON II

You have advanced along the path - to learn of the Brain of Spirit and the <u>initiating</u> or <u>operative</u> powers, which you will later learn to use to make your body <u>continually</u> responsive to spirit, not only improving it but transforming it.

Here I give proof of the power of the <u>initiating</u> powers - the powers which initiate responsiveness of all cells of every vital organ of the body, and of every muscle and nerve.

Even the muscles must be tuned up, to receive the spiritual energy of the universe, and to manifest it more fully.

With such manifestation through muscles, you will possess enduring energy, and experience much less fatigue.

Thus you can add many hours to your life, and ultimately many years, as well as doubling attainment and joy every day.

These initiating powers <u>INITIATE</u> <u>responsiveness</u> of the body, so that it is tuned-up to receive and respond to spirit.

They include the <u>unknown</u> powers of sound and light and color and rhythm and cosmic rays, et cetera.

There are many of them, but it happens that God so made the body that <u>only</u> <u>one</u> of them is both beneficial to every cell of the body, and also able to penetrate to every cell.

It is the one which includes unknown overtones of sound.

Perhaps you doubt that overtones of beautiful sound - overtones of power - <u>can</u> sing <u>in</u> and all through your body.

So I ask you to make TWO simple TESTS, to PROVE to yourself that beautiful overtones CAN vibrate through your entire body, even though quite unheard and unknown to you.

Make these tests NOW. In each test, use FOUR things.

In the FIRST test you will use - a table, a spoon, a piece of string, and AIR.

2-8

In the SECOND test, you will use the same table, spoon and string; but instead of **air**, you will use your FINGER TIPS.

Hence, ANY difference in tones will be due to using FINGER TIPS instead of air.

Any table, made of wood, will do for both tests.
And any soup spoon you choose, solid silver or plated.
For the string, choose any kind of wrapping twine or cord, - about 4 feet long.

What follows now is the first test:

Tie the middle of the string around the small part of the handle of the spoon.
This leaves about two feet of string at one end, and about two at the other.

Now, hold up one end of the string in one hand, and the other end in the other hand, so that the spoon - tied in the middle of the string - will hang down and sway.
See the illustrations on next page.

Next, stand near a table, and sway your hands a little, so that the BOWL of the spoon swings AGAINST the table edge - just 'tapping' the EDGE of the table top.

LISTEN to the tones! EVERY tone you hear is produced by the singing qualities of the table and spoon and string!
Their combined tone is carried to your ear by AIR!

And what DO you hear? A pleasant "JINGLING" sound!
That is all, is it not?

Now, carry out the SECOND test.
It is done differently.
In the second test, you use your FINGER TIPS.

Wind one end of the string two or three times around your RIGHT forefinger, back a little from the tip, so your thumb can hold the string from sliding on the finger.

In the same way, wind the OTHER end of the string around your LEFT forefinger.

Then put the tip of one forefinger in one EAR; and the tip of the other, in the other ear.
Keep the string far enough back on each forefinger, so the string does NOT touch your ear.

Three factors ARE the SAME - table, spoon, string.

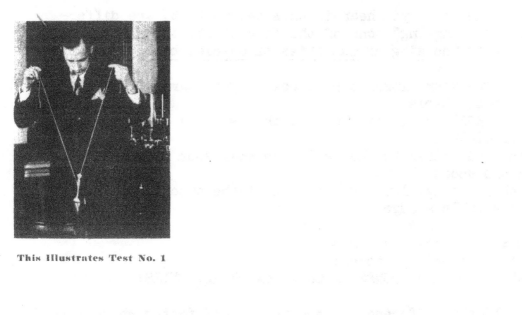

This Illustrates Test No. 1

This Illustrates Test No. 2

In the first test, tone traveled along string and then through AIR to reach your ear.

But in the second test, the sound travels along the string and then THROUGH the blood and bone and muscle of your FINGER TIPS And your fingers are composed of muscle, blood and bones!

So IF the tones you hear in this second test, are different from the "jingling" tone of the first test, the difference MUST be due to the singing qualities of muscle, blood and bone.

NOW, with your finger tips stuck in your ears, STEP BACK a little from the table.
BEND FORWARD a little, so that the swinging spoon will NOT touch your clothes.
Then bend nearer to the table and sway your body a little, to swing the spoon.
Do this easily, letting the bowl of the spoon again hit against the table's edge.

AND what DO you hear, NOW?
No mere "jingling" tones!
Instead you hear TONES OF GREAT CATHEDRAL BELLS!

And ALL the difference is due to the ONE factor which IS different, - that is, to the singing qualities of MUSCLE, BLOOD and BONES in your own FINGER TIPS!

More astounding is the fact that ALL the difference you hear is caused by ONLY a HALF-INCH of finger tip.
What then must be the silent songs of your entire body?

Just as a great 6-foot (72 inch) bell produces greater tones than a half-inch bell, so ALL your body - 10,000 times larger than your finger tips - produces tones 10,000 times MORE POWERFUL than those you have just heard.

There IS a means of producing powerful tones in your body.
It is your own voice. Each voice tone produces silent and UNHEARD overtones within your body - mystic INNER tones - which work tremendous changes.

If the tones of your voice, are disagreeable or weak or edgy they produce friction in your body.
If they are tones of love - they harmonize cells, TUNE-UP the spiritual quality of your body; OPEN it to the INFLOW of spirit!
These silent overtones can make the cells of your body sing in harmony with the mystic songs of stars and atoms!

Certainly, the test you just made did NOT prove that the tones you heard were "THE" tones of songs of atoms and of stars.

But there IS proof that they are like those of stars, -
provided the tones of your voice are tones of love.

Stars of universes and electrons of atoms ARE held together
by ATTRACTIVE power - the most titanic power of earth and heaven.

Out in space, billions of stars have been held together, circling in harmony for trillions of years.
In the atom, electrons have been held together since creation,
and even million volt power in laboratories can not pull them apart.

There is ONLY ONE great attractive power!
Whether out in space, holding stars together; or in an atom,
holding electrons together; or in the body holding cells together;
or in the human society, holding people together in love and attainment of great ideals - there is but one holding-together power!

There is but one such power, and IT IS LOVE!

So if you use the deep loving tones in your voice, particularly in the work I give you to do in these Lessons to tune-up
your body, you will produce unknown and unheard overtones of beauty
and power vibrating all through your body.

Such tones will create harmony among cells, and lift them up
in love, to be ready to receive spirit and respond to spirit.

Do not doubt the existence of these overtones.
You can not hear them just as you had never heard the tones
that sing through the tips of your fingers until today, and did
not know that such beautiful tones vibrate in your body.

Be certain that the powers which work alike, produce results
that are alike. The overtones of your body will be like the overtones of stars and atoms, and you will begin to respond to the
harmony of the universe, IF your tones are tones of love.

Do you, my friend, now begin to realize how useless it is merely to repeat words and thoughts, to produce harmony?
There must be actual response of the entire body, before your
body can respond to the harmony of the universe.

The songs of stars and atoms ARE overtones of the ONE attractive power; and the inner body overtones produced by your tones of
love ARE tones of the SAME attractive power.

I know you want to reach great spiritual heights - attain super
consciousness of Spirit!
I know you want a body thrilled with energy, ever flowing into
free and full action, for perfect manifestation.
But you cannot attain the first, without the second.
Unless you tune-up your body to spirit, you cannot become

truly conscious of spirit.

You have PROVED that overtones like those of great cathedral bells DO sing IN the tissues of your OWN body.

You now know you can NOT use light's unknown powers to awaken the Brain of Spirit, because light rays do not penetrate even through the skin!

You know you can NOT use mind to awaken spirit.

You know there is but ONE great power which HARMONIZES and HOLDS all things together.

You know that power is love!

You know that the SAME power which harmonizes and holds stars together, IS the power that holds cells together!
Otherwise one would work against the other, and tear the universe apart - tear stars apart; tear your body apart.

To inspire (take-in) spirit energy, you KNOW you must tune-up your body to spirit!

Moreover, you know you want more than mere theories about spiritual power; you want the actual awakening of the Brain of Spirit, and spiritual responsiveness, here and now.

So YOU are now ready for the next lessons - to begin to tune-up the body to spirit.

In every silent moment - visualize the two HEAVENLY CONDITIONS you most desire.
First, abundant energy, flowing into your body.
Second, all power in you, FLOWING fully into action.
Attainment of these two, is perfect manifestation of earth.

I know you have read so many things that have been just masses of words without much meaning, that you have come to believe that Truth is difficult to understand.

Free yourself of that idea. It takes no education to understand spirit. Simple souls oft attain the greatest power.
DO the work I give, and the results will make it clear to you. You, born of God, CAN understand.

So let us begin now, with great insistent desire, to UNDERSTAND the means of AWAKENING the body to respond enough, so it can in-spire spirit, - millions of times more powerful than Mind.

THE GREATER SPIRITUAL RESPONSIVENESS OF BODY

AND

AWAKENING THE BRAIN OF SPIRIT

by Brown Landone

FOUR BRAINS and IMPROVEMENT vs TRANSFORMATION - - - - - LESSON III

SPIRIT is the most powerful ENERGY of the universe.
The physicist calls it, cosmic-energy, The biologist, life.
We call it spirit - the radiancy of God.
ADRENAL is the name of one of the tiny organs of the body.
It enfolds a medulla of brain cells. The substance of these cells
is the most powerful SUBSTANCE known on earth.

Since spirit is the highest energy of the universe and the actual matter of the adrenal is earth's most powerful substance, they
form the union of the highest power in the most spiritualized matter.
It is the mystic-wedding of spirit and matter!

Transformation differs from development or improvement.
No matter how highly you develop a grub-worm, it's still a worm!
But transformation changes the grub into a butterfly.

We have improved the body for ages - by diet, breathing, baths,
exercise, developmental training, mental control.
We have attained a high degree of thought consciousness.

We have also been taught 'mind-power' - teachings of the occult; and also consciousness of inner light, use of the violet ray,
the vibrant Om, realization of the absolute, et cetera.
In these Lessons we retain ALL that is helpful of these means,
and then ADD the use of Spirit itself.

We also use the power of spiritual desire!
Desire is not spirit itself, but it is the activating power
of Spirit. It puts spirit into action.
It also awakens and greatly augments the activity of each
one of the seven creative powers which I teach you in later Lessons.

Before discussing desire, I wish you to know what and where
the Brain of Spirit is. It is the brain, which mystics knew long
ago, but knowledge of it had long been lost to modern man.
It has been recently re-discovered.
It is NOT the brain in the skull, for that is the mind brain.
It is not the solar-plexus, the emotive or love brain.
It is not the sacral plexus; that is, life or sex brain.

3-14

The power of each brain works marvels; but their power is as nothing compared to the spiritual power of the Brain of Spirit.

Even the substance of the Brain of Spirit is powerful.
Matter which lacks power, lacks spirit.
Matter which is powerful, throbs with spirit.

The actual substance of this hidden brain of spirit is so FILLED with spirit, and hence so powerful, that we dare not inject a drop of its pure substance into the blood of a human being.
We first dilute one drop of it in 100,000,000 drops of water.
Science proves that this substance of the Brain of Spirit is more powerful than any other substance known on earth!

This brain is the brain of brains!
Surgeons can remove a third of the brain of the skull, and the individual can still live on. The solar-plexus can be injured, yet the person will not die. The sacral (sex) brain can be inhibited, and the testes or ovaries removed, and yet the health of the body may even be improved.
BUT IF Brain of Spirit is seriously injured, there is DEATH!

This brain is THE center of spiritual desire.

Man waited 300,000 years - before a Teacher appeared who proclaimed the power of desire - by promising "What things soever ye desire - - - ye shall have."
Then, man waited nearly 2,000 years more, before he discovered in his own body, the secret brain of spirit, the brain which is moved only by spiritual desire.

By desire, man's energy - even in ordinary life - can be multiplied four-fold or forty-fold in a few minutes!
We have known of such results in the past.
But we have not known how to affect them at will!

For example, when I was seventeen I was ill in bed.
I had been an invalid all my life. I was so weak that I had to be carried up and down stairs. Yet when I was awakened by 'a fire' one night, I got up alone, dragged two heavily loaded trunks down two flights of stairs and across the street!
It was my desire to save the treasures in those trunks, which awakened in me, that astounding energy.

Yet one hour later - using all my faith in thought power, and physical energy, I could not lift one end of either of those trunks!

Why? By that time, the desire to save the trunks was gone, - because they had already been saved!

Each new discovery of a different brain in the body has initiated a great new advance.

3-15

Herophilus, some 300 years before Christ, recognized the brain in the head as the center of thought.

Then for almost 2,200 years, man mistakenly assumed that all other soul powers also manifested through that one mind brain.

When a young man, new in medical science, my observations as a neurologist, convinced me that two of the great plexuses of the nervous system, were not merely plexuses, but that they were actual brains which functioned individually as brains.

Later, I performed 1,400 experiments and tests which proved it. At that time my conclusions were ridiculed.

Today, however, in every medical college, there are textbooks - often three-volume reference books - on this same subject - giving proof that these plexuses are brains.

By 1922, man had definitely differentiated the functions of three great brains in the body!
(a) the mind brain in the skull.
(b) the emotive brain of solar plexus, on an approximate level of the stomach, but back in torso, in front of the spine.
(c) the sex - or sacral brain - lower in the torso.

Now a FOURTH brain has been discovered - that is, fourth in the order of discovery!
It is not a mind brain; or love brain, or life brain.
It IS a brain of SPIRIT power!

The ancient mystics seemed to know of this brain of spirit, and even knew its location, - for they wrote of the spirit of man being centered in his reins. Reins is an old word for kidneys.

Their inspirational knowledge of long ago has now become proven fact. Today it IS proven that such a brain does exist, and in the particular part of the body designated by the mystics 3,000 years ago. It is just above the kidneys.

The kidneys are also called the renals, and hence anything above them is super. Therefore we have the word suprarenal.

In lower animals which do not stand upright, the glands are not above the kidneys, but in front of the kidneys.
Hence in lower animals, they are called ad-renals.

For many years, I had been intuitively certain of the existence of a brain of spirit, because I could not believe that the miracles wrought by hormones, were produced by mere 'juices' of glands!

Now my faith and intuition are justified.
Physiologists have now proven that the cells of the medulla of the suprarenal are NOT gland cells!
They have proven that the cells of this medulla are brain cells - similar to cells of the sympathetic nerve plexuses.

The outer part of each suprarenal is composed of <u>gland</u> tissue and functions as a ductless gland.

But the <u>inner</u> part is <u>brain</u> cells; functions as a brain!

It is so phenomenal, that I wish at once to prevent you from confusing it with another gland - the pineal - which some writers who are sincere, but lack physiological knowledge, have <u>mistakenly</u> assumed is the seat of the soul.

The pineal is composed mainly of a <u>few flakes of lime</u> sand held together by connective tissue! Amazingly fantastic claims have been made for it, but it is silly for any educated person to believe that lime sand is the kind of substance, through which spirit effects its supreme manifestation.

Each of the four brains in the body is fitted by the Creator to manifest one power more dominantly than all other powers.

Hence there are four brains and four basic soul powers.

<u>Mind</u>, which idealizes and directs.

<u>Love</u>, which attracts and harmonizes!

<u>Life</u>, which unites and reproduces!

<u>Spirit</u>, which inspires, impels action, and creates!

<u>Each soul power has a brain for its own particular function</u>!

The brain of spirit is the inner center of the suprarenal. It is a brain of spirit-energy. <u>And only spirit spiritualizes all cells and all tissues! Only spirit creates and re-creates!</u>

<u>Only spirit can transform the body!</u>

<u>Only spirit can transfigure the powers of the soul!</u>

This newly-discovered brain, <u>IS</u> the <u>brain of spirit</u>!

The word <u>spirit</u> designates the Supreme Energy, because all energies which move in spirals are supremely powerful - that is, much more powerful than the energies which move forward in straight lines or in wave lines.

In all early languages, the word for spiral and spirit, are the same! So I use the word spirit - in the same way the ancient mystics used it - to designate the supreme power - whether of the material or of the spiritual world.

This helps you to understand <u>in-spiration</u>! It is the act of supreme energy <u>spiraling-into</u> physical structure. Since the very substance of the <u>brain of spirit</u> is super-powerful, it can respond enough to in-spire (take-in) spirit-energy of the universe.

We are now almost at end of the path which leads to the seven steps which lead to the portico of the Temple of Transformation.

THE GREATER SPIRITUAL RESPONSIVENESS OF BODY

AND

AWAKENING THE BRAIN OF SPIRIT

by Brown Landone

TWO STUPENDOUS TRUTHS - LIFE AND DEATH REVERSED - - - - LESSON IV

This Lesson and Lesson VI contain three stupendous truths.
So far as I know, they have not been previously presented,
except in private courses of my own.

The first stupendous truth is the true understanding of our
life here, compared with the life of those who have passed on.

Death is the word we use for passing on.
(In all I write here, death refers only to the body.)

Usually we speak of those who have passed on, as dead!
And very strangely, we think of ourselves as the living.

Yet both of these statements are NOT true!

When the sperm and the ovum unite in the womb of the mother,
there is life, impelled by spirit!
The cell lives, and multiplies and increases its life, and
if life means anything, it means increase of life and growth.
This process of increase and growth of the human continues
within the womb of the mother until the child is born.
It continues after birth until the 21st or 22nd year.

THEN, every human individual BEGINS TO DIE.
There is no more youthful growth or increase in life of the
ordinary human individual after his 21st or 22nd year - except
in a few very exceptional cases.

Day by day, the body of every adult slowly dies!
Some die more rapidly than others.
So it is WE are the ones who live in the realm of death!

Even those of us who are happy that we have retained vitality
and youthfulness through a number of years - after all, the best we
can say for ourselves, is that we have NOT been dying quite as
rapidly as other people have.

All adults on earth live in the realm of death, because they
are dying individuals.
And strange, as soon as one passes on, he is free of this

4-18

dying condition, and hence he lives in the realm of the living

It is a stupendous truth!
We on earth are always slowly dying in this realm of death.
Those who have passed on, are the ones who are truly living.

From this, we can take the step in clear thinking
It leads to the second stupendous truth of life.

The second stupendous truth is that our condition of continuous dying here, is due to the destructive energies which we mistakenly think are energies that support life.

The biologist or physiologist has never found the primal cause of death in any study of the chemistry of the body or any study of the physiological activities of the body.
Please note that physiology does not mean the anatomy or structure of the body, but its activity and functioning.
Each thinking biologist or physiologist says there should be no reason why the human body can not live forever.
YET we are very certain that the body does die.

To live, man depends on the use of certain energies.
He depends on them for the functioning within his body.

Now we come to my second stupendous truth!
Every one of these energies on which man depends for life is a DESTRUCTIVE energy; it always tends to destroy whatever it temporarily builds up.

We have been so stupid, in our scientific study of energies, that it almost warps our faith in science, and our own intelligence, when we learn that every energy which we have considered to be a constructive energy is basically a destructive energy.

For a time each such energy may stimulate and produce a temporary growth, but in so doing, it already starts the process of death because of its own destructiveness.
Even all of our therapeutic sciences and efforts to heal the human body depend upon use of destructive energies.
In fact not one medical physician or naturopath in ten million knows what a constructive energy is.

For healing we use heat, light, electricity X-ray, radium rays, and chemical energy as in food and medicines.

We generally expect these energies to heal the body and give us life, - yet every one of these is destructive, always destroying whatever it temporarily builds up in us.

For instance, we depend on light for life.

Some people are great fadists of sun bathing, and even boast about how healthy they are, because so darkly tanned.

But light is absolute death to the inner human body.

It is so deadly to the human body, that nature provides that it shall not be allowed to penetrate the body.

Light can not get into the skin, more than 1/100th inch.

Nature is very wise and man is often very very dumb.

When dumb man exposes himself to too much light, nature knows enough to protect him from killing off his own body.

So nature puts up a black-out curtain between layers of the skin - little particles of color through which light can not pass. That color is called tan.

Nature deposits this shade of tan so light shall be kept out from the cells of the inner body, because light will kill any cell of any organ of the body except the skin, in about two seconds!

And if nature does not build up a tan to keep light out of your body so that it will not kill you, then the light cooks your skin - that is, blisters it - until you do stay out of the light, until your skin has recovered enough of life, to be able to stand another dose of killing light.

Light even destroys the cells of the retina of the eye, if it is exposed to pure light such as sunlight. Explorers in Arctic or Antarctic regions - where light is often continuous for months, and reflected from the snow - go blind, because light destroys cells of the retina, unless the explorer protects his eyes by colored glasses, to shut out most of the light.

Light even destroys the very qualities of its own nature. Light broken up into its different vibrations produces colors, but light destroys colors. It fades them.

I am not writing this to oppose the use of light, but I am writing of a stupendous widely unknown truth.

The light - on which we depend for life - is a killing enemy of our bodies; it is one of the destructive energies which even destroys that which it itself builds up.

We also depend on heat for life, - for if body temperature drops befow a certain degree, it is truly dangerous to life.

This is the reason we must eat foods, which free a certain amount of heat (calories) in the body.

We need heat to keep up the temperature of the organs, so that the energies of the mind and the soul and spirit - that radiate from brain centers and nerves - can easily manifest in and through the tissues of the body.

But heat itself is destructive. It destroys the human body; destroys (burns up) wood and other substances; even melts steel.

I am not here fully discussing any one of these energies.

4-20

I am merely telling enough so that you will recognize that each of the energies on which we depend for life, is destructive.

Consequently all adult human beings - depending on such energies for life - live in a realm of death and slowly die, every day from the 21st or 22nd year.

Sound also - although beautiful to our ears as music, can actually drive man insane; and it is proven by laboratory experiment, that sound vibrations that approximate 8,000 vibrations per second disintegrate bones and teeth, and even the hardest substance found in the human body - gall stones.

Now it might be considered beneficial to use such rays of sound to dissolve gall stones in the human body, except for the fact that if we placed the human body in the path of such sound waves, the entire body would be disintegrated!

Even higher silent vibrations of sound, of laminated crystal stones - are deadly to several forms of life.

If you drop a pebble of laminated crystal into a tank of milk, within a few minutes, every germ in the milk is dead.

Or drop a pebble of a laminated crystal stone into your goldfish bowl, in half hour, every goldfish in the bowl will be dead.

Since these sound vibrations are absolutely silent, their destruction of life, is "the mystery of the silent death".

And electric rays can shatter glass, shrivel plants, and kill animal life from tiny cells up to the human body.

X-rays are also destructive; they actually burn up organs of the body. So terribly destructive that even the physician who uses them to cure others by such a destructive energy, protects himself with gloves and stands behind a lead screen.

And radium also is a destructive energy. A tiny bit of it in your body disintegrates all organic tissues, even bones.

It is stupendous truth, is it not, that here on this earth we depend on these energies for life, although each of them is a destructive energy, and destroys with absolute certainty the human body to which it is supposed to give life.

I am not leaving this subject here, for I have another stupendous truth to reveal to you in Lesson VI.

It is the truth of the seven great powers - the spiritual powers, which I have discovered - or rather re-discovered.

Every one of these is a constructive power.

These are the seven powers God used to create the earth.

Each day's creation reveals that a different power was used each day, and that each produced a different result.

Since those results are eternal they reveal that the powers which produced them must be eternally constructive, otherwise God's creation would not have lasted.

THE GREATER SPIRITUAL RESPONSIVENESS OF BODY

AND

AWAKENING THE BRAIN OF SPIRIT

by Brown Landone

"SPIRITUALIZED" MATTER and RESPONSIVENESS - - - - - - - LESSON V

It is now wise that I sum up for you, the bases on which we
are to proceed for your greater development:
(1) the awakening of the brain of spirit; and the
(2) increased spiritual responsiveness of your body.

You now know that man's body begins dying at 21 or 22, and
continues slowly dying for the rest of its life on earth.
You know that all the powers on which man has depended for
life, are destructive energies, rapidly killing his body.
You also now know that something more than improvement is needed for man's greater advancement here on earth, - for neither man's
body nor mind of today surpass the body or mind of the ancient
Egyptian or Greek.

Man must now make transforming changes in his body, otherwise
he will stand still, or even slip back.

Since man begins dying at 21 or 22 years, something must be
wrong with our methods, as well as our choice of powers used.

Man has prayed and idealized, striving earnestly both for physical and spiritual growth - using many means and methods.
Yet he has often failed to attain all he has tried to attain.

We should face the truth, and find out why we fail.
Nothing is gained by our hush-hush method of not saying
anything about those who after claiming that they have found the
truth, still die while young.

Let us face truth, and truth itself will give us the answer.
Truth itself has never failed, but our understanding has!
And our mistaken applications of truth have often been wrong.

Neither the most hygienic life combined with the best physical
training, nor the most ideal life in accord with Truth of mind, has
added to man's length of life.

The facts are these: Every professional strong man has died
before he was 50; most of them before their 35th year!
I am writing of those who took good care of themselves - not

drinking, not smoking, not using foods supposed to be detrimental.

Likewise, most of our great leaders of Truth whom we have admired, have died before they were seventy years of age.

This does indicate a failure, because there are more than 4,000,000 people in our country who have never heard of truth, and yet they are more than seventy years of age.

Even the one leader whose keynote of mentalized truth, is that there is no matter and no possible death to the physical body, died before she was ninety years old.

This is neither criticism of individuals, nor of truth!

But it is honest recognition that we do not yet use the powers of the soul that make the body spiritual enough to live as youthfully as many other forms of life!

Man's body dies - as an old body - even when young in years.
Some lower animals, even birds, love as long as man!
And some animals live twice as long!
Any animal that can keep his body vital and healthy and active for 200 years possesses something which man has missed!

It is shocking that man really lives only until he is 21 or 22 years old; and then begins dying and continues to slowly die, week by week, and actually ends life here while yet young in years!

Since man's soul is made in the image and likeness of God, and since God is eternal - forever living, never dying - it seems man should have accomplished more in making his body responsive to spirit, so that it would live longer and more youthfully.

It is strange that man still depends for life, on destructive energies, which tend to destroy his body, so that he dies young.

But now that we have discovered the brain of spirit, there is certainty that you can awaken your body to respond more fully to spirit and to the creative powers of God, so that you may actually work a transformation of the body.

The degree of change depends on two factors:
(1) the power of the energy of the brain of spirit; and
(2) the degree of responsiveness of your body tissues.

The brain of spirit is deep within the suprarenal gland.
The suprarenal (adrenal) is the supreme endocrine gland.
In making this statement, I do not discredit opinions of other scientists, although I seem to disagree with them.

Many endocrinologists assert that the pituitary endocrine is the master gland of all the endocrine system, because it can make the hormones of other glands, if they fail to do so.
I do not contradict them, for I know this is true, - that is,

that the pituitary is the master endocrine <u>factory</u>.

<u>BUT</u> all evidence proves that it is the suprarenal which IS the <u>master</u> <u>BRAIN</u> <u>of</u> the <u>master</u> <u>FACTORY</u>.

The very <u>substance</u> of the brain of spirit in the adrenal <u>is</u> <u>practically</u> <u>SPIRIT</u> <u>itself</u>!

It is no longer possible to draw a clean cut line, between matter and spirit, but we can truly say that some substances are not powerful, and that other substances are very powerful.

When we say that a substance is not powerful, we mean <u>there</u> <u>is</u> <u>NOT</u> <u>as</u> <u>much</u> <u>spirit</u> <u>in</u> <u>it</u> as in other substances.

When we say, another substance is the <u>most</u> <u>powerful</u> <u>substance</u> on earth - whether in or outside of man, in air or depths of the earth - we mean that that <u>substance</u> <u>IS</u> <u>so</u> <u>like</u> <u>spirit</u>, that it is practically spirit itself in manifestation!

The <u>very</u> <u>substance</u> of the brain of spirit is so saturated with spirit that it <u>is</u> practically spirit itself.
It is the purest form of manifesting spirit <u>in</u> matter - perhaps it is 1 part matter, and 999 parts spirit.

From this brain of spirit, spirit itself can be radiated to every cell of man's body to transform every cell - to change man so that his body shall live instead of die.

For this, there is a need of greater <u>responsiveness</u> <u>of</u> <u>body</u>.

Your body is now responsive to the destructive energies - to light, sound, electric rays, ultra-violet, radium, et cetera.
But all of them tend to destroy the body so rapidly, that your body begins to die just about the time it ought to begin to live as an adult, able to attain great things in life.
There <u>IS</u> great need of the body becoming more responsive to the seven great powers of spirit - the constructive powers which God himself used in creating the universe.

<u>And</u> <u>what</u> <u>do</u> <u>I</u> <u>mean</u>, <u>by</u> - 'responsiveness'?

When I say that matter is responsive, I mean that energy <u>can</u> <u>flow</u> through it, with little friction, so that the substance is <u>not</u> worn out, and the energy is <u>not</u> used up in merely forcing its way through the matter.

To illustrate the value of responsiveness, let me use an electric dynamo, a motor, and a wire connecting the two.

The dynamo radiates 1000 units of energy every minute.

To carry that energy from the dynamo to the motor, you use a connecting wire.

If you use a semi-iron wire - which is <u>not</u> responsive to electricity - to link up your dynamo to your motor, <u>the wire itself will use up 950 units of the energy</u>.

Then your motor will receive only 50 units of energy!
This makes it a very weak motor - a failure in life.

But if you use copper wire - which <u>is</u> responsive to electricity - <u>it uses up only 80 units</u> of the energy radiated by the dynamo.

<u>This leaves 920 units of energy for you to use</u>.
This gives you a very strong motor - a successful life.

Soul is infinite, and there is <u>no</u> limit to its powers.
So, if the body were fully responsive, the energy of the body would also be limitless.
But an <u>un</u>-responsive body uses up so much energy, that your energy for the activities of life is greatly reduced.

Tune-up the body so that it is <u>more</u> responsive to spirit - more responsive to your soul powers - and much more of the power of your soul will manifest - not only in energy but in health and in vitality and attainment and love and charm and friendship and abundance and spiritual illumination and realization!

The soul is limitless; nothing can prevent its limitless expression, except an <u>un</u>-responsive body.

Since we have now discovered the seven great constructive powers of spirit - the very powers that are enduring and do not wear out structures through which they manifest - we should try to make the body responsive to them.

As your body becomes more responsive, you will more fully express the divinity within you, and realise that you <u>are</u> made in likeness of God - to live like a god on earth.

But be very certain, my friend, that you can <u>NOT</u> increase such responsiveness, by any direct effort of the conscious mind - whether by affirmation or concentration or visualisation.

Mind always hinders expression of spirit; because the limitations of conscious mind can not remove their own limitations.

If however, you rise to consciousness of the power of spirit, and make your body more responsive to spirit, then transformation is possible, and all the other things will be added unto you.

THE GREATER SPIRITUAL RESPONSIVENESS OF BODY

AND

AWAKENING THE BRAIN OF SPIRIT

by Brown Landone

THE SEVEN 'GOD RAYS' OF CREATION - - - - - - - - - - - - LESSON VI

Practically all work of science has been concerned with the study of the destructive energies of earth and the universe.

But from geology, we know that earth has existed for billions of years.
From biology, we know that life on earth has existed for tens of millions of years.
So there must be energies that are not destructive, - for nothing but constructive powers can create that which lasts.

Scientists now call energies, - 'rays' or powers.
There are seven rays which are God-powers.
These are the constructive powers of the universe.
They have never yet been investigated by scientists.

It is these powers, which make body responsive to spirit.
And we CAN discover what kind of energies they are, because God used them one at a time - one for each day of creation - and tells us exactly what he created each day.
The greatest Bible truth is found in its first 34 verses.
They tell just WHAT seven powers God used in creation!
They tell us the result of using each power, each day.

Another illuminating truth is that the word, translated God in the first chapter of the Bible, is the word Elohim!
You know that in different foreign languages, plurals of nouns are formed in different ways.
In English, we usually form a plural, by merely adding "s".
In the Hebrew, one sign of the plural is im.
Eloh-im is plural in form; it means SEVEN powers of God!
That is, the seven powers or energies, or seven rays of God which he used to create heaven and earth, in seven days.

ON THE FIRST DAY, God used his IN-SPIRING Power or Ray!
He radiated his light - to in-spire energy into his ideal of creation to give it power to become real.

ON THE SECOND DAY, God used his EXPANDING-UPLIFTING Ray.
In the margin of the Revised Version of the Bible, you find
that the word 'firmament' is the translation of a Hebrew
word which means uplifting or expanding.
This reveals what God did on the second day of creation.
And the uplifted expansion, God called heaven!

Scientists know there is such a power, yet they have never
even studied the power itself.
They know that gasses expand, and that other substances
expand when heated.
And they know that this power works independently of heat;
and you know it also, if ever near a raw cut onion!
Particles of onion oil move outward by expanding power, so
rapidly that you smell it even though several feet away!
God's power of expansion exists in all things - onions or
universes!

ON THE THIRD DAY, God used his FORMING Ray.
To 'form' means to put things together into shape.
That is what God did on the third day of creation, as
revealed in Genesis 1:9-13.
He formed the heavens; he formed the waters; he gave form to
dry land. All these 'forms' appeared on the third day.

I devote many later Lessons to these powers; but here, I
give you only their names; read first 34 verses of Genesis.

THE FOURTH constructive power God used in his CLARIFYING
Ray - the purifying power which eliminates non-essentials, and
clarifies one thing as different from another.

THE FIFTH DAY, God used his VITALIZING Ray, - to harmonize
all things. This power even harmonizes elements in water, so
that out of them, life is created.

THE SIXTH DAY, God used his RE-CREATIVE Ray, - the power
that gives each thing the power to multiply after its own kind.

THE SEVENTH DAY, God used his HOLDING Ray - the power 'to
hold' all things created - keep them from being dispersed.
I might as truly call this God's Sabbathizing Ray, because
the word sabbath often means 'capture' or 'hold'.

These are the only constructive powers in the universe!
And scientists have made NO study of them.
Every scientist knows that there is an expanding power.
But he never studies it, and when you mention it, he merely
shrugs his shoulders, and says, - "Yes, all things expand."
It is strange, that scientists have never been impelled to
recognize that if 'all things' expand, there must be an expanding

POWER which expands them!

Every synthetic chemist knows that when certain molecules of one kind are brought near certain molecules of another kind, they rush into a new form - a new chemical.

Yet when questioned about this, the scientist again shrugs his shoulders, and says, - "Why, that's affinity!"

It is amazing that not one scientist has even tried to find out what power causes affinition - the one process of forming all new things.

The above are THE constructive powers of the universe.
They impel all the lesser powers - such as heat, sound, light, electric rays, x-rays, radium, cosmic rays.

All the minor powers destroy or tend to destroy, and their effect on the human body always leads to death.

But there IS something in creation of man which - FOR A TIME - is NOT affected by these destructive powers.

It is the SPIRIT! It gives to man - when conceived within womb of mother - something which gives him life!

And for the first few years of life after birth - for about 20 years - so long as man depends on this spirit - even unconsciously - he LIVES, and his life increases and grows.

But when man begins to use his 'mind' too much - particularly as the dominant power of his life - then man STOPS growing and increasing life, and BEGINS DYING!

So from about his 21st year - dominated by mind, instead of spirit - man slowly dies year by year!

Mind does something to spirit, that hinders the free flow and manifestation of spirit. It clamps down and limits!

Conscious mind limits man to time and space; and restricts every impulse of love, life and spirit.

Yet the soul of man IS limitless! It is spirit, created in the likeness of God, and knows NO limit of time and space!

Conscious mind will not even let you believe that you can expand in spirit o'er all the world in a second!

Or instantly change from one age to another. Or be here one second and half around earth in another.

Yet your soul CAN do all these things!
In sixty seconds of a DREAM, your soul CAN do all these things and a thousand more, because when you dream, your conscious mind is asleep, and can not limit your soul.

This means your soul is free for the time, although you have not yet learned how to use this freedom when you dream.

The soul experiences this freedom also in near-drowning.

At such a moment the conscious mind unconsciously gives up its control, and the soul is free to live limitlessly.

Hence at such a time, the soul experiences more in a minute, than it lives in a life time of conscious thought.

I do not expect you to understand all this fully now.

I write of this here, as a <u>basis</u> of future understanding.

<u>Study</u> this Lesson many times, as a basis!

I shall ask you in succeeding Lessons, to make your body so responsive to spirit, that conscious mind shall <u>no</u> longer limit your soul or bind your body - so that the Creative powers can transform your body and transfigure your soul, as you become more responsive to spirit.

<u>COMMENT ON SLIGHTLY CHANGED NAMES</u>

Finding names for things which have never been known on earth, is one of the most difficult problems for the human mind.

For example, I tried for thirteen years, to find a name to designate the work of my friend, Luther Burbank. But there is <u>no</u> English word, which defines his kind of work.

It has been very difficult to find English names for the Seven Creative Rays. The mystic names which I have had to translate, in writing for you, are - shamayim, apheriam, caroceliam, armonian, godeshian, meolanian, and many others.

Sometimes three different names are given to the same ray.

These had never been translated into English, until I first wrote this course some years ago.

I <u>AM</u> now changing my first English translation a little bit, to make the names simpler and meanings clearer for you.

For example, what I previously called the Conforming Ray, I now call the <u>Forming Ray</u>, because 'forming' is sufficient, as the name of the power that gives <u>form</u> to things.

And what I previously called the <u>Purifying Ray</u>, I now call, <u>Clarifying Ray</u>, - for it is the clearer meaning of the power God used - symbolized by making sun and moon - the light that made it possible to clarify all things.

But no matter what little change I may make in names, each Ray remains the same, and its power remains the same.

THE GREATER SPIRITUAL RESPONSIVENESS OF BODY

AND

AWAKENING THE BRAIN OF SPIRIT

by Brown Landone

'SPOKEN WORD' - SILENT MYSTIC SOUND OF SPIRIT - - LESSON VII

My insistent purpose is that you get results in attaining the two MOST important goals in all you life - first, full in-flow of spirit; second, full out-flow of expression of spirit.

I had a basic reason for those tests of Lesson II.

First, they PROVED to you that tremendous overtones CAN vibrate in your blood and bones and muscles - through every cell of YOUR body.

Second, they proved magnification of overtones - that even the ordinary jingle of a spoon DID produce sounds of cathedral bells in your finger tips.

Third, they indicate that great harmonious overtones vibrate in your body, for the tones you heard WERE beautiful and harmonious, hence workers of good in your body.

These same overtones vibrate in atoms! I emphasize ATOMS, because every cell in your body IS composed of atoms.

An atom is a tiny sun center of infinite energy of God.
We call the protons and electrons of which atoms are made, the smallest 'particles' of matter.
But since matter is energy, a proton or electron is really a 'particle of energy', - not a particle of matter.

Although infinitely small, the atom has a sun center.
Its electrons whirl around that center, just as our earth and the other planets whirl around our sun.

The whirling is so rapid that the power is TITANIC!
IF scientists could free the energy locked up in the atoms of one teaspoonful of mud, its energy could toss all navies of all nations from the Atlantic to the Pacific in one second of time!

Your body IS made up of such ATOMS of tremendous power.

The power within them is the SAME attractive power which

holds stars together to form universes.

The attractive power <u>is</u> <u>the</u> <u>same</u>, because it produces like results.

In the past, many of our hopes have <u>not</u> been fulfilled!
Faithful souls have tried earnestly – tried and tried again – and yet not attained the results they desired.

We mistakenly taught that Divine Mind is all power.
This <u>IS</u> a mistake, for mind is the <u>means</u> which God has given to us to use the still greater powers of spirit.

The goal of life is (1) <u>incarnation</u> of spirit INTO the body;
(2) <u>transformation</u> of the body BY spirit; (3) out-flow of spirit;
(4) to transform <u>everything</u> in life!

In our efforts, there has often been a SLIP in our work – a slip between the effort we make and the result we attain.
This slip has often been due to lack of understanding of listening to the "Inner Voice" and our use of the "Spoken Word."

This "INNER VOICE" is called 'conscience' by some.
But its messages do <u>NOT</u> come in words!

The Inner Voice is truly the mystically silent overtone of God – whose power ancient mystics knew and used.

Just as there IS an "inner light" in your body, which the eye can not see, – so also there IS "inner sound" – the voice of absolute silent – which the ear NEVER hears!

I am revealing holy truths to you – <u>stupendous</u> <u>truths</u>!
They are usually misunderstood; seldom truly understood.

"THE SPOKEN WORD" is <u>NOT</u> a word or words spoken aloud.

Our past teaching has been only PARTLY right.
The 'spoken word' has great power.
But the mentalists of our Truth movement have <u>materialized</u> it, and used it to designate words or phrases, to be spoken aloud as affirmations or declarations of being or power.

Sometimes you have been helped, when you yourself have awakened the <u>true</u> spoken word of spirit within yourself.

In other cases, it has failed a hundred thousand times.
Many practitioners have 'spoken the word' of abundance for others, and there has been no abundance.

They have spoken abundance for themselves, and are in want.

They are not to blame!

The lack of results has been due to the materialization of the high ideals of the true word, into crude sounds which the ear can hear.

The true word is NEVER a word or a phrase, spoken aloud.

"The Spoken Word" IS Spirit - a mighty silent harmonizing overtone of God pulsating THROUGH your body.

Speaking it aloud with your lips kills its true powers.

In ancient texts, "spoken word" means the "HIGHEST POWER, ISSUING OUT" - issuing or radiating AS A POWER!

Hence, our use of it as a truth spoken aloud by our human voice is a materialistic desecration of the real spoken word.

The TRUE 'spoken word' vibrates in silence!

It UNIFIES you WITH the essence power of stars which issue out from God.

It vibrates IN all things on earth, and IN all the eternal circling of stars; it TUNES-UP the body, so that the body itself becomes more RESPONSIVE to spirit.

It PENETRATES to every cell; reaches to Brain of Spirit, and frees the silent power of spirit.

Please do not think that awakening the Brain of Spirit is complex and difficult. It is VERY SIMPLE!

And the means are SO simple, that un-thinking people often miss both the understanding and the awakening.

Only un-thinking people teach complex truth.

That is why they are always failures!

Thinking souls soon learn that basic truths are simple!

So also, the SIMPLEST means are always the MOST EFFECTIVE.

A great uncut diamond may lie in a gutter for a year; 1,000,000 people may pass it by, missing its wealth.

THEY think it is only a SIMPLE pebble without value.

They are the un-thinking people, who fail to realize the truth that the value wealth of a diamond resides in its quality, NOT in the complexity of facets cut upon its surface.

In this course, I give you VERY SIMPLE means of awakening the Brain of Spirit, - so simple you may at first wonder how they can produce the marvelously great results.

These simple means produce results, because they UNIFY divine power WITH the silent power of movement; WITH harmonious unheard tones; WITH your deepest soul desire!

THE GREATER SPIRITUAL RESPONSIVENESS OF BODY

AND

AWAKENING THE BRAIN OF SPIRIT

by Brown Landone

INITIATING THE MIGHTY OVERTONES - - - - - - - - - - - - - LESSON VIII

ALL your body is ALWAYS vibrating with mystic sound.
(1) there are ordinary tones which you can hear;
(2) OVERTONES of these tones which you sometimes hear;
(3) higher overtones, absolutely SILENT to your ear;
(4) mighty overtones which have UNIMAGINABLE POWER, and unite with the higher silent overtones of your body.

In the laboratory we have proved that all tones have power!
That sounds you can hear, can DISINTEGRATE bones.
That silent overtones of singing STONE crystals can sterilize milk.
That still higher overtones can increase the energy of animals, so they increase their activities ten times, without increased fatigue!
Then in human life we have proved, that silent overtones initiated by bones of love in your own voice, can awaken TITANIC energy, increase activity, without increase of fatigue.

Let me explain simply, what an overtone is.
When vibrations of a tone are DOUBLED, its simplest over-tone is produced. These can be doubled again - MULTIPLIED and MULTIPLIED! These are over-tones!
A few of these can be heard by the ear - as in music.
The 19th overtone of an initial violin tone is exception-ally beautiful, and can be heard by some ears.
But thousands of the higher overtones are absolutely SILENT to our ears; yet they possess mighty power.

You already know that overtones can ring in your finger tips.
Now, please learn that overtones - produced by your own voice, CAN and DO vibrate in ALL PARTS OF YOUR BODY.

Often a person, when talking over a telephone, wishes to say something to a person standing near by, which he does not wish the person at the other end to hear.
So he foolishly puts the receiver of the telephone to his chest, while making the side remark to the person nearby.

8-33

This is silly; if you put the transmitter against your chest while talking - the person at the other end CAN hear what you are saying - sometimes more clearly than when you talk into the phone, - for tones of your voice DO vibrate through your TORSO as well as in your voice.

If you hold the palm of your hand flat on the UPPER BACK of a deep-voiced man when he is talking, - you CAN feel the overtones of his voice even in the MUSCLES of his back; and HEAR them, if you place your ear against his back.

If you place a microphone against your UPPER CHEST, you can broadcast through its muscle and bone. When another person is telephoning you, if you place the ear-piece of your telephone flat against the sides of your head, you CAN hear by means of your HEAD BONES!

Moreover, even YOUR ABDOMEN often feels deep overtones.
You have FELT such tones many times, when listening to a mighty pipe organ, either at church or at a movie theatre.
Even the FEET can both feel AND hear tones!
Deaf people at a concert hear music by feeling its tones vibrate through their FEET on the floor.

Every tone produces overtones. When you speak, the tones of YOUR VOICE produce marvelous overtones.
You hear them only when they vibrate through air to your ears.
But your voice produces thousands of the higher overtones IN your body. These you never hear.

These SILENT overtones - produced by YOUR OWN voice - always vibrate in your body - when you talk or hum or sing.
They actually pulsate in every nerve and brain cell, and activate ALL cells and EVERY PART of your body.
They produce AMAZING POWER in your own body.

You can USE such overtones of your own voice to tune-up your body's vibrations, to make it RESPONSIVE to spirit.
Every mediumly LOW tone, starts thousands of silent overtones of great power vibrating in your body.
Every low tone you HUM, produces mighty UNHEARD overtones of mighty power IN your body. They are always SILENT to your ears, but their AMAZING POWER can transform your body.

And every deep LOVING tone of your speaking voice produces unheard overtones of ATTRACTING and CONSTRUCTIVE power - the same power which holds electrons together in atoms, cells together in your body, and stars together in space.

ANY tone you speak or HUM or sing - IF somewhat LOW for your voice and IF it is a LOVE tone - can produce unheard silent over-tones which can work miracles in your body - IF you unify them with strong DESIRE and Love and Action!

In this alone, you possess power - as of a king or a god!
On earth there are 2,000,000,000 people!
In your body there are 800,000,000,000,000 cells.
Every cell is a very intelligent individual.
And all these billions of cells live IN the overtones you
initiate by the tones of your voice or your humming.

No stretch of imagination can visualize the tremendous
power you possess in your tones, not only to heal the body, and
harmonize its cells, but also to give you power, increase endurance, and augment activity with lessened fatigue.

These silent overtones - which your ear never hears, although
produced by your own voice - are the true spoken "Word".
The 'Om' that is hummed aloud, is only the materialized,
devitalized, despiritualized substitute of the true word!
The true higher 'word' is always silent!

It is silence that gives power.
You already know that the two-cylinder auto that chugs along
at 8 miles an hour is very noisy and has little power; while the
16 cylinder auto which can speed 90 miles an hour, is almost
silent, and has comparatively great power.
The nearer to silence, the greater the power.

Think what one complaining tone can do to your body!
No wonder "winners" are always failures.
In contrast, vision a thousand silent overtones of harmony
initiated by the love and power tones of your voice creating peace
among 800,000,000,000,000 cells - giving them power of unified
action. The ease that is vibrant health!

Prove to yourself that humming DOES produce overtones in
your body; place your hands flat on your chest, and HUM!
ANY low overtone, which your hands feel, IS POWERFUL!
As you hum such tones, they first produce overtones you can
hear. Then, the SILENT overtones which PENETRATE to every cell,
and reach even the Brain of Spirit itself.

You do NOT need to sing to initiate such overtones.
Just HUM - humming produces very POWERFUL overtones!
And IF humming tones VARY from day to day, that is good.

LEARN to hum, mediumly low and loving tones.
NOT back in your mouth, but in your chest and then far forward on your teeth, just as though you were a boy again, playing
on a comb covered with tissue paper.

Do NOT try to hear the tones you hum!

Instead, try to FEEL their mystic silent overtones - vibrating through EVERY CELL of EVERY ORGAN of your body.

The tone you hum is only an ordinary tone.
But its mystic OVERTONES vibrate UNHEARD through your body; they TUNE-UP its tissues, so that every cell actually sings the silent harmony that pulsates among the stars!

Use this TRUE 'Inner Voice' and the TRUE 'Spoken Word'.
They ARE of spirit, not of mere words.
They are vibrant inner overtones of silence.

Use the Divine Mind God has given you, to guide you.

Use the Divine Love God has given you, to transform your soul attitude; and initiate tones that will harmonize 800,000,000,000,000 cells in your body, so that they will work together in perfect harmony without friction.
This means health, and also tremendous power and energy.

And use the Divine Spirit to awaken the deeper desire, to be unified WITH the overtones of love, your own voice, and WITH movement of your body - to break down its old and crystallized stiffness - to open it up to spirit, so that it will respond to spirit and let spirit flow fully.

The means I teach is so simple, it has tremendous power.
Even if it did nothing more than break down the stiffened crystallization of aging, - that alone would be a MIRACLE!

At least twice daily - at ANY time, and for AS MANY minutes as you wish - stand up, FEELING at ease, and as adjustable to the spirit as a willow tree is to the wind.
Gently SWAY your body, as a willow tree in a gentle breeze.
Sway from your ankles; away from your waist line - forward and back a little, then side to side - and always EASILY!

I know that this alone is NOTHING new; BUT the UNITY of high thought, WITH deep feeling, WITH mighty overtones, WITH easy movement - IS new - true ONENESS in expressing spirit.

So let the body sway, sway, sway - just a little; and easily and with rhythm.
Sway rhythmically as you hum, hum - low and lovingly.

The ancient mystics knew this secret of UNIFYING the mighty power of silent overtones with movement!
BUT they knew very little about the human body.
So they made two errors: (1) they insisted on IMITATING the tone of a master - their teacher; and (2) because of the restrictions of their religious ceremonies, they used an ERECT SITTING position while humming.

The first error is an error; your soul is YOUR soul, and your body is YOUR body. Hence you should use your own tone.

The second error results in fixation - and hence they spend years in trying to attain, what we can now attain quickly.

In the NEXT Lesson, I carry this work further - teach you a prayer of actual unification of spirit with action - the true wedding of the spirit and the substance in each cell.

Let ALL you do, be SIMPLY done, and power WILL come!

It works like this: the silent overtones of the humming, TUNE-UP 800,000,000,000,000 little cells of your body to vibrate with power.

The silent overtones are harmonious, so the love quality in the humming TUNES-UP ALL OF THESE CELLS to vibrate in harmony.

Then the easy swaying rhythmic movement breaks down the stiffened and aged conditions of years, and lets spirit flow.

Your desire of what you want to attain, awakens impulse to attain - resulting in action by all cells of your body UNIFYING all powers of your soul, awakening the Brain of Spirit itself, and opening the body to spirit energy.

One thing more in this Lesson!

Please in all work of awakening the Brain of Spirit, begin PRAYERFULLY and LOVINGLY.

Do NOT try to secure quick results.

If you could awaken the Spirit Brain instantly, its power might destroy your body. Even its substance is so powerful that if a physician should inject one drop of its pure substance into your blood, its power would tear through your body, even rip muscles apart.

In this work, you are NOT working with mere Mind, which merely 'thinks' about power.

You are NOW awakening power itself - SPIRIT - the greatest power of the universe.

IF you do the work as I give it to you to do, the awakening will be normal, and the results TRANSFORMING!

THE GREATER SPIRITUAL RESPONSIVENESS OF BODY

AND

AWAKENING THE BRAIN OF SPIRIT

by Brown Landone

THE MYSTIC 'WEDDING' OF SPIRIT AND MATTER - - - - - - LESSON IX

Use all your powers - actually USE them, and use ALL of them!

Use them to unify the deepest desires of your soul with its
highest ideals, with mighty mystic overtones of spirit, with
actual movement of the body itself, for the most complete expression.
Thus, you bring the power in you, into actual manifestation.

I give you an Action-Prayer for such Actual Unification.
It unifies the spirit that moves the stars, with the spirit in
you, with the substance of every cell of your body.

There are many prayers of words and thought and feeling.

But this prayer is four-fold communion with God.
Its silent tone tunes your body to vibrate with spirit.
Its movement frees the body of its tensity of years.
Its aspiration awakens the brain of spirit.
Its desire impels spirit to flow into every bodily cell!

This supreme unity is attained ONLY when soul realizes, and
then actualizes its own unity in spirit and action.
This prayer of high ideal and deep soul desire is unified with
body movement and unheard tones in perfect harmony.

To prepare for this, I ask you first to learn WHICH tones to
use in such a prayer, to actually wed matter and spirit, to create
a holy oneness in each cell of your body.

You have already heard the quality of overtones vibrating in
the flesh and blood and bone of your finger tips.
But in this prayer, you initiate even higher overtones to
vibrate through the cells of your body.

In this prayer, you initiate these higher tones by humming.

But in your humming do NOT IMITATE any tone of any other per-
son, or of any musical instrument.
NO two souls or human bodies are alike in manifestation.
The finger prints of NO two finger-tips are the same.

9-38

Even bone cells differ with EVERY person!
NO two people have the same cellular structure.

Since all overtones vary with the spirit of the person and
also with the structure of the body, NO tone of any other person
is as beneficial to you as your own tones.

This fact is basic truth - YOUR tones are best for you!
Please do NOT try to imitate tones of any teacher or master.

To attain the amazing results we desire, the tones you hum
must be mediumly LOW for your voice, and they must express LOVE!

Such tones will tune-up every cell of your body, by the unknown powers of inner sound - vast, silently throbbing overtones
initiated by your own voice.
These silent overtones possess mighty power, even though your
ear never hears them.

So learn to HUM - hum - HUM! Learn to hum such tones - low
and loving - before you begin to use the action-prayer.

First, determine the approximate pitch of tones to be hummed.
And do NOT try to imitate the pitch of any tone of a piano, or
the pitch of any tuning-fork.
Make the pitch of your humming, like the tone YOU would use,
to express your greatest love to the one you love the most!
Then it WILL respond to mystic overtones of stars and atoms.

Make the tone - pleasing, easy to hum, low and loving.

Remember, the swaying and humming in Lesson VIII.
In that, the purpose of the easy sway was to free the body of
tensity, and to prepare it for inflow of spirit.
In this prayer of action, the purpose is different; it is to
TAKE-IN spirit, and WED it to matter.

Learn this movement next: BEND forward and down, just as you
do when you try to touch your toes with your fingers.
Do NOT bend far down; bend only as far as is easy for you.
Merely bend forward and downward, and up again, EASILY.

This bending is NOT like the gymnastic or military exercise
in which you try to keep the legs straight, while bending to touch
your toes. This bending is not for goose-step efficiency.

DO NOT try to keep the legs straight as you bend forward.

This bending should free the body to respond to spirit.
So let the hips sag backward.
This is what I mean by bending easily.

By itself, there is NOTHING new in this, EXCEPT that - in bending forward, as you do in this prayer - you push _out_ the lower part of your back a little.

This gives more vibrating space for unheard overtones to multiply near the sacral brain of life!
And these overtones increase their POWER astoundingly with increase of torso space.

Hence with this easy bending movement, you _unify_ use of silent overtones, with their power multiplied many times!

The preceding nine lines, contain the key to the power of the organ tone quality of the voices of the mystics!

What follows is - The Tonal-Action-Prayer.

EACH MORNING when arising, and EACH NIGHT before retiring, use this simple-powerful tonal-action-prayer.

Slowly bend forward easily, and as you bend, hum!
Hum a _low tone_ - a tone that is easy for you to hum, pleasing to your ear, with all the feeling of LOVE you can put into it.
Then straighten up, humming the same tone while doing so.

Stand erect a second - quiet, looking forward and upward - to mountain tops of vision of the goal you desire!

Then bend again; straighten up again, always humming.
Stand a second - eyes to mountain top of your desire!

Repeat this, until you bend down and straighten up, SEVEN TIMES each morning; and seven times each evening.

Please do not 'time' your movements - that injects thoughts of mind into it - stiffens action, opposes spirit.
Instead, let spirit in you direct you - joyfully, freely.

Move slowly or not, just as you feel like doing; and certainly, time of movement may vary each morning, each night!

Then after one week's use of this action-prayer, follow the above - each night and morn - by expressing your high ideal and deep love in words - as given in verses which follow.
But do NOT speak the words distinctly; always keep something of the HUM in your tones, as you speak.
The humming tones are more powerful than speech, in silently multiplying the unheard overtones of mighty power in your body.

Stand easily erect, and look to spirit power sublime; and vision what you long to be, and thus repeat or read the following, with vibrant hope and certainty divine:

"I STAND expectant here; my aspirations reach unto the stars;
My soul is longing now, to in-spire mighty energies divine;
My body too is hungry for the vibrant mystic power sublime;
And every cell awaits the thrill of energies of silent songs;
That permeate all atoms here, and all the universe afar."

Then next, BEND easily and low, and use these words:

"I BEND, and bending, feel the vibrant spirit power
Of mystic harmony, inspire itself into each cell -
Into eight hundred thousand billion cells -
Into each cell of which my body is composed!
I urge each cell to joyfully respond unto the power
That swirls from God to me - a great transforming stream
To permeate and flow throughout my body NOW - this very hour!"

AND NOW, LIFT UP your body once again, and pray:

"I RISE again, a-tuned to all the power of worlds of space -
Each cell a-thrill with silent energies divine -
Each cell alive with mystic harmony sublime -
Awakening in me, the power that meets God face to face."

Each factor of this prayer, ALONE by itself - that is, its
words, or thought, feeling, or movement - may not accomplish much!
    BUT WHEN they are UNITED, as I ask you to unite them in this
prayer, they MULTIPLY each other's power a thousand fold!

Yet since it is so simple, please do not pass it by.
It is the simplest means, which has the greatest power.

When unified, these means in-spire (take-in) the silent
powers of stars, to vibrate in and through your body!
    And then, the unheard overtones of your own humming voice will
unify themselves with powers of God and all his universe!

They open up the channels of your body, tune it up to full response to spirit, so that the inflow shall reach down into the Brain
of Spirit deep within, and awaken it to free UNDREAMED of power for
you to use.

Of course, you've oft awakened powers of Mind!
    But THIS IS SPIRIT - far more POWERFUL - a million times -
perhaps a billion times - more powerful than mind!

In succeeding Lessons, I teach you to use the Holy Spiral -
to awaken the IMPELLING power within, to FLOW OUT - freely, fully -
into action, to create the actualities of life.

THE GREATER SPIRITUAL RESPONSIVENESS OF BODY

AND

AWAKENING THE BRAIN OF SPIRIT

by Brown Landone

MYSTERIOUS "LIKENESS" OF MOVEMENT - BODY AND SPIRIT - - LESSON X

In this work you are awakening response to spirit!

Spirit is neither a stagnant nor a theoretical power.
Spirit is the cosmic moving power of ALL the universe.
Spirit is the ONE moving power of atoms and cells and stars.

In all ages, savages as well as mystics, have sensed the true nature of the movement of spirit.
In our language today - and in all ancient writings - the words 'spirit' and 'spiral' come from the same basic word root.

EVERY mystic uses these two words as the same. The truth that spirit means spiral, reveals the WAY in which spirit moves!

I have taught you to tune-up the cells of your body by use of mystic overtones of silent sound; and taught you to blend vibrations of substance and spirit in rhythm to movement unified with the power of silent tone.

Now, I teach you the movement of spirit - the holy spiral!

But please carry on this work prayerfully and lovingly.
Do NOT try to secure quick results, either in awakening the Brain of Spirit, or securing spiritual responsiveness of body.

IF you should awaken the spirit brain instantly, its freed spirit power would destroy your body.

This is no mere scare line, - for even the pure SUBSTANCE of this brain has titanic power.
If a physician were able to secure one drop of its pure substance, and inject it into your blood, its power would act like a bolt of lightning, rip all muscles from your bones, rip them into shreds, and make even your heart a mere mass of fringe.

But do not worry about the possibility of this happening to you. If any physician ever obtains a drop of this pure substance, he will hire a body-guard to protect it, for it is worth many million dollars a drop - much more precious than radium.

10-42

I cite its power (1) only that you may recognize how many billion times more powerful spirit is than mind, (2) that you may recognize the immensity of power that can thrill a spiritually responsive body; and (3) I write of the greatness of this power, so that you shall never try to rush the results of attainment of response to spirit.

Work LOVINGLY, to tune-up your body, first!

And remember you can not awaken spirit, by mind action.
So start first, with mystic silent sound, then rhythmic movement, and then spiral movement.

There are great unknown powers in such means.
You have already heard marvelous overtones of cathedral bells ringing in your finger tips.
There are a thousand other unknown powers of sound!
And there are many other initiative powers of God.

Spirit power is millions of times greater than mind power, because spirit is spiralling power, and all spiral powers are magically greater, than powers that vibrate forward in straight lines.
You remember that an electric current of 25,000 volts kills the body; but that when it is lifted-up to a million volts and its frequency increased, it thrills and transforms the body.
So it is, with all spiral powers.

Please read the following paragraphs on vibration of power IN substance, many times!

First, no power can move beneficially through a substance, unless the vibratory movement of the substance is lifted-up until it is like the movement of the power.

Second, UNLESS the vibration of the substance is thus lifted-up, the power either destroys the substance, or else it does not even manifest in it.

For example, electricity will either shatter glass to powder, or it will not manifest through glass, because the vibratory movement of glass is not lifted-up to the vibration of electricity.

So also light can not shine through iron, because the vibration of iron is too slow for the vibration of light.

Third, a power can NOT manifest beneficially through a substance UNLESS the vibration of the substance is lifted-up TO the vibration of the power.
This IS absolute law. You can NOT attain great manifestation of spiritual power, unless your body vibration is lifted-up to vibrate in the same way spirit vibrates!

Fourth, you can NOT do this with thought; for thought always vibrates forward in a straight line, while spirit speeds forward in spirals!

This is why thought or mind has always hindered free expression of spirit all your life.

Fifth, spirit can exist without a body, but it can not manifest without something to manifest through - a body of substance lifted-up to the spiral vibration of spirit.

Sixth, spirit can manifest in a part of your body, without being radiated throughout the rest of your body.

For example, spirit may manifest in your brain, and make you conscious of it, without manifesting throughout the body.
This makes it possible to 'think' spiritual ideals, even though the rest of your body lacks spiritual power.
This leads many a person to think he is spiritual, merely because he thinks about spiritual ideals!

Seventh, when spirit actually manifests through your body, it transforms it. To attain such transformation, your body must be lifted-up to the spiritual or spiral vibration.

Eighth, the movement IN any substance is always LIKE the movement of the power, which is moving that substance.

Ninth, when you see anything moving forward in a straight line, you KNOW it is being moved by some power that vibrates forward in a straight line.
And when you see anything moving in a spiral, you know that it could not move in a spiral, unless moved by a power that is a spiral moving power.

Tenth, the movement of the power moving a substance of body must be like the movement of the substance or the body, otherwise the substance is disintegrated and its form destroyed.

This is the most important law of physics.
It has never yet been taught in colleges.

Eleventh, we know that mind moves in a straight line vibratory movement, because it always tends to make the body and every part of the body move in straight line movements.
So also we know that spirit is a spiral moving power, because the power of spirit always tends to make parts of the body move in spiral movements.

Hence, you can easily determine what kind of soul power is moving in your body, at any particular time.

If some power moves your arm in straight line movement, then that power must be a straight line moving power, otherwise it could not produce straight line movement.

And if a power tends to move your body in half spiral movements, then the power which is producing such movements, must of itself be a spiral-moving power.

PROVE these truths for yourself, before a mirror.

Twelfth, stand before a mirror, and imagine yourself directing a stranger, how to reach a place he wishes to find.

Tell him to drive four blocks straight ahead, then three blocks to the right.

Gesture with your arm as you give him these directions.

Watch your movements in the mirror.

You use your mind to direct the man, and to move your arm; hence it is mind which determines the kind of movement your arm makes at such a time.

As you point the way the stranger should go, your arm tends to move in straight lines; even your fore-finger is straight as you point the directions.

Thirteenth, now express the LOVE of your soul, and watch your movements as you look in the mirror.

Your little grand-daughter comes into the room and rushes to you. You smile, and take her in your arms.

Every straight line in your face, changes.

Every line tends to be curved. You can not even smile in straight lines.

Now stand before the mirror, and imagine yourself trying to embrace someone lovingly, by moving your arms in straight lines only. It is grotesque, burlesque!

Fourteenth, since love moves in WAVE lines, it makes your body tend to move in curved movements.

I use the phrase "tend" to move, because there are bones in your body, and no body movement can be a perfect curve or a complete spiral.

Fifteenth, love tends to make your body movements curved, and spirit tends to make them spiral movements.

Sixteenth, even strong efficient physical power, tends to move in spirals, just as spiritual power does.

To throw a ball with power, the baseball pitcher twists his body into a half spiral from his feet to his head, and even moves his arm in a half spiral as he pitches.

Seventeenth, standing before the mirror, imagine yourself pitching a ball by straight line movements.

Imagine you have the ball in your hand, lift your arm in a straight line, to throw the ball STRAIGHT forward.

Do NOT twist or spiral your arm in THIS test.

If you move it in straight lines, you will look like a wooden man, with hinges at wrist, and elbow and shoulder.

And the movement is so weak, it makes you feel weak, and look like a sissy to others.

Imagine what your habitual straight line tendency of movement, has been doing to the cells of your body for years - vibrating through every tissue, every organ, and every cell.

Eighteenth; now test the power effect of spiral movement on your body.

Twist your body to throw a ball as a baseball pitcher does!

Imagine the great increased power that will come to you, by changing from habitual weak-feeling straight line movement, TO spiral movement of spirit power.

Nineteenth, commit these four truths to memory!

Mind always tends to produce movement in straight lines!

Love tends to produce wave and curve movements.

Life and power always tend to produce spiral movements.

Spirit is the supreme spiral power of the universe.

Twentieth, every power moving in a substance, adapts the particles or cells of substance to the nature of its own power.

If it did not do this, the substance would be destroyed.

Twenty-first, mind always moves in straight lines, hence it tends to make the cells and tissues, through which it vibrates, like unto itself - that is, straight-lined!

Twenty-second, when mind vibrates through a cell, the inner particles of the cell form in straight lines. This leads to crystallization - a mentalized, stiffened, aged cell.

Twenty-third, it is impossible for the spiral whirl of spirit to flow freely in a body, if its cells are crystallized by mind.

Twenty-fourth, watch your movements in a mirror, and even though you have lived Truth for twenty years - ask yourself if you have been using mind truth, or spirit power.

Twenty-fifth, spirit is the ONLY spiral-moving power.

It is the holy spiral of the universe - the Holy Spirit of the Mystics.

Twenty-sixth, mind can awaken mind to illumined ideas; but it can also produce the hallucination that you possess spiritual power, when you do not.

Spirit is the only IN-spiring power of the universe.

Twenty-seventh, for the greater awakening of the Brain of Spirit and greater spiritual responsiveness of the body, the body itself must be lifted-up to the highest spiritual vibration of the universe - lifted up to respond in movement to the holy spiral.

Twenty-eighth, for inflow of spirit, the vibratory movements of your body must be changed, FROM straight line vibrations of mind, TO the spiral movement and spiritual vibration of spirit, - that is, the vibratory movement of your body must be lifted-up so that it is like the movement of spirit itself.

Twenty-ninth, the change from straight line movement, to use of the holy spiral, IS the change from death to life of your body - from slow dying day by day to the in-spiring of new life hourly.

Thirtieth, since the purpose of this work I am giving you is to secure actual manifestation for you, - then mere "contemplation" of spirit power is not enough, and too much affirmation and meditation of thought, may so crystallize the body that inspiration of spirit, is hindered.

Nothing but actual manifestation of spirit, changes and transforms the body and creates heaven for you here and now.

Thirty-first, movement of any power in a body prepares the body for greater inspiration of that power.
Every movement of your body is the expression of some power producing the movement.
And every movement sets up its own kind of vibration in the cells of your body.

Straight movement prepares the body for greater mentalization and crystallization.

Wave movement opens the channels for greater inflow of love.

Spiral movement prepares the body for greater inflow of the holy spiral of spirit.

THE GREATER SPIRITUAL RESPONSIVENESS OF BODY

AND

AWAKENING THE BRAIN OF SPIRIT

by Brown Landone

TRAINING MUSCLES TO SPIRAL MOVEMENT - - - - - - - - - - - - LESSON XI

To realize the necessity of changing your body, to an habitual tendency to spiral movement, stand before a mirror, and

(1) Imagine that you are a very old man - so very stiffened that you can not even turn your head, except in straight line movements.

(2) Imagine yourself to be a youth playing baseball or tennis (or watch a youth playing such a game) and note how many different twists there are in the movement of the body.

Old age is largely restriction to straight line movement, because as man restricts his body to straight line movement, he shuts off manifestation of spiritual power, and limits the body to pure mental effort to move.

Moreover, if you watch any 100 people, you find that every movement which gives charm and attractiveness and vitality to a personality, tends to be a spiral movement.

But please, use common sense both in your judgment of what I mean by a spiral movement of the body, and as well as in your work of carrying out the activities suggested below.

Use sense with spirit; never twist, or attempt any spiral movement which does not appear to be a graceful, and which does not feel easy and powerful.

Anything that looks grotesque in movement - as you watch yourself in a mirror - is evidence that you are over-doing the effort to awaken easy spiral movement.

I suggest seven different activities to help you change your habitual tendency of movement.

But first, I give you a basic spiral movement (BSM) that is the basis of each activity, one to seven, given below.

11-48

The BSM is this:
Stand easily with feet a little apart, and with your weight
on one foot.
Twist your body easily in a part spiral to the left; then
back to front.
Then in a part spiral to the right, and back to the front.

The above is the BSM, to which I refer below.

And please remember - any twist of body suggested in this
work, must not be grotesque, but easy and graceful.

There are reasons for this training in spiral movement:

(1) Each spiral movement gives you increased feeling of
manifested power!
(2) It lifts up the vibratory condition of your body to be
ready to respond to spirit;
(3) Since it is spiral in movement, it turns your consciousness from feelings of weakness, to a certainty of power in action.

The following are the seven spiral activities to use to change
your body from its present habitual action, to more youthful, more
inspiring, more powerful activity.

These begin with slow and gentle twisting of body, and proceed
to stronger and more viril spiral movement.

FIRST, carry through BSM (see top of this page), and think
of a vine climbing upward - reaching to spirit and to sunlight.

During the BSM, either repeat or at least think, the thought
of these lines:

I thrill to the surge of life
As tendrils are thrilled at sunrise
I thrill to the surge of life
As tendrils are thrilled at sunrise
Sunrise, Sunrise!
As tendrils are thrilled at sunrise.

SECOND, make the twisting of your body a little stronger now,
and think of another form of life - the wonderfully beautiful twisting of a young panther.
Think only of the beauty of its movement - the grace, the ease,
the suppleness.

Using BSM, twist your body as a panther at play, and while
doing this, think the thought that follows, or commit it to memory
and repeat it:

I twist myself slowly 'round
As lithe as a panther at play
I twist myself slowly around
As lithe as a panther at play.
As lithe, as lithe!
As lithe as a panther at play.

THIRD, now increase consciousness of spiral power.
Use BSM, and think of yourself as a wire spring.
Imagine you are twisting you body up as a spring, and then
letting it untwist a little more rapidly than during the twisting.
FOURTH, use BSM, and put your body into position to throw
a ball as a baseball pitcher pitches a ball.

Pull your arm behind you, and half twist your body to the
rear. Then let your body untwirl as a spring untwirls, and
throw the imaginary ball with a feeling of power!

This helps to adjust every large muscle of your body to a
spiral movement, and to make every cell of such muscles responsive to the movement of spirit power.

FIFTH, now add thought and feeling to the BSM of twisting
spiralling, to develop a tendency of such movement of your body.

For a minute each night and each morning - with use of BSM
- move your arm forward and upward, imagining that you are a
public speaker, proclaiming a great truth to audiences.

With this BSM body and arm action, use these words:

The power of spirit rules this earth;
And war shall pass, and peace shall reign, -
For holy spirit is supreme
On earth and in the universe!

In proclaiming this, do NOT move your arm upward in a
straight line gesture, as a prim old woman, or a stiffened old
man.
Instead, move your arm and hand, out and up, in a half-
spiral, - in a gesture of power.

SIXTH, use the BSM now, with a consciousness of youth,
instead of that of age.
Imitate in your twisting, any activity you have seen in
the movement of a child at play, or a youth in games.
Don't 'think' of being a child or a youth, but feel the
spirit of the child or youth in you - expressing in movement
as the child or youth expresses the power of life in them -
the newness of life.

All these seven activities do initiate a new tendency of
spiral movement within the body.

Do NOT try to make a whirling spiral of your body!

Instead, establish an habitual tendency to spiral movement -
to free you from the dominant and habitual straight line movement
which ages the cells, lessens free movement, and stiffens muscle
action.

This work brings back the spiral movement of youth!
The spiral movement is dominant in youth.
The straight line movement is dominant in old age.

The ancient mystics knew the power of the holy spiral. It
affects every cell of your body, and prepares the body for greater
inflow of spiritual power.

And spiritual power is different from mind, - a million times
greater than mind power.

SEVENTH, think of the spiral movement as symbol of life, -
ever tending to spiral up from earth toward heaven.

Using the BSM, respond to the feeling of life within you,
moving upward through your body, and outward through the fingers
of your uplifted hands, using just such arm motion as you did when
proclaiming the power of a great truth to an audience.

Repeat several times, spiralling a little faster each time,
to break down the stiffened straight-lined, mentalized, crystallized,
old-aged condition of your body.

But please understand that none of these seven activities are
evidence of spiritual power in your body.

These activities are given to train the muscles of the body to
a tendency of spiral movement, so that the body will be fitted to
respond to spirit, ready for the power of spirit to move through it.

Do this work, and you shall begin to manifest spirit - the
highest power of the universe, changing your body from an aging
structure, to one thrilled by youthful spirit!

A few souls in all ages have risen to this height! And now,
thousands - because of our new knowledge - can change their bodies
to greater manifestation of spirit in action.

I am praying, friend, that you shall be one of them.

In the next lesson, I teach you to unify the holy spiral of
movement, WITH the mystic powers of silent tone, WITH the power
of rhythm - and to blend all in the oneness of spirit.

THE GREATER SPIRITUAL RESPONSIVENESS OF BODY

AND

AWAKENING THE BRAIN OF SPIRIT

by Brown Landone

THE RHYTHMIC MULTIPLYING POWER - - - - - - - - - - - - - LESSON XII

The strangest thing in life to me is our stupidity!

We fail for years, to recognize the great astounding means of
powers all around us all the time - e'er waiting to be used.
You know rhythm has power - just a few minutes of flowing
RHYTHMIC music which you like - IS a rest.
And no matter how fatigued you are, you can oft dance for an
hour to RHYTHMIC music, and be rested by it.

We have known this truth for centuries, and yet we have not
recognized that rhythm IS a power of God - an operative power to
be USED to multiply our energy 100 fold!

You also know your little heart does work each hour, which
would exhaust 4 husky men, each weighing 175 pounds.
It is strange that a RHYTHMIC beat can perform such a miracle!

We know gigantic stars have circled on for eons of time!
We know God moves them RHYTHMICALLY; we know that their titanic
energies, are TIRELESS for many billion years.

We know that jerking movements exhaust us, and rhythm rests us!
We know we can dance to rhythm without fatigue; but that JERKING
the same muscles about spasmodically for the same length of time,
would nervously exhaust us.

We know that RHYTHMIC music in cigar factories INCREASES production more than 300% - increasing energy of workers, three times!
But have you thought of using rhythm, to increase your energy
300% every hour?

We know that engineers found that husky steel plant workers
were exhausted from carrying $12\frac{1}{2}$ tons of pig iron a day.
And that the same men - when taught to move rhythmically -
carried $47\frac{1}{2}$ tons a day with LESS fatigue!

We have been stupid, in not realizing that rhythm - which gives
your heart the power of four husky men - IS a power!

Think of your little heart, and the SECRET of its amazing energy.
There is NOTHING extraordinary about its muscle fibers or its
nerves. Yet its power transcends anything purely muscular or physical!
It weighs about 12 ounces; Yet each hour, it does work enough,
to lift 2.1 TONS of concrete one foot off the ground!
It works every hour, day and night, for sixty or a hundred
years!

What ARE the TWO secrets of its power?
(1) your 'mind' almost completely lets it alone;
(2) its RHYTHM nears PERFECTION!

It makes us ashamed, that we have been so stupid, that we have
not recognized that rhythm IS a POWER to be USED.

Rhythm is one of the great operative soul powers.
It banishes fatigue; and multiplies power a 1000 times!

Think of your heart, and then vision what rhythm can do for
all your body - increasing energy many times, and transforming the
activities of every organ of your body!

Rhythm possesses its titanic power, because it is of spirit.
Spirit itself is RHYTHMIC!
If Spirit were not rhythmic, it would have caused so much
friction, that it would have disrupted the universe eons ago!

Since Spirit IS rhythmic, you cannot greatly increase your
body's response to spirit, unless your body is made more rhythmic.

NO, I do NOT mean that you must dance rhythmic dances; or frequently skip about on toe-tips - waving your arms!

BUT I DO mean that your body will NOT respond to Spirit in its
fullness, UNLESS it moves with an INNER rhythm, from the soles of
your feet to top of head and tips of fingers!

The phenomenal power of rhythm is proven to be titanic even in
ordinary work. Remember the husky steel workers.

To attain the greater MANIFESTATION of spirit you desire, you
must tune-up your body to rhythmic movement.

Energy is energy; and energy in rhythmic action is tireless!
Rhythm in action is the "lost chord" of our use of our powers!

Most people, as you know, use up "lots of energy" without attaining great results, because they lack the power of rhythm, and
try to live contrary to the spirit power of the universe!
UNIFY your desire with movement, with silent tone, and with
rhythm, and you attain the perfect ONENESS of power.

Even my instructions of this Lesson, I soon give in rhythm, so that - if you but read them every day - and LET your body respond in rhythm to the words - with beating throb of INNER rhythm - it will prepare your entire body to respond to spirit.

In this, it makes little difference whether or not you can carry the tune of any particular musical air.

Just sort of chant or sing or hum the words; to any kind of a song or chant - or use a tune that you make up - and e'en a different one each day or hour - if that appeals to you.
Tap out the rhythmic beat of the words; or move your entire body with it, - for rhythm is VIRILE power of earth and heaven.

It is not necessary to learn the sections which follow.
But keep the words by you, and read them several times each day and let your body MOVE a little with the rhythm - entire body or a part of it - e'en tapping out the rhythm with your foot, or swaying with it.

Do NOT be afraid to let your body feel the virile rhythmic power of God.
It is the ONLY means of manifesting tireless energy - of stars, or atoms, or of body or cells.

As overtones tune-up vibration of the body cells, so rhythm tunes up the MOVEMENT of the body, to throb with spirit power, and then multiplies the power, 1,000 fold!

So read RHYTHMICALLY the words which follow, until their rhythm is HABITUAL to you - habitual to every organ, every cell, - so each will feel the rhythmic beat of every other cell, and multiply your manifested power a thousand fold.

I wish you now to feel, and strongly feel the rhythmic beat of marching men!

I want you to feel the rhythm, within your consciousness; pulsating in and through your body, till it throbs with rhythmic power in every cell.

I want you now to let your body move in full response to the simple rhythm of the words which follow below.

I want you to feel the virile rhythmic power of God that multiplies all other powers a thousand fold!

I want you to "think" of this, as little as you can; but to feel so much that it will thrill you through and through.

I want you to live the Master's word, to "take no anxious thought" for anything; but to live each hour so that his joy shall be fulfilled in you.

"This hour, I put myself in rhythmic tune
With all the harmony of all the universe!

"I close my eyes and vision all my body cells -
Eight hundred thousand billion cells -
Alive with rhythmic harmony
That comes from distant stars sublime,
To penetrate to deepest depths
And 'waken both my body and my soul to holy power divine!

"I let my body feel the rhythmic beat of stars!

"I let my body move in rhythmic harmony,
And dance with life that throbs in every cell!
I let each cell respond to music-movement born of stars--
That multiplies all other powers a thousand fold,
And makes of man, a god on earth -
And gives to him a life sublime
Of peace and love and joy and power divine.

Rhythm IS a divine operating power of the soul.
It is the means which God uses to make all great powers manifest the greatest good!

The proof is certain!
Use mind jerkily, and you set every cell in your body on edge,
and stir up antagonism of people around you!
Use love jerkily, and people will pity you, but not love you.
Use the life power jerkily, and you wreck your body!

Sometimes it is wise to use some light gay rhythmic movement,
as a start, in breaking down old fixed conditions - so that the
body will respond more easily to the higher rhythms.

If you have need to break down the old stiffened conditions,
then use some jaunty tune you know - such as "My Bonnie Lies Over
the Ocean" - and chant the words which follow, to that tune, -

"My body is thrilling to rhythm (rith-um)
And dancing to music of stars;
My body is dancing to rhythm
That multiplies pow-er in me.

"Rhythm, Rhythm,
Rhythm and power in me, in me
Rhythm, Rhythm,
That multiplies power in me.

"I thrill to the dancing of atoms
That dance to the rhythm of joy;
I dance to the rhythm of atoms
That multiplies power in me."

I wonder, if I hear you say, "Some people may need such work but I do not - for I dwell in the consciousness of Divine Mind, and all of truth is included in it!"

Certainly, all is included in what you term Divine Mind and that is why you should not shut out the Rhythm of God and His Holy Spiral and the Mystic Overtones of His creation!

Let me caution you, my friend, If you hold to the thought that all you need to do, is to "think" of the high ideals of God, then you are taking an ANTI-CHRIST attitude!

Christ positively taught that you can not add one cubit to your stature by thought, and he added that God is spirit, and that man must worship him in Spirit!

God conceived all things with infinite Love!

He used the holy spiral of spirit to whirl his stars into universes, electrons into atoms, and atoms into cells.

You can not deny the means God used, without failing to attain what you desire.

God used the mystic power of silent overtones to tune-up all manifestations to be at-one in divine harmony!
God used divine rhythm to bring all things he created into harmonious activity.

You can not neglect the use of these operative powers of God, without suffering the loss due to such neglect.

To become God-like, you must manifest as God manifests!

Tuning-up the body to constant inner rhythm, tunes-up the consciousness to constant feeling of peace and love and joy and power!

THE GREATER SPIRITUAL RESPONSIVENESS OF BODY

AND

AWAKENING THE BRAIN OF SPIRIT

by Brown Landone

THE <u>POWER</u> <u>OF</u> THE <u>HOLY</u> <u>UNITY-IN-USE</u> - - - - - - - - - <u>LESSON XIII</u>

I write this Lesson that you shall <u>not</u> <u>think</u> too much of the information given, but <u>feel</u> <u>more</u> - to get into the feeling of spirit - to be more ready to respond to spirit.

When you study the use of each power separately, it leads to much thinking and thought of mind.
But unity-in-use leads to a feeling of inspiring attainment, because as soon as they are in use, you have a <u>feeling</u> <u>of</u> <u>doing</u> <u>something</u>, and do not think so much about them.

It is like learning a new dance step. You think of its separate movements while learning; then stop thinking, and lose yourself in the joy of the music, and the movement, and the rhythm.

So in this, I lead you to unity-in-use, for joy in use.
This unity-in-use is the only means of attaining <u>actual</u> <u>oneness</u> of powers which makes you God-like, so that there shall be <u>no</u> failure in your efforts to attain whatsoever you desire.

Such oneness is a spiritual blend of all soul powers - of all CONCEPTIVE powers of <u>mind</u>, <u>love</u>, <u>life</u> and <u>spirit</u>; blended with use of all the OPERATING powers of the mystic unheard overtones, the silent spoken word, the holy spiral of spirit, and rhythm that multiplies the power of all.

<u>And</u> <u>the</u> <u>ACTIVATING</u> <u>power</u> of all soul powers is soul DESIRE!

Remember when I was seventeen - an invalid too weak to walk! Yet, when there was a fire, I dragged two heavy trunks of treasured manuscripts, down stairs and across the street.
The power to perform that feat was activated for the moment; and it was NOT awakened by 'thought', for if I had stopped to think about it, I could not have done it.

<u>My</u> power was activated by intense DESIRE to save the trunks, <u>WITHOUT</u> any thought of my illness or lack of strength.

13-57

Desire _is_ the spiritual catalyst of the soul, and the less
'thought' there is about it, the more powerful desire is!
So do not confuse desire with more "wish" or affirmation.

A wish of mind - or an affirmation - whether wishy-washy or
intense - is a head light, which - whether dim or brilliant -
merely reveals what you wish for.

But desire is different; it is spiritual ENGINE power!
It is always MOVING you to GET what you want!
It is the only power that turns all other powers into action!

Desire MOVES mind - not only to think, but to DO something
about what you think.
Desire moves love - not merely to love, but to do something to
win love and attain what you love.
Desire moves life - to multiply and reproduce results.
Desire MOVES spirit - to inspire man with God-power to work
transforming changes!

We have missed the use of this power of desire in the past,
because we have tried to awaken it by mind; and mind hinders it.
Now however, with new knowledge of the brain of spirit, a
new world is opening to us - the possibility of using desire at
ANY time to activate all the other soul powers, so that its use
will not be incidental, as in my dragging those trunks to the street.

Use the divine MIND in you to vision (1) your present status
in life, (2) the goal you wish to attain, (3) the powers you can
use to attain it; and (4) the means of using each power.
Use mind as a searchlight to seek out the goal!
Use it as a headlight to illumine the way to it.

And USE divine LOVE: Lovingly love all the billions of cells
of your body, so they will have their being IN your love, and so
love one another, that they will work in perfect harmony resulting
in enduring energy without fatigue!
And love every quality of every thing - its form, color,
sound, hardness or softness, roughness or smoothness, lightness or
weight; and - if a scientist - its chemical qualities; and then
you will find new abundance of which you have not dreamed.
Use love to love your fellowman; use it as the power that
holds all things together - stars in their courses, electrons
together in atoms, and you and others together, so it will be
impossible not to love and not be loved.

And use LIFE - to whirl old cells into mystic weddings of
energy and substance, to form new cells for a youthful body.
Use life to give new form to things you desire in life,
multiplying them limitlessly into the abundance of life.

And use SPIRIT! Open to it; let it in-spire into you the

God-powers of the universe to transform body and transfigure soul.

I ask you to use __ALL__ powers of your soul - the conceptive powers, and the operative powers of mystic silent overtones, and of the holy spiral in movement, and of the rhythm of the stars.

__Do as God does__ - use the operative powers to __initiate__ the use of the higher conceptive powers in your body and your life.

Vision first, the transformation of your body, thus:

"I vision cells conceived a-new in me - each cell re-born -
A-tuned to all the spirit power of rhythmic songs of stars;
Eight hundred thousand billion cells,
Embraced in love divine, as tenderly
As mothers hold their babies to their hearts of love!
Each cell inspired by thrill of life divine
To wed and multiply a million fold,
To be re-born, and born again, to live forever youthfully."

And second, intensify desire in you;

Each time you hum a tone of love to start a thousand silent overtones of mystic power, each time you move with holy spiral power of spirit energy, each time your body feels the rhythmic beat of stars, - __DESIRE__ whate'er you want, with all your heart!

And third, lift up your soul - to use of all your powers in harmony with rhythmic beat, with mystic overtones, all whirled into expression here by God's divinely spiral power, which God himself has used to whirl creation into actuality.

Lift up your soul to unify all power with strong desire, - for in the blend of all, there IS the one-ness we call God!

And fourth, make this your prayer of unity-in-use:

"I LONG - as I have never longed before - with deep desire,
Of deepest depths within the feelings of my soul!
I LONG to unify all powers that God has given me to use:
So that God's mind reveals whate'er it has conceived for me;
So that God's love in me, shall dare to love as it has long desired to love;
So that God's life in me shall multiply all things abundantly;
So that God's spirit shall e'er blend with spirit of my soul,
To make me like to God - with power to turn desires of heaven unto actualities of earth!

Oh listen, friend, unto the mystic music of the stars,
And feel the mighty swirl of spiral power;
And let your body feel the mighty rhythm of the universe,
And you shall know the oneness that is God,
And enter heaven here and now."

THE GREATER SPIRITUAL RESPONSIVENESS OF BODY

AND

AWAKENING THE BRAIN OF SPIRIT

by Brown Landone

SEVEN GOAL POSTS AND GUIDES - - - - - - - - - - - - - - LESSON XIV

This work is so new, its basic discoveries so astounding, its results so nearly miraculous, its means so simple and different from those usually taught, that it is wise to clarify the seven bases of progress, by which you attain most quickly.

First, work for actual MANIFESTATION of what you want, - not for mere thought about it.
Second, truth is NOT yet complete in man's manifestation, but is forever seeking fuller expression.

Third, accept and use the operative soul power - that is, those powers which help to initiate the use of greater powers.
Fourth, mighty silent overtones of stars, can vibrate in and through your body, IF you initiate them by low and loving tones.

Fifth, spirit has movement, and the spiritual energies of the movement of the universe are always rhythmic.
Sixth, spirit vibrates spirally, and the holy spiral of God's universe IS an operative power of your soul.

Seventh, today IS God's age of transforming change for man, and your progress can increase mightily now if you realize that you are chosen to effect a transformation now.

The first goal is visioned clearly, when you consecrate your-self to attain the two heavenly conditions man wants:
(1) free flow of spirit into man;
(2) free radiation of spirit out into every activity of life.

Second, be certain that the ideal of what you want, is dif-ferent from the process by which you will attain it!
Be certain also, that the process is just as divine as the ideal.
Just as ideals of Truth are perfect, although we have not yet attained one-tenth of those we affirm, - so also in essence the soul is perfect; although we have NOT yet perfected its manifest-ation.
I wish to teach how to attain greater manifestation - to be

14-60

more responsive to spirit - for more complete **expression of life.**

Third, use all four conceptive powers of your soul - Mind, Love, Life, and Spirit - for they are born of God, radiate to man, to make man like unto God.

There are other powers - the great initiating powers.

These initiative powers are just as divine as the conceptive powers - for "all are of God."

It is silly to select one of God's powers, and insist that it is the power of God, and that all other powers are not of God.

Mind and Sound, Love and Light, Life and Electronic Rays, Spirit and Cosmic Rays - each IS a power of God!

ALL energies are powers of God. God created all of them; and commanded man to use all He created.

Use each to produce after its own kind, but do not expect good results, if you try to substitute one for another.

Fourth, increase your energy by (1) daring to recognize your likeness to the divine source of energy in its limitlessness, and (2) by tuning up your body to harmonize all its billions of cells, to work together without friction.

Fifth, increase the flow of energy into action, by divine rhythm of action in use of all powers.

Sixth, do NOT let Mind hinder the awakening of Spirit.

Every fussing thought about details DOES interfere.

Thoughts of what the soul should or should not do, HAVE hindered free expression of spirit, to limitations of time and space.

Be intelligent, but take no anxious thought of any thing.

Use common sense! In one of my booklets, I have written of the inner light of cells; of inner foods - hormones produced within the body; of the marvelous magicians within the body - the endocrine glands; of phenomenal changes of weight; restructuring of organs and tissues by the hormones produced within the body.

Yet, in spite of all those words of 'inner' and 'within' - a few students always write asking why I do not tell them where to GET such inner foods - where to BUY them!

Please understand - you can NOT buy the highly spiritualized substances of inner foods produced in your own body.

They are created within, by spiritual responsiveness.

Seventh, do NOT LIMIT your development. Limit your effort, and you get limited results; but multiply power, and respond greatly, and you manifest greatly.

CONTENTS - PART TWO

* * * *
* * *
*

THE GREATER SPIRITUAL RESPONSIVENESS OF BODY

AND

AWAKENING THE BRAIN OF SPIRIT

by Brown Landone

THE NEW RESPONSE - LESSON XV

This Lesson XV is the first Lesson of Part II of this Course.
It is entitled The New Response!
By this title, I mean: (1) spiritual response; and (2) response that is new in your life!
New to every cell of your body, as well as to your soul!

In the past, you have probably thought of spiritual responsiveness of motives, desires, and ideals of the mind.
But I teach you the BASES of ALL response.
I teach you the spiritual response of the body itself - of its very tissues, and particularly of its activities!

And that means the activity of the MUSCLES!
You will never attain the highest degrees of spiritual consciousness until you lift up your mind to recognize that the cells and tissues are just as divine as the most ideal thought your mind can conceive, - for God created all things!

Moreover, there is NO way on earth by which your soul can express anything, EXCEPT through your muscles.

There is NO expression possible, except by movement of the large muscles of your body, or movement of small muscles for facial expression; or expression by the words and tones you use.
And you can not speak one word, or utter one tone except by muscle action - of chest walls, cheeks and lips and tongue.

There can not even be a gleam in your eyes, except little tiny muscles change the thickness of the lenses of your eyes.

Read the above, if necessary, a hundred times.
I mean it, a hundred times - once a day for three months!
That may not be too much, to open your mind to the great illumination - that ALL expression of soul depends on your muscles!

And all expression increases in power, as you tune-up the muscles to spirit. Thus only, you attain godhood in action!

Expression of spirit is THE highest attainment in this life; it is manifesting as God intended you to manifest in his likeness!
And only when body tissues are responsive enough to receive infinite energy, can spirit manifest freely and fully.

15-64

Certainly you now recognize that YOU are a radiation of the divine rays of the universe - of the marvelous powers that are forever constructive - the very powers which God himself used during the seven days of creation when he created all things which have existed for hundreds of millions and even billions of years.

And that which has continued for billions of years must be right, for evil always destroys itself, and all it creates!
Hence the seven creative powers of God - manifesting IN man - MUST be the very constructive essence of God himself.

Manifesting these powers is different from merely 'thinking' the thought that you are made in the likeness of God! This differs from affirming or declaring it, or meditating about it.

I teach manifestation, NOT thoughts 'about' manifestation!
And these Lessons teach you, the EASY approach to becoming more responsive to these spiritual powers - by the simplest and most effective means you can use in this life on earth, so that you can enter the Temple of Transformation.

Cosmic energy CAN penetrate your body, so that you feel the thrill of it, IF your conscious mind does not block it.

So I ask you, to think as LITTLE ABOUT this work as possible.
That is, think just enough to get the information necessary, to tell you what to do. Then LIVE in response to the urge of spirit - to carry out the exercises that may be given - NOT as exercises, but as means of easy response of body - free expression of the soul!

Some Lessons will be long; other Lessons will be short. Each WILL contain ALL that it is essential for you to know in order that you may learn to respond to the fullest degree possible.

Infinite spirit forever surrounds you, and from it you receive all the energy you can ever manifest on this earth!
And spirit IS the source of everything you can ever attain on this earth or manifest in heaven!

The meaning of spirit is the essence of all power.

For example, the light you see on earth - that is, light of the sun, NEVER comes from the sun, as light!
Instead, it is the spirit of light which radiates from the sun - it is pure light - light that is NEVER seen by the human eye - the perfect light of God.

The 'sunlight' which you do see on earth is NOT pure light!
In actual fact, it is nothing but the friction that is created

by the AIR, as the PURE sunlight tries to get THROUGH it.

There is proof; when scientists rise high in a balloon, even at midday, it is almost dark in the upper atmosphere!
There is very little crude light up there, because there is very little air up there, and hence little friction.

And when man mounts still higher, there is absolute darkness.
That is, what we call 'sunlight' is crude friction of true black light, passing through air! And since air does not exist out in space, there is no light out there, which the eye can see!
There is only the pure UNSEEN light of God!

So I make a real distinction, between this crude light on earth, and the spirit "of" light which is the essence of light - the holy unseen light - light such as God knows.

There is also a spiritual essence "of" x-rays and of ultra violet rays, and of all radiant rays. All we know of them on earth, is the crude friction - due to pure rays trying to plow, either through air or more solid substances here on earth.

Likewise, I make a distinction between 'mind' as manifested by man on earth, and the spirit 'of' mind.
All those who dwell in mind, dwell in the realms of thoughts, and thoughts are forever changing and forever dying!
"Not by might - but by my spirit," saith the Lord of Hosts; and the Hebrew word translated might means strength of mind!

At this point, I caution you again, against trying to classify or mentalize - and thus kill - the essence of this work!

A few months ago, I received an outline, made by a student - an outline of two lessons of this Course.
This woman wrote that she was re-writing this course, so it would be "RIGHT". She said she had classified and numbered the exercises, so she could do all of them - efficiently, practically - in only eleven minutes each day!

In essence, what this woman says, is this: "I have classified and numbered expressions of love, so that I can get all expression of my love for my loved ones, out of the way in eleven minutes each day, and thus my life becomes efficient and practical.
What she calls 'practical', is killing the spirit of love; killing the response of mind and body to spirit, and SUBSTITUTING mere thoughts of mind, FOR the love and life of spirit!

Assume that you are a young sweetheart, and that your lover comes home, after two years across the sea in military service.

15-66

He enters your home, and as you walk toward the door to greet
him, you stop half way, and say, -
"John, since you've been away, I've worked out very efficient
and practical means of expressing our love.
"I have scheduled a plan for our manifestation of it!
"We will take exactly ½ of a second for one kiss; no more!
"Then 3/4 of a second for an embrace; after which we will sit
on the sofa and hold hands for 2 minutes and 10 seconds."

I do not need to explain; you <u>know</u> that any such attempt, will
first dampen <u>response</u> to your love; then freeze it; then kill it!
<u>Mentalization</u> of expressing love, can <u>completely</u> <u>kill</u> <u>the</u> <u>love</u>
<u>within a month</u>! So also with expressions of spirit!

<u>IF</u> this woman has "worked out" response to spirit, just right;
then it's not worth teaching; certainly not worth living it!

So I caution you, my friend. <u>Think</u> <u>just</u> <u>as</u> <u>LITTLE</u> <u>as</u> <u>possible</u>
<u>about the information</u> of these Lessons!
Give only enough thought to them, to <u>know</u> what you should do.
Then forget the thought, and <u>live</u> the love and life of spirit!

Keep always these two truths in mind, my friend:

First, life and love and spirit <u>are</u> <u>completely</u> <u>different</u> from
the much lesser powers of the thoughts of conscious mind;

Second, conscious mind is a mechanized skeleton in activity -
an actual hindrance in manifesting life and love and spirit.

You know this <u>is</u> true - for you know that nothing has ever
interferred so much with the full and free expression of your life,
<u>as</u> the 'thoughts' of conscious mind which have forever been saying -
you can't do this, you can't do that, you haven't the strength to
do this, or what will people say if you do that!

<u>All</u> <u>hindrances</u> <u>to</u> <u>response</u> <u>to</u> <u>spirit</u> are due (1) <u>to</u> <u>thoughts</u>
<u>of</u> <u>conscious</u> <u>mind, or</u> (2) <u>such</u> <u>slowness</u> <u>of</u> <u>body</u> vibration <u>that</u> <u>its</u>
<u>tissues</u> <u>do</u> <u>not</u> <u>fully</u> <u>respond</u> <u>to</u> <u>spirit</u>.

One of our great inspired English poets whom I intimately knew,
compared the <u>place</u> of conscious mind and thought in our lives, to
the box of tools which a carpenter uses!
Except when using thought, thought should be laid quietly aside,
as a carpenter puts his tools aside, when he is through with them.

But up to this time - living in a world of thought - you have
become a slave to mind; you even take your thoughts to bed with
you, and cannot sleep; or if you do sleep, your mind unconsciously

races on all night, and you awaken tired in the morn.

Be as wise as the carpenter is wise!
Put aside your box of tools of the mind, each time you are through with them, and then live love and life and spirit.

"I am the poet of hitherto unuttered joy.
"I see the heavens laughing - - - yet I dare not say what I see - - - lest I be locked up.

"These things I say - not to excite thought in you, - but rather to destroy it. Or if it does excite thought, then to excite that which destroys itself.

"Spirit is not born of thought.
"And whoever dwells among thoughts, dwells in the region of delusion and disease.
"Although thought should gird you 'round about,
"Forget not to disendue it.
"As a man takes off his coat when hot.

"As a skilled workman lays down his tool when done with it, so shall you use thought
"And then lay it quietly aside again when it has served your purpose."

Yet you do go about through life carrying a box of thoughts on your back; the carpenter is wiser, he does not sit down to eat, or go out to court the girl he loves, or come home and go to bed - with a box of tools always hung on his back!
Thoughts are tools of the mind; use them, and put them aside.

This is the first step in learning to let your body respond more fully and freely to spirit.

Forever avoid teachers and instructors and lessons and books which teach you 'exactly how' to do things in a definite fixed way!
Fixity of operation is good for a machine, but death to initiative, death to inspiration, death to responsiveness!
'Just how' can help you to be a good machine.
But a machine always wears out - and is soon thrown aside!

You are more than an efficient machine; you are a creator, created in the image and likeness of God - a living soul - with power to manifest continuously, with increasing activity, increasing youthfulness, increasing life and love and power and spirit!
ALL of which come ONLY BY RESPONSE to spirit!

THE GREATER SPIRITUAL RESPONSIVENESS OF BODY

AND

AWAKENING THE BRAIN OF SPIRIT

by Brown Landone

IN-SPIRING MATTER WITH SPIRIT - - - - - - - - - - - - - LESSON XVI

The new response of the body to spirit, starts with something
which may perhaps surprise you.

It must begin with the means by which the spiritual energy of
the infinite enters the body.

There are great dynamos of spirit power in your body - within
your actual physical body. There are great motors of tremendous
power in your body.
But the energy which they radiate - the energy that flows
over your nerves - comes FROM OUTSIDE your body!

From the word spirit, we derive our word - in-spiration!
Inspiration is the act of in-spiralling energy; that is, the
activity of energy spiralling itself into your body!

It is impossible to find any illustration that is fully true,
for the soul is greater than anything else man knows on earth, and
the human body is the most marvelous organic mechanism of all God's
creations! Hence there is nothing to which soul and body can be
truly compared!
Soul and body transcend all other things on earth, and nothing completely illustrates that which takes place, when infinite
spirit which surrounds you, flows into and through your body.

But in some factors, comparisons are true; Great generators
in a power house can generate no electricity, unless there is
electronic energy flowing to them from all the universe.
Such energy surrounds every power house, penetrates it, and
fills every inch of space in and around every machine!
It is the electronic energy of the universe that makes it
possible to IN-spire energy into the generators, so that, when
they operate, they can radiate electricity out along wires.

So also, ALL the power that radiates from your soul - or in
and through your body - is first in-spired INTO the structure of
your body, by infinite energy which forever surrounds you.

And in proportion, as you increase responsiveness of tissues of your body - lift them up to respond more fully to the higher vibrating energies of the universe - in that degree, will you manifest more spiritual energy in every activity of life.

In beginning this new response, let me again emphasize that ALL power first comes to you FROM OUTSIDE your body!
It is in-spired into the structure of your body, either to be used at once, or else stored up as titanic power to be released later and radiated out into manifestation.

BUT WHERE does this energy in-spire into your body?

What is the MEANS used?
The means must be some part of your body, whose cells are more sensitively responsive to spiritual energy and all higher energies of the universe, than any other cells of your body.

To this time, you have thought of your ears as miraculous receptors, because they are able to receive vibrations of tones, vibrating up to 24,000 times a second!
It IS marvelous that nerves of the ear can respond, so amazingly to such high overtones of sound!

Also your eye seems to be the most amazing organism ever developed!
It is a camera that adjusts its own lenses to different amounts of light.
Then its retina adjusts its nerves instantly to different lengths of light vibrations!
Some of the little nerve cells of the rods and cones of the retina of your eye, can receive vibrations that range from 400 trillion times a second, up to 700 trillion a second! That is, - from lowest reds to highest violets the human eye can see!

It is marvelous - the delicate responsiveness of the nerve cells of the rods and cones of the retina of the eye!
YET, the nerves of the ear and the nerves of the eye can NOT equal another tissue of your body in responsiveness.
"IT" is the most receptive organ of all your body!
Some physiologists now call it the mirror of the soul.

And what is it of which I am writing:
It is your SKIN - the most miraculous organ of your body!

It is different from all other organs.
It is a physical body by itself.
It is composed of cells that are the opposite of the cells of all other organs of your body.

ALL other body cells can live ONLY in DARKNESS and WATER!
And most of your body is three-fourths water.

BUT if skin cells are put in water, they die.
And if they are put in darkness, they die.

It is your spiritually responsive body! It is your skin,
composed of cells which MUST have light and air, although all
cells of the inner body die if exposed to light or air, even
for a second!

Cells of skin originate from the same kind of cells as
do cells of the brain and nerves and endocrine glands!
They are the MIRACLE cells of the body. One physiologist
even calls the skin the 'miracle organ' of the body.

The skin is the in-spiring organ - the ONLY organ that can
take-in the energies of God, so that they can be embodied in the
brain dynamos, and then radiated to all parts of your body!

In your skin alone, there are two billion "RECEIVING SETS"!

If this seems strangely impossible to you - that is, that
there are billions of receiving sets in your skin which 'receive
power' from the universe, realize that scientific engineering has
already developed power sending and receiving apparatus here on
earth, for use in a practical mechanical engineering way.

Towers can be built to send out power, just as we have towers
that broadcast radio waves which are carried to your radio set and
turned into sound.

It IS possible to build towers that radiate power, so that if
you are within 500 miles, with an automobile with a 'power-receiving
set', you can tune in to that tower of wireless power, and receive
power for the engine of your car - sufficient to run it anywhere
within a radius of 500 miles.
And of course this radiance of power may - in a few years - be
so improved that it can be used anywhere within a thousand miles or
five thousand mile radius of such a tower!

I cite this only to illustrate four great truths:
(1) all great power first exists outside of the structure;
(2) it is inspired or taken into the structure;
(3) it can be inspired or taken-in only if the structure is
responsive to the power; and
(4) the degree of power taken-in depends on the degree of
responsiveness of the structure of your body.

To receive such power, your physical structure must be TUNED-
IN to it - must be RESPONSIVE to it!

16-71

AND YOU - in this most marvelous organ of your body - YOUR skin - have more than two billion RECEIVING sets, CAPABLE of receiving the highest powers of the universe.

The receiving sets in every area of your skin are infinitely MORE responsive to higher energies than the nerves of your ear, or even those marvelously delicate nerves of the retina of the eye.

The PROOF that the skin is MORE RESPONSIVE, is the fact that it DOES respond to much higher powers than eye or ear.

Your eye can not perceive x-rays, yet your skin can respond to them and in-spire them into your body, even all through your body except through your bones.
And nerves of the eyes are so dull compared to skin cells that they can not receive ultra-violet light.
But skin cells are so responsive to spirit that they CAN receive ultra-violet rays, and transmit them to all inner organs.

In preparing for this new response to spirit - this response even of your body to spirit - clearly vision the truth that your skin IS the ONE most miraculous organ of your entire body.

Look at it in a new way - reverence it, for it is the bridge - between all that is manifesting as you, and all that is not you!

It is the receiving inspiring organ of incarnating spirit!
It is the bridge between the infinite power that surrounds you, and the energy of all the inner structure of your body.

There are 800,000 billion cells in your body.
That number may not mean much in words, so I put them in figures - 800,000,000,000,000 cells, - that is, 400,000 times as many as all the people on earth!

Each cell is a LIVING INDIVIDUAL! And the very life of each one - the vitality of each one, its every impulse to act and move, to live and love, and to respond to spirit - depend on how much energy is in-spired into your skin by your skin, and then carried into your inner body.

So look upon every skin cell as an angel from God - an angel to take-in the powers of God, and transmit them to all the body.

This is the very basis of the new response to the physical structure of your body to the infinite energies of God.

The skin is MEANS of the inspiration of matter by spirit, and the inspiration of matter with spirit.

The vibration of matter must be tuned-up to that of spirit, otherwise the matter is destroyed by spirit entering it.

ONLY as the rate of vibration of matter approaches that of spirit, can spirit flow into it, in its infinity.

It is this full IN-flow of spirit which lifts you to living in the image and like to the likeness of God.

If I have not previously written of this 'likeness', I write of it now, so you will understand what we mean when we accept God's statement that he made man in his own image and likeness.

The Hebrew language is confusing to those who know only the English. It differs greatly from our English language. Often it uses the same root word, to form the noun and adjective and verb and adverb - all in one sentence.

It does this often, for powerful emphasis!

For example, consider a Hebrew word, like - play!

In using this word, an ancient writer might have written, - "The player played the play playfully."

This is what was done in the original Hebrew sentence, that is translated - "God made man in his own image and likeness."

Root words of similar meaning are used as the basis of the words translated made, own, image, and likeness!

The meaning of the root words is 'ACTIVITY'.

So the full meaning of this great truth is this: God, the infinite activity, activated the activity called man, by his own activity to be like unto God's own activity.

It is IN activity, that man is like God!

And since the meaning is repeated four times - in made, own, image and likeness - realize the great emphasis God gave to this truth, to help you to comprehend it in its full significance!

It is response TO this activity which guarantees attainment of all that is worthwhile in earth and in heaven.

This is the ultimate attainment desired of the new responsiveness - greater activity by means of spiritual response, so that the body may become more like spirit, and manifest spirit more fully and more completely, like unto a god on earth.

Now, in the next Two Lessons, prepare the skin as a mystic organ, for higher response to spirit, to inspire more of spirit!

THE GREATER SPIRITUAL RESPONSIVENESS OF BODY

AND

AWAKENING THE BRAIN OF SPIRIT

by Brown Landone

ASPIRING SEEKER AND ADJUSTER

AND

THE NEWLY DISCOVERED UNITY-IN-RADIANCE - - - - - - - - LESSON XVII

I teach you SPIRIT and its expression THROUGH the body!

Spirit is the God-Urge of expression!
It is the out-pouring and out-pushing of God Himself!

It fills all spaceless space, and surrounds and permeates
every star and atom of creation with infinite power!

It FLOODS the universe - including YOU - with titanic energy!

Moreover, spirit is ready to thrill your body - yes, even
your physical body - with such a flood of energy, that ill health
and fatigue and weaknesses of old age will be impossible!
Spirit is ready to contact you intimately and continuously.

I know your earnestness - hoping, praying, trying again.
And yet, although you HAVE for years, and faithfully - still,
mind and body are NOT YET fully responsive to spirit.
Yes, even after the years, there are lacks - your body is NOT
yet vitalized; it is not yet fully in-spired by spirit; there IS
lack of that abundance; and there is lack of full joy; and lack of
constant contact and communion with the all knowing spirit.

I am not criticizing! But my heart feels for your efforts,
which up to this time have not yet been fully fulfilled! So I
wish to help you discover the cause of the failure of your efforts,
so you shall attain response, so the lacks will disappear.

The cause is this: in the past, no matter how consecrated
you have been, your mind has tended to move in one direction, while
spirit is ALWAYS moving in the OPPOSITE DIRECTION!

Spirit is always radiating outward - even OUTWARD! And all
spirit is always IN-SPIRING itself into whatever responds to it!

Think clearly! Mind is always reaching-out to GET ideas and perceptions, and take them back into its self.

Instead of radiating outward as spirit does, mind is always seeking to take-in information to within itself.

Even in meditation, mind tends to look within the self to find power, instead of recognizing that supreme power is outside the soul, and available for use only when inspired into the self.

So when you use mind too much - even when you think too much of what you are doing in this work - you use the power of mind, which works in the opposite direction to that of spirit, - for spirit is radiance from God - the OUT moving power of God!

So with mind always tending to pull ideas TO itself, and spirit radiating OUTWARD, there IS subconscious CONFLICT.

Oh, see the significance of this! It explains WHY you have failed, even when trying earnestly, to attain your desires!

So, I FIRST teach you to be an "aspiring seeker and adjuster", to stop thinking enough, so that you can respond enough to spirit, so that spirit can in-spire itself into your mind and body.

Without inspiration all effort ends in disappointment.

BUT response to the divine IN-SPIRING RAY brings heaven to earth, it brings the divine energies of heaven into YOUR desires and into the earth of actualities for you, even into your body!

The Inspiring Ray is the first RAY used by God in creation.

Respond to it, and you create as God creates!

Respond to it, and for the first time, you will begin to unify body and mind and spirit to move together in the same way at the same time - with power of unity you have never known before.

Then ills of body and lack of energy disappear!

Failures turn to success! Feelings of being separated from God, and from those whom you love, vanish.

I teach you to RESPOND to spirit, and to its SEVEN Sacred Rays of Creations! These rays are called the Elohim Rays.

The word Ray is now used by scientists to designate each distinct group of radiant energies.

The word Elohim - you will remember - is the Hebrew word in the first chapter of our Bible which is translated God.

But its ending 'im' in the Hebrew, means that it is plural; hence it should be truly translated "God's powers". There are seven of these creative powers - seven holy Elohim rays of God.

The Elohim Rays are much higher than any radiant energy yet known to scientists - vibrating far above septillions times per second.

Each ray has a particular vibration of its own, AND whenever it vibrates THROUGH any substance, it produces a particular RESULT of its own IN that particular substance. That IS creation!

Even common earth rays possess this transforming power!
The common HEAT ray, for example, has such power. You've seen it work; a chunk of hard butter in the presence of heat rays soon CHANGES its FORM, and becomes just melted yellow grease.

Sound is also a very common ray - so common you do not realize that it also has transforming power.
But sprinkle a thin layer of sand on a tin platter, and tap the edge to produce sound, so the sound rays make the platter ring, and the layer of sand IS transformed.
It forms beautiful designs - circles, squares, diamonds, stars!

BUT ELOHIM RAYS have power, MILLIONS OF TIMES GREATER than any of the ordinary rays known on earth!

I have already stated that the main cause of your LACK of attainment, is the INNER CONFLICT between your MIND and SPIRIT.
Of course, you may not consciously know of this conflict, for mental mind seldom knows the mystic workings of spirit.

But certainly, you DO know that your body is not yet CONSTANTLY THRILLED with the power of spirit, and you do know that your communion with spirit, is not yet CONSCIOUSLY CONTINUOUS.

Conflict is NOT in ideals, but in OPPOSITION of ACTIVITY.
Your mind tries to make the powers of your soul move one way - inward; while spirit moves in the OPPOSITE way - outward!

But when mind and spirit work TOGETHER, results are as CERTAIN as God, and as wonderful as miracles!

Since it is mind that is to blame, there is but one way of solving this conflict. It must ADJUST its old ideas.
This is attained, only when you make the activity of both your mind and body LIKE unto the activity of spirit.
Then you respond to the divinely Inspiring Ray of God.

To help you in this, learn the NATURE of spirit's ACTIVITY.

First, spirit is NEVER passive, but always infinitely ACTIVE!
Second, spirit NEVER turns inward on itself!

These two truths are known to all scientists, and to many spiritual thinkers; and hundreds of books teach them!
Yet few students use them; and most teachers urge you to dwell in attitudes which oppose spirit - to be passive instead of active;

17-76

to look within, instead of looking outward for inspiration.

What is YOUR mind doing? Working with or against spirit?

First, spirit IS ever active, yet your mind - because of mistaken teachings - tries to make you become PASSIVE in the Infinite Silence in order to be at-one with spirit's activity.

This opposes spirit, for spirit is infinitely active!
Passivity may make you into a good SPONGE to soak in a little more spirit. But the soaking process does NOT make you active as spirit is active. It actually prevents you from being at-one with spirit and its activity.

Second, spirit always moves out to in-spire all its contacts.

Yet your mind has been taught to look WITHIN for spirit, to awaken spirit IN you.
Be very certain that you can NOT fully attain what you want, so long as your mind CONTINUES acting one way, while spirit radiates in another way.

Lovingly teach your mind to move WITH spirit.

FIRST, STOP being passive!
NO matter WHO has taught you, or WHAT MISTAKEN psychology or mysticism you have been taught, realize now and forever, that any attempt to be passive in order to be more active, IS a CONTRADICTION!
There is only one way of becoming unified WITH spirit!
That way is to become ACTIVE as spirit is active.

SECOND, ABANDON all methods and all the means you have used, of withdrawing within the self.
Great peace is due to unity of action. Spirit is always moving outward to in-spire itself into all things.

As an inspiring seeker and adjuster, move outward with spirit, even to infinity - even to feeling you are up among the stars!

The PEACE OF SUCH EXPANSION IS a THOUSAND-FOLD GREATER than the peace of with-drawal; and this peace of unity with God's inspiring power opens the soul to illumination! When your body and spirit ARE in perfect unison, there is no blockage of memories of the past, and no dimming of knowledge of the future.

In this there IS limitless vitality from inspiration of the body by spirit; and at the other end of the gamut, intimate communion with spirit by inspiration of spirit itself.

THE GREATER SPIRITUAL RESPONSIVENESS OF BODY

AND

AWAKENING THE BRAIN OF SPIRIT

by Brown Landone

GREAT PEACE-MAKER and INSPIRATION OF POWER - - - - - - LESSON XVIII

When the activities of your body and mind and heart and spirit
are at peace - that is when their activities work TOGETHER - then
your desires become holy actualities.

This brings us to another factor in making peace with spirit.
To be responsive to spirit and create with absolute certainty
of results, you MUST use the SAME powers which God uses.
And in the same order - one after the other.

God needed seven days for creation, each day to create a DIF-
FERENT result, and with divine certainty, because use of a different power must produce a different result.

The secret of this great hidden mystery, resides in what I
taught you in the preceding lesson, or the meaning of the word
translated 'God' in the first chapter of Genesis!

Remember it is ELOH-IM and the 'im' at the end is the Hebrew
sign of plurality, - just as 's' is a plural form in English, which
tells us that the word boys, means more than one boy.

Elohim means the SEVEN holy impregnating POWERS of God!
WITHOUT USE of these powers even God's own conceptions of
creation were without form and void, - see Genesis 1:2.
"In the beginning God created the heaven and the earth, and
THE EARTH was without form and void."

Isn't that exactly what has happened to thousands of creations
you have conceived in your own mind?
You have created them in the heaven of mind, but as actual
manifestations on earth, they have remained 'formless and void'.

Many teachers of the last 90 years have mistakenly taught that
all you have to do to create what you want, is to hold a thought of
it in mind.
They however do not know the process of God's creation!
They fail to realize that even God's mind creation of earth
WAS VOID, until he used other powers!

Let us repeat: "In the beginning, God created the heaven and earth, and THE EARTH was without form and void." That is, the actual manifestations was empty (void), and had no actual form!

So also, our creations in mere thought, have in 99 cases out of 100 - remained IN consciousness, FORMLESS and VOID - never coming into actual manifestation!

That is why I give you this work of the use of the Seven Creating Powers of God - THE powers which God used to turn the formlessness and emptiness of thought, into actualities!

It was only when God used these seven powers, that he created the ACTUALITIES OF creation. Read Genesis 1:7-2:3.

You also, in the past, have created many desires and ideals which have never taken form and become actualities.
BUT NOW, with your use of seven powers of God, your desires and ideals CAN become actualities - just as God's did.

These powers are the SEVEN sacred rays which God used in ALL his creation, and they were first symbolized by the Seven Days or processes of creation.

Through the ages mystic men have tried to lift mankind toward manifested perfection, by use of EACH ray predominately for thousands of years at a time!
This has already created six great civilizations of the past, EACH with at least One Great Temple as the symbol of the spiritual urge of its own civilization.
Now we are in the seventh civilization.

These seven powers of creations - creating actualities - are:

The First is the Great IN-SPIRING Ray or power of spirit - the "let there be light" of the third verse of our Bible.

The Second great power is the EXPANDING Ray - the Ouranian Ray as Jesus called it - the Heaven from Within.

Third, the great FORMING Ray.

Fourth, the CLARIFYING or CATHAYAN or Purifying Ray.

Fifth, the VITALIZING or Shamean Ray.

Sixth, the RE-CREATIVE Ray, creating new atoms and new cells.

Seventh, the Great HOLDING Ray - by use of which man is beginning the completion of man's attainment here on earth.

These lessons teach you responsiveness TO these rays.
In THIS Lesson, I teach you of the Great IN-SPIRING ray!

Such response can come only from an attitude of openness of the soul - free from restrictive thoughts of mind, so that the soul is open for the inflow of spirit, for inspiration.

The use of the in-spiring power of the first great ray of creation is proclaimed by - "LET there be LIGHT."

But it is certain that this 'light' is not the light seen by the human eye, because what we call light was not created until the fourth day of creation. It was then, that symbols of the sun and moon were created - creation of light which we call light - seen by the human eye.

The word 'light' in the phrase - "let there be light" literally means, - "Let there be a SPREAD of spirit fire."
This means, a SPREADING or radiation of spirit, moving out into all things, and consequently IN-spiring itself into them!

This is closely linked up with the use of the Second Great Ray - that of Expansion - because when spirit moves into anything, it expands it into new activity and new attainment.

Now return to a truth I taught you in a preceding Lesson - that the physical means by which all energies which manifest in your body and in your brain structure, are received!

Preparation for response to this Inspiring Ray, is simple.
But do not try to do it, by 'thought' of mind.

Remember that mind always tends to take things to itself, to store them up within its own consciousness.
That is, mind never gives attention to anything, except to perceive something it wishes to take into its own thoughts.
No one would ever study anything, except mind wishes to gain information to take into its consciousness.

Mind is self-ish, grasping ideas to enrich itself.
Hence mind has become a ruthless dictator, interferring with the manifestation of love, and even of spirit itself.

But spirit is radiant, flowing out, always to inspire itself into something else, always to uplift that something else!
You want spirit to FLOW into your body and THROUGH IT!

Remember clearly, that ALL in-spiration of power into your physical structure, comes through the skin.
The skin possesses the only cells which are tuned to vibration high enough to respond to infinite energy.

Moreover, in its very structure, it has over two billion 'power' receiving sets, which can and do receive the infinite energies of the universe - the energies of God.

Even physiologists now call it, the 'miracle' organ, and write of its mystic activity!
YET YOU give it very little chance to inspire the divine energies of the universe!
In fact, you usually actually HINDER its activity for 23 hours, 59 minutes and 59 seconds every day.

So at least for seven minutes each morning and night, alone by yourself, give the cells of your skin, freedom!

Remember also that your skin cells are DIFFERENT from all other cells of your body.
In origin they ARE like brain cells!
But functionally, they DIFFER from ALL other cells.

ALL skin cells MUST have LIGHT AND AIR, to live!

In contrast, ALL cells INSIDE your body, DIE the moment they are exposed to light or air; and this is true of ALL cells of all the INNER organs and tissues of your body.
This is why - in growing heart tissues cells outside the body - as Dr. Carrel does - the laboratory room must be dark, and laboratory assistants dress in BLACK gowns!
The ONE great life-need of SKIN cells is AIR, and MORE AIR!

Most benefits 'supposedly' due to sunlight, are due to air.
Only a little sunlight is beneficial!
More than a little IS deadly detrimental.

God and nature know more than faddists do.
If you expose your body to just a little too much sunlight, divine intelligence knows it is so very detrimental, that nature blisters your skin to make you keep out of the sunlight; OR it builds up a dark curtain of tan below the outer skin to keep out the light.

But skin cells need air and MORE air, and STILL more AIR!
AIR is the GREAT ACTIVATOR of all BILLIONS OF skin cells.

They MUST HAVE AIR TO LIVE!
Yet, you do NOT give them EVEN a 1% normal chance to live!
Your body lives 1,440 minutes every day!
14 minutes is only 1% of the 1440 minutes of the day.
But you do not give your skin cells a chance to live in DIRECT CONTACT with air, even for 14 minutes each day!

Will a plant grow well, if given only 1% of the air it needs?

All life breathes to live. Even an apple in the cellar breathes. And a tree breathes. It even perspires – about 400 quarts of water on a hot day. But what would happen, if you kept its leaves swathed in clothes?

Even to live, your skin cells must have MOVING air!

Yet you deprive them of it, 99% of the time!

This is a great physiological CRIME of this age!

The activity of the skin IS mystical and mighty!

It affects even the inner body.

The body itself DIES, if only a part of its skin is injured.

Science has recently made a remarkable discovery.

If one-third or more of the skin is burned, even liver and kidneys begin to DISINTEGRATE.

And although the skin may heal, yet death results because of its indirect effect on the liver and kidneys.

This is but one proof that the skin – in addition to its own inspiration work – helps to maintain normal activity, and even the structure of kidneys and liver.

Skin activation is essential, so that other organs can do their part in responding to spirit.

Co-operate with your mystical skin cells; and FREE THEM from the sodden condition in which you have kept them.

Give them AT LEAST a 1% chance to live – to contact air freely for at least 14 minutes EVERY day!

I ask you to expose your skin FREELY to AIR!

And to MOVE about when doing it!

SEVEN minutes each MORNING and SEVEN minutes each NIGHT.

Certainly these two periods – 14 minutes in all – less than 1% of the 1440 minutes of the day – are not too much, for the activation of the miracle cells of YOUR body – the only cells which MUST have AIR to live.

Choose a seven minutes period convenient to you; and be certain that the temperature of the room – in cold weather – is agreeably warm.

Then when you first awaken in the morning and also just before you retire at night – take a piece of WHITE SILK CLOTH about a yard square, and gently fluff – very very gently fluff – the entire skin surface of your body.

Fourteen minutes of exposure to air – which skin cells MUST have to live – PLUS this light fluffing of the skin with a dry soft white silk cloth – will do MORE to activate your skin, than twenty-four hours out in the sunshine.

18-82

Give the MYSTIC cells of your skin just a little chance, and the SPIRITUAL responsiveness of body will increase TEN-FOLD!

Awaken your skin to receive the IN-Spiring power of God!

This ray has a peculiar vibratory power of its own.
When it passes into a living substance, it inspires it.
How long should you continue this activation of the skin?
Continue it for life, IF you wish to continue to inspire the energy of the universe - the energy of God - to the limit.

Yes, the instructions I have given you are VERY simple.
I want them to be simple, so you will scarcely think of them.
All you need to do, is to secure about a square yard of white soft silk and then use it with the skin free to the air, for at least seven minutes each night, each morning!
Do not lie down for this, but move about - move around in your room by yourself, alone.

There are many proofs now, that movement of air ON the skin counteracts much of what we used to think were detrimental results due to lack of sufficient oxygen in breathing.
We now know that it is ionization which is THE essential in the breathing of air and in action of air on the skin.
We also know that the electronic energy of God is the energy which CONDITIONS the cells of the body, so that they become more responsive to the essence of all powers of God.

Let us clearly understand this, even if it is necessary for me to repeat something I may have previously written.

All energies of God work together IN HARMONY, unless your conscious mind interferes with their working.

For mind and love and life and spirit to manifest through your body, the body must be conditioned - that is, brought up to a certain state of vibration - before even the all-powerful energies can manifest!
The words 'all-powerful' mean only that energies are all-powerful according to the harmony of all powers of God.

It is necessary for the body to be conditioned by the energy we call heat, BEFORE any cell can function at all. You already know this, for if a human body is frozen stiff, no power of life or mind can manifest through it.

So also the body MUST be conditioned by the electronic energy of God BEFORE its cells can respond to spirit.

But energies which condition the body, are NOT life!
They merely put body in condition, so life can manifest.

18-83

Hence, scientists who conclude that heat is life, or that electricity is life are completely mistaken.

All such energies are merely the conditioning energies which make it possible for higher God-energies of spirit to manifest.

Nevertheless, all the conditioning energies are essential for all manifestation of life; and the greatest manifestation of life in the body is due to the ionization which takes place because of electronic energy.

So it is wise - when you use the square of silk to fluff the skin of your body - to stand: (1) on a tile bath floor, or (2) on a large piece of glass, or (3) on a rubber mat - on anything which prevents electrical energy from passing away from the skin.

There is proof of the value of this, for electronic energy can be induced to accumulate on the surface of the skin.

You know that merely walking over a thick carpet, barefooted on a cool day, charges the skin with electricity, so that when your finger tips touch an object made of metal, there will even be a flashing spark of electricity.

The life or death of every cell of the body depends on a major positive electronic charge at its center, and a lesser negative electronic charge on the outside of its little body.

We also know that if these charges tend to equal each other there is death; and that the vitality, energy, endurance depend on the in-spiring of the positive powers of the universe.

Your skin is a mystic organ - the miracle organ, as mystic as anything you have ever dreamed of in occultism!

It is the only body tissue which contains billions of little receiving sets, to take-in the spiritual energies of God.

I do not wish to instruct you much about this. I have told you all that needs to be done.

I do not wish you to think much about it, - but to feel - all the time you are fluffing your skin with the white silk cloth and leaving it uncovered free to the air - to feel that your skin is awakening to responsive vibration of a higher rate.

Remember the skin's delicacy of response to vibration of higher powers, is finer and greater even than the response of the most delicate nerves of the eye.

The skin's mystic activity is to receive power - to in-spire energies of God; and then to transmit those energies to all the billions of cells of your inner body.

This in-spiration of power, IS the true 'breath of life'.

18-84

THE GREATER SPIRITUAL RESPONSIVENESS OF BODY

AND

AWAKENING THE BRAIN OF SPIRIT

by Brown Landone

THE LIMITLESS EXPANSIONIST - - - - - - - - - - - - - - - LESSON XIX

Ouranos is the word ALWAYS used by Jesus for 'heaven'.
It means infinite EXPANSION!
And Jesus taught response to the Expanding Power of God, as
THE means of the awakening heaven here and now, of expanding life
into a heaven of attainment, of bringing heaven to earth.

This Expanding Ray was called the Huanacan Ray ages ago!
It was defied in the Tiajuanacan Temple of the God-in-Gold in
the sacred eastern Andes = thousands of years before mystic wise men
went to Thibet.

IT LIFTS UP and EXPANDS the soul!
God used this second step in creation.
And by the use of this Expanding Ray, God wrought the Second Day
of creation, = "the FIRMAMENT in the midst of waters."
In the revised version of the Bible, notes at bottom of page
indicate that the word translated firmament, means expansion, and
God himself called this expansion, heaven. See Gen. 1:8.

To respond to this Expanding Ray, I teach you a new attitude!
It is NEITHER relaxed nor tensed, but expectantly expanding;
and hence it is in harmony with spirit's ever expanding activity.

You do NOT relax your body to become more responsive!
No matter what you have been taught, any and all slackness of
relaxation is NOT 'like' the activity of spirit.

Slackness or relaxation is LACK of energy in action.
It makes both mind and body non-active!
Non-activity does not and can NOT respond fully to activity.

There have been strange teachings given to you, to help you
attain greater spiritual consciousness.
Spirit is the highest activity of God, yet these strange
teachings tell you to stop activity in order to become active.

To respond to spirit = the greatest activity of the soul =
first quiet the slow chugging action of body and anxious thoughts.

19-85

But you should not try to quiet their activity by trying to stop their action.

Rather you should INCREASE their activity, so that you rise above the slower action.

Get the full significance of this.
When you run your auto very slowly, it chugs and jerks.
And you can overcome this by increasing its activity - increasing the speed!

You respond to spirit, only as soul increases its activity!
When activity is lessened, responsiveness is lessened.
When activity is increased, responsiveness increases.

In your past efforts, you have tried to lessen the activity of your body in order to increase the activity of spirit.

That is, a contradiction carried into active opposition!
I teach you to unify the activities of body and of spirit, - for only in unity of activity will your dreams and desires come true.

I teach the STEPS by which you become responsive to spirit.
These I call the steps to SACRED RESPONSE.

The work of each subsequent lesson, starts with the expanding attitude given in this Lesson and the next.
For the present, use the five steps given here.

What follows is the positional body attitude for SPIRITUAL responsiveness - harmonizing mind and soul with spirit!

This IS the one divine attitude - the only divine attitude - which unifies activities of your body with activities of your mind with activities of spirit, with the EXPANDING Ray of God!

FIRST STEP: Sit in a semi-easy chair, resting your back easily against the back of the chair.
Elevate your chin a little; hold up your head!
Look a little upward and outward - easily and without strain - as though peacefully looking up and out to the stars.

Since spirit is radiantly active, do NOT bow your head!

And do not close your eyes, and do not let your body sag - either forward or downward, for such attitudes are in opposition to the uprighteous attitude of spirit itself.

Do NOT look within, for spirit infinitely radiates outward!

God's world of spirit is infinite!
Even your soul, is NOT confined inside of your little body.
God does permeate your being, but the greater truths are:
(1) you are IN God, and (2) your soul is greater than your body.

Your soul is not IN your body, - for body is limited and soul
is limitless.
The light in your room radiates out from an electric bulb,
and is all around the bulb. Only its focal point is inside the bulb.

So also, your body is the focal point of your soul it is no
more inside your body, than light in your room is inside the bulb.

SECOND STEP: SIT seven minutes in this RADIANT EXPANDING
attitude, and do this each night and each morning!

Feel yourself expanding: look out as at night, over the
tops of trees; out over far away hills; out, far above the horizon,
even TO the STARS!
Say unto thyself, - "I will lift up mine eyes to the hills," -
for it is from the heights of God, that strength cometh!

THIRD STEP: Feel as though you were OUT in the midst of all
infinite spirit, OUT beyond any thought of limited body or mind.

EXPAND out and out, until you know that the infinity of your
own soul is NOT confined to your little body.

Your soul IS spirit, and DOES actually live in spirit among
the stars, as well as on this earth of God!

FOURTH STEP: Vision what you want, with NO restrictions!
Spirit is infinite. So, vision fulfillment WITHOUT LIMIT!
ADJUST your old thoughts to new ideals!
You are IN spirit, so vision yourself IN spirit!

FIFTH STEP: As you sit in this expectant attitude, and as
your mind expands so it IS like spirit in action - DESIRE what you
want with all intense spiritual longing of your soul.

This makes your soul reach out, not inward; and this is in
harmony with all the activity of spirit itself!
And as your activity becomes LIKE the activity of spirit, con-
flicting opposition disappears, and desire IS fulfilled!
EVEN YOUR BODY - in this expectant attitude - becomes responsive and is transformed - flooded with vitality of spirit.

As you expand, your consciousness intimately contacts spirit
itself and all its manifestations.
You become continuously guided by spirit.

All mental barriers to past memories, disappear!
And with your activity, like the activity of spirit, you
constantly commune with it.

Practice easily now - the first five steps, given above.

Often clarify in your own mind, the Seven Holy Powers of
God of the Seven Days of Creation!
There is nothing else like these powers in all heaven and earth.
They never destroy; they are always constructive.
And each always produces a result after its own kind.

For the First Day of the process of creation, there is the
In-spiring Ray - the radiation of energy into the ideal of what you
desire, or into the substance or thing or condition you wish to create.

For the Second Day of the process, there is the Expanding
Ray; which starts the creating of something different from that
which was inspired by the First Power.

For the Third Day, there is the Forming Ray which begins to
give form to what is expanding, to actualize the ideal of what
you desire.

For the Fourth Day, there is the Clarifying Power. You may
also call it the Purification or Differentiating Power - each
part taking its own place, being harmonized so that each part
works together harmoniously to produce what you most desire.

For the Fifth Day of our process of creation, there is the
Vitalizing Ray to be used.
It is mystic and mysterious in its power; it gives life even
to that which does not have life - just as God on the Fifth Day
brought forth life out of water which in itself is not living.

For on the Sixth Day, the Re-Creative Power - the power of
each thing to reproduce itself, like to its own kind - the source
of all abundance of earth - whether abundance of energies, or
life, or of things of material wealth.

And for the Seventh Day, the Holding Ray - that is, the power
that keeps what you have created for use for yourself and for
others, and also keeps what you have created in the form or condition in which you created it, so it does not lessen, or deteriorate, or disappear.

THE GREATER SPIRITUAL RESPONSIVENESS OF BODY

AND

AWAKENING THE BRAIN OF SPIRIT

by Brown Landone

EXPANDING TO CREATE - - - - - - - - - - - - - - - - - - - LESSON XX

I write for you of "The wisdom of God in a mystery, - even
the hidden wisdom which God ordained before the world!

"The powers that be, are ordained of God!"
"Let every soul be subject (responsive) unto them!"

Spirit IS forever infinitely expanding; hence expansion is
the only way by which you become like spirit, and responsive to it.
It is THE way of 'heaven', taught by God and the Christ!

It is the mystic secret of the expanding ray!
We have not yet comprehended what Jesus meant by heaven, any
more than his apostles and disciples and followers did.
What they later taught proves that they did not understand!

Yet Christ tried to make it very clear!
He taught what he meant by heaven again and again, and used
illustration after illustration! Yet they did not understand!

Even in the Old Testament the ideal of heaven is defined,
and the meaning is exactly the same as that which Jesus taught.
If you have a Revised Version of the Bible, turn to the first
chapter of Genesis, and look at the foot notes. (I tell you this
again; just as Christ repeatedly repeated it to his followers.)
The Hebrew word translated 'firmament' means heaving up,
and expanding and expansion! And God himself called that, heaven!

Then the only word for heaven in the New Testament - the
ONLY word which Jesus himself used for 'heaven' - means LIMITLESSLY
INCREASING AND EVER EXPANDING ACTIVITY!

Jesus said, "Heaven is like unto a grain of mustard seed."
One single mustard seed CAN soon produce enough other seeds -
expand in one season into a thousand seeds - so that its progeny
will cover an entire field with mustard plants in one season.

And Jesus said, "Heaven is like leaven." Leaven is YEAST!
And there are very few things we know on earth, which expand
so rapidly and amazingly as yeast.

20-89

And Christ said, - "The kingdom of heaven is within you!"
That is, - that the CENTER of expanding power is within YOU!

Be certain to understand this clearly, for there have been
many mistaken teachings which confuse the truths of Christ.

There is NO statement whatever, that 'heaven' is within you.
All inspired and mystic statements of all ages reveal that it
is not heaven, but the kingdom of heaven that is within you.
The word translated kingdom is basilica, - meaning stronghold
of power, or center of power!

Heaven is expansion; and it is the center of this power - the
kingdom from which expansion takes place, that is within you.
And since your soul is made in the likeness of God, you are
the center of that expansion; you are the Limitless Expansionist!
By use of God's EXPANDING RAY of spirit, you enter into
its heaven of infinite expression and attainment, here and now!

Remember, the FIRST steps of the SACRED RESPONSE:
(1) the physical attitude;
(2) expanding far out in consciousness, as TO the stars;
(3) feeling that you are in the midst of stars; and
(4) visioning what you want while feeling this expansion.

HELL is being forced to shrink, - when you want to expand!
Heaven is expansion out beyond your present consciousness.

God used the expanding power the Second Day, to begin the
change of the formless and void earth - which resulted from the
creation in mind only - into an actual and spiritualized earth.

The first power, used on the First Day, is INSPIRING power.
It in-spired itself into substance and into all energies.
It inspires itself into each soul and each body!

Now another great truth. I have taught you that Elohim
is the word which is translated 'God' in the first chapter of our
Bible, and that it is plural in form - meaning God-powers.

In its spelling, a strong 'A' instead of a weak 'A', is used.
The strong 'a' is aleph, and aleph is the word for bull in the
Hebrew language - the sacred symbol of divine HE-powers of God.

The Inspiring Power which God used the First Day of creation,
is the impregnating power of God, by which he impregnated all
energy and all substances with power of continuing creating and
growth during the next six days or processes of creation.

Certainly, AFTER the use of the Inspiring Power on the First
Day of Creation, something more was needed to grow into reality.

Compare this with God's divine process by which woman gives birth to the child. First male power _impregnates_ woman. This is in-spiration of power into that which is to be created.

BUT the human being is not yet born! For development and birth, the use of _another_ power is needed!
The tiny _impregnated_ cell in the mother's womb, is still _FORMLESS_, and _VOID_ of the form of a human body.

So, for this, God uses the Expanding Power; and within the mother's womb, the one tiny ovum cell, _EXPANDS_ into a million cells, ten million cells, ten billion cells - the most amazing expansion of earth and heaven. Thus, the child's body is ready to be formed.

I am teaching you Truth, far beyond mere thoughts of truth!

Statements of Truth are crystallized; they have _lost living_ power; they stimulate, but their effect always wears _off_.

What I teach you is true of _everything_ God has created!
Just as new life of the human being is born by use of the two powers God first used in the creation of earth - the First and Second days of Creation, so also these same two powers must be used in the _initial birth_ of everything you desire on earth, if you wish to _become_ an _actual creation_.

Conception of the plant is created within the seed.
But as a plant, it is still formless and void; it is merely the idea of a plant which exists in the seed.

Then something is _in-spired into_ the seed - the warmth of heat, or the energy of _sunlight_. This awakens life in the seed.
This is the use of _inspiring power_ affecting the seed.

Next comes the use of Expanding Power - Expansion within the seed breaks its outer covering, and expands the infinitely small substance of the seed, so that it multiplies itself millions of times as it grows to a plant, or even to become a tree.

Everything you attain in life, can be attained with the absolute certainty of God, if you _begin_ with the use of the Inspiring Ray, and continue with the use of the Expanding Power, and then follow on with the powers of the other days of creation!

In this, _you_ are the Limitless Expansionist!

And expansion, please remember, _is_ heaven!

THE GREATER SPIRITUAL RESPONSIVENESS OF BODY

AND

AWAKENING THE BRAIN OF SPIRIT

by Brown Landone

REVIVING PURIFIER and BALANCE WHEEL - - - - - - - - - LESSON XXI

Yes, you have been able to 'get along' - body, slowly dying - every day - from your 21st year to the end of your physical life here on earth.
BUT NOW, with new Expanding Power awakened, this can change.

The Expanding Ray is also called the resurrecting ray.

This Ray was known to holy men as the Caracolian Ray in very early Maya times, and symbolized in their Temple of the Stars.

But 11,000 years before the Mayans, it was defied in ancient Tiayura by holy mystics who built the most mysterious temples of earth, near the highest waters under the southern cross; and by them, it was called - the Ray of the Mystics of the Southern Cross.

From what has already been excavated and discovered, it seems certain that their civilization excelled all other civilization in at least nineteen different ways.
Their holy men later went to Thibet, but have now again return-ed to the mountains and high waters under the southern cross.

This Expanding Ray is also the Reviving Ray, and as you be-come responsive to it, you are continually, being reborn.

Instead of the usual slowly dying process after the twenty-first year, life of the body becomes a process of continuous hourly resurrection!

Resurrection takes place by purification AND by inspiration.
That is, to restore life in the body, the body must be puri-fied so that more spirit energy can be taken-in (inspired).

By purification, I mean MORE than mere cleansing of body - more than the processes which physiologists teach.
I mean an actual change of quality of the substance of the cells - like the change, when coal is changed to diamonds.

And I am NOT writing now of purifying your soul.
You do NOT need to purify it, because it IS pure.

21-92

God made the soul perfect in the beginning - in his own image!
Only two things interfere with its perfect manifestation.
One is the opposing activity of your conscious mind.
The other is the NON-responsive condition of your body.

In this Lesson, I write of your BODY - to make it responsive.
For just as pure light cannot manifest its glory of color
through a lump of coal, so your soul cannot make its power manifest until the substance of your body IS transformed - as coal
is changed to diamonds - so that it can respond to spirit.

No mere material physiological means will do this.
So, to attain true responsiveness, you BECOME a spiritual
physiologist!

As there is spiritual salvation, so there is bodily salvation.
To continue living, your body must expand in spirit, and be
resurrected physically from death, each four minutes.
And UNLESS you do this, spirit ceases to manifest through it!

The process, which the infinite has given you for this redemp-
tion, is the Sacred Breath of Resurrecting Expansion.

This is more than mere physiological breathing.
A pig breathes physiologically, but you need something higher
in breathing - something that awakens the mystic relationship between life in your body and your breath and the energies of spirit.

MANY modes and methods of breathing have been taught.
Some vitalize the body temporarily, and yet lead to early death.
Others awaken brain centers unevenly, so that the mind becomes
unbalanced. Others actually burn out the lungs.
Others produce results, - directly opposite to that which is
claimed for them. Others unbalance blood circulation!

I have studied and faithfully practiced all methods of breathing usually taught - physiological, athletic, hygienic, mystic -
some learned in America, some in Europe, some in the Orient, some
of mystic Tibetans.
And there is one test above all other tests, which will determine whether any one of these systems is beneficial or harmful.

The primal essential of breathing is to free the body of
fatigue poisoning - that is, to rest the body, minute by minute.

Hence, ANY method of breathing which you can NOT continue for
ten hours without increasing fatigue, IS detrimental.

Test this: Go to an open window, and take a few deep breaths -
as you have often been taught. If permanently beneficial, then
you can keep up that breathing for hours without fatigue.

But try it, and you find it so fatiguing, that it is difficult to continue even for ten minutes. Hence, it cannot be beneficial breathing, for the primal purpose of breathing is to rest,
not to fatigue the body - rest it by removing the poisons of fatigue!

Here I discuss ONLY the Breath of Resurrecting Expansion!
It keeps your body pure, as spirit is pure!
It continually frees your body of the non-responsive substances!

There is need of this breath, for although there are only 2
billion people on earth, there are 800,000 billion cells in your
body; and all of them must be 'redeemed' from death each 4 minutes.

Normally, you exhale 16 quarts of carbon dioxide each hour.

This is necessary to exist! But eliminating only 16 quarts
of carbon-dioxide each hour, lets your body slowly die.

It alone, does NOT make your body any more responsive than
that of a pig; it does not resurrect the cells to new life.

If for one hour, you allow even a little extra carbon-dioxide
to accumulate in the body, - that is, if you breathe out only 15
quarts instead of 16 quarts, - then, all your vital organs - endocrine glands, nerves, brain - become numbed and non-responsive.

In contrast, IF you breathe out a little more than usual, -
that is, 18 quarts an hour - then, YOUR BODY is changed as though
by mystic magic!

If then I teach you the Sacred Breath, which will eliminate
19 quarts an hour, you can work MIRACLES of increased vitality,
resurrection of cells, expansion of energy, and continuance in life!

With such breathing, more spirit will flood and permeate your
body; cells will respond more fully to spirit energy, radiate more
of their mysterious inner light, and your body will be sensitively
awakened, so that you can intimately contact spirit and all its
manifestations.

The process is very simple, and the results are amazing.

We now know for a certainty HOW to transform breathing.

Nature, spirit, a little child, and mystic masters - teach us!

Here is nature's proof: When you exercise vigoriously, extra
impurities are produced, and nature urges you to breathe in such
a way, that you will more quickly get rid of the extra impurities.

SO, what do you do? YOU PANT!

And how DO you breathe, when panting?
Each in-going breath is shorter than usual!
Each out-going breath is longer than usual!
With NO pause after each in-going breath!
But with a pause after each out-going breath!

Where is spirit's proof? How do you breathe, to free your
body of the extra emotive wastes due to sadness or sorrow?
You SIGH, or sob!
And a sigh can not be a sigh, unless its in-going breath is
short; and its out-going breath long.

The proof of a little child, asleep - breathing as spirit
impels it to breathe.
In-going breaths are short; out-going longer!

Proof of the mystic masters depends on the perfect Teleois
balance of 4 to 7 in breathing! This cosmic balance of in-going
breath to out-going breath, was taught in Ancient Tiayura.

It is very simple - so simple, it is mysterious!
Breathe-in for FOUR counts; breathe-out for SEVEN counts.

This 4 to 7 ratio is not based on mere theory or supposition!
It is the law of perfect spiritual form AND movement!

All perfect movements resolve into 1, or 4, or 7.

"Perfect numbers" are always determined by addition, - BE-
CAUSE it is the only arithmetical operation which is ALWAYS
BASIC in ALL other secondary operations of mathematics.

Multiplication, subtraction, and division are secondary!
For example, multiplication is merely repeated additions.
Multiplying four times five, gives the same result as adding
five, four TIMES.
And subtraction is nothing but UN-adding numbers!
And Division is a process of subtraction.
When you say, - that 4 is contained five times in 20, you
mean that 4 can be subtracted five times from 20!

I write of this now, so you shall know: (1) that there is
ONLY ONE BASIC arithmetical process; (2) that it is addition;
that (3) only by addition can we test numbers to determine both
perfect form and movement in the universe; and that (4) perfect
harmonic movement is essential in breathing.

If a number is perfect, it can be resolved - by ADDITION of
its digits into 1, 4, or 7.
For example, 13 is 1 and 3. ADD 1 TO 3, and you have 4.

Hence 13 IS a perfect number, because it resolves into 4.

Now test 26. ADD its 2 to its 6, and you have 8. Hence 26 is NOT perfect, because the 8 is NOT 1, or 4, or 7.

Next test 16. ADD its 1 and 6. You have 7. It IS perfect. So also 31. Its 3 plus 1 make 4.

And 142 is perfect, - for 1 plus 4 plus 2 is 7.

Except for two actual proven FACTS, these numbers of 1, 4, and 7, might seem fantastic!

The first great factual truth is, that these are the ONLY numbers found THROUGHOUT the universe, in ALL form and movement!

The second factual truth is, that they are the ONLY proportionals, which ARE found in ALL the structure of universe.

They determine proportional distances of stars, widths and length of paths of comets; and distances of planets from the sun!

And on earth, these same numbers determine EVERY beautiful geometric design ever used in art or architecture; the intervals of our musical scales; the proportions of the human body! They are even found in the inner designs of snowflakes.

From my use of these sacred numbers - 1, 4, and 7 - you may ask - "Do YOU believe in numerology?"

My answer is, - NO and YES. I do NOT believe in fantastic systems of numerology worked out by man, for they ARE wrong!

But I DO believe in the Teleois numbers which ARE found in all snowflake designs, in intervals of colors in the spectrum; in our musical scales, in forms and relational distances and even in speeds of meteors, comets, planets, stars of the universe.

With such evidence, I accept the SPIRITUAL basis of 1, 4, 7.

And hence I teach you the Resurrection-Expansion Breath, as the SIXTH step of the Sacred Response, based on 1, 4, 7.

Use this breath ONLY when resting in an easy chair; after making your peace with spirit, and after the fourth step of Lesson 1.

AFTER the Fourth Step of visioning what you want, immediately proceed with the Sacred Breath of this Lesson.

And never, use this breath when standing; although, if an invalid in bed at present, use it when lying down.

Use it 4 minutes each morning, and 7 minutes each evening!

Breathe-IN for four counts. And do not hold your breath! Then breath-OUT for 7 counts and pause for 1 count of rest.

Again breathe-IN 4 counts; breath-OUT, 7; and rest 1 count. Continue FOUR minutes each morning; SEVEN minutes each night.

Follow this, by again DESIRING what you want, intensely.

NB: Do NOT ask me or anyone, HOW LONG each "count" should be!

NEVER 'time' your breathing to a clock, or to anyone's advice.
Your breathing is YOUR breathing! Spirit IN YOU will determine how long each count should be FOR you at this time!

The SPIRITUAL law is the law of EASE! So always breathe so
that the FOUR counts of YOUR in-going breath and the SEVEN counts
of your out-going breath, are EASY for YOU.
Ease is the proof of spiritual harmony in action IN YOU!

This sacred Breath IS in tune with the universe.

Its 1, 4, 7 ARE the proportional distances of planets from
the sun and of interstar spaces!

They determine our musical scale - one primal tone; four
base tones - do, mi, sol, do; seven intervals in major scale.
Then other Teleois numbers - 13 (4) and 19 (1) - determine
respectively, the 13 intervals of the perfected chromatic scale,
and the highest beautiful overtones of purest violin notes.

These same 1, 4, 7 are found in designs INSIDE of snowflakes;
in the whirls of flowing water; in curve of a bird's wing, and in
the perfect proportions of the human body.

These mystic relations of one to four to seven were used in
designs of all great temples - in the ancient Temple of Heaven in
Cathay; the Great Pyramid; the Inner Chambers of Thibet; the Temple
of Eleusis; Holy of Holies; Maya Temples; and in the most spiritually symbolic Temple of God-in-Radiancy.

They balance, the proportional movements of the universe.
In the Sacred Breath, they become the balance wheel of life!

Although physiological breathing lets your body die in a few
decades, yet the 1 to 4 to 7 Breath, continuously redeems it!

Use this breath, and you spiritually resurrect your body.

The apostle saith, "All flesh shall see the salvation of God."
And since death and life are conditions, death can be turned to life.

"The Lord God BREATHED -- and man became a LIVING soul."

This turns death to life; old cells into new ones.

With such life, "Thy youth is renewed like the eagles!"

THE GREATER SPIRITUAL RESPONSIVENESS OF BODY

AND

AWAKENING THE BRAIN OF SPIRIT

by Brown Landone

THE SPIRITUAL PHYSIOLOGIST - - - - - - - - - - - - - LESSON XXII

There are FOUR basic means provided by God, for purifying the cells of the body, to make it more responsive to spirit.

The intelligence of the cells is so great that they TRY to carry-on their mysterious functions, even when you neglect them!

And if you spiritually cooperate, their activities transcend mere physiological functions, and become redeemers!

Your blood is the living fluid of life. Mystics speak truly when they call it the "living blood of the lamb of God."
It rushes through your body, quarts of it every minute, purifying every cell, for greater responsiveness to spirit!
Other intelligent activities - of intestine and kidneys - carry off quarts of other un-responsive wastes every day.
Your skin squeezes out impurities, through two thousand million little tubes; and your lungs breathe out 30,400 quarts of impure air each day - 2,532 pints every minute!

God and nature work for you hourly - intelligently, lovingly. They keep these processes active, even when you neglect them. Even when you do not give them half a chance!

Oh, I realize what you may be saying to yourself, - "WHAT? Is this course, just attention to kidneys, intestines, skin, lungs? Why, that is the same old physiology - nothing more."

Ah, but there IS something MORE!
Mere physiological processes let your body DIE even before you are a mere 100 years old!
They let it begin to die when you are only 21.

BUT WITH spiritual cooperation, they can make the body so spiritually responsive that it tends to PHYSICAL IMMORTALITY!

This is the difference between slowly dying for most of your life, or inspiring the structure to increasingly live.
The spiritual is linked with the physiological, - the body which must be made spiritually responsive - lifted up to vibrate like spirit, to continue its life, vitally and youthfully.

22-98

Another factor should stun you with amazement.

For many decades scientists have been trying to find out WHY the body dies, - for physiologically the body should not die.

Although birth is a miracle, and yet we can understand that when spirit enters into anything, it lives.

And after a body is given birth, we know it should grow to adulthood, because it is created, responsive to spirit.

Such growth is proof that the human body, at birth and during childhood, IS responsive to spirit.

And then comes the mystery, for - even when growing - even while it is still responsive, it begins to STOP being responsive!

And even when healthy, it begins to die in its 21st year! WHY? That has been the mystery.

For, since growth is proof of the body's responsiveness to spirit, WHY does it not keep on being responsive - living forever?

Today one phase of this mystery is solved.

Scientists know that the primal cause of aging and death of the body is accumulation year by year - of impurities in the body.

We know that these impurities are NOT responsive to spirit.
(1) that as they accumulate, legs of spirit manifests;
(2) that if you free the body of them, MORE SPIRIT MANIFESTS. This much is simple truth, understandable and proven!

Now one step more: spirit is life; and hence, if you spiritually purify your body, spirit will continue to manifest, and the body will not wear out, but will continue to build new tissues - continue their youthfulness, FOREVER!

WE NOW HAVE PROOF OF THIS: Dr. Alex Carrel has proven it.

He has proven that (1) perfect food is not enough; that chicken heart cells, even when fed perfectly, DIE in a few hours.

But also (2) he has proven that when chicken heart cells are purified - when non-responsive wastes are washed away every day - they live on and on, continually reproducing NEW CELLS.

Instead of dying in 48 hours; they HAVE lived 227,760 hours! And the cells of that tiny piece of heart tissue - purified daily - have been so responsive to spirit, that - if all of them had been kept growing - they would have produced enough NEW heart muscle every year to cover 546 ACRES, a FOOT DEEP!

Note the SPIRITUAL significance of this!
Your body is composed of cells!
The ultimate life or death of those cells depends on purifying activities of kidneys, intestines, and skin, and on the continued

resurrection of life by the holy breath!

If you but help their purifying process only a little, your body can become so much more responsive to spirit than at present, that it will approach the conditions of physical immortality.

For daily spiritual resurrection of the body, purification is the first essential! This is proven, - for if you stop one of its purifying processes for a few minutes only, your body becomes so NON-responsive to spirit, that it dies.
Yes, the body dies, when breath is shut off for 4 minutes.

Each purification process is a means of spiritual resurrection, of the life of the cells of the body - resurrection each hour!

Life is of spirit, and life itself is eternal.
If nothing interfered with spirit, the body would be immortal!
Spirit never stops spirit.
Nothing but NON-responsive substances IN the body make its cells so NON-responsive to spirit that cells begin to die!

Physiological purification keeps body alive a few years.
But SPIRITUAL cooperation makes the body like spirit!

Spirit itself is ever ready to manifest in continued life. but your body - in its present condition - cannot stand up to the vibration of spirit.
Only SPIRITUAL help will make it more responsive to spirit.

If you but purify your body just a little MORE than is done by the usual physiologic processes, you can WORK a MIRACLE!

Purify your 800,000 billion cells - change them from tiny particles of dirty coal to diamonds of spirit!

Resurrect the cells of your body so they will become so responsive to spirit, that mind will work with spirit, and respond to its power of continuing life!

Become the Spiritual physiologist of your life!

Clarify again the first two great rays of creation:
First, the Inspiring Ray - in-spires energy into your body, to energize every cell with the 'fire of spirit'.
Second, the Expanding Ray breaks down the fixed conditions and resurrects activity, purifying the body of in-activity expanding power in structure, to new and greater attainment.

THE GREATER SPIRITUAL RESPONSIVENESS OF BODY

AND

AWAKENING THE BRAIN OF SPIRIT

by Brown Landone

GIVE ACTUAL FORM TO YOUR CREATION - - - - - - - - - - - - LESSON XXIII

"The heavens declare the glory of God!
The firmament sheweth his handiwork!"
And man is "reverently and wonderfully made" in God's likeness.

I now teach you the FORMING Ray - the ray of the Third Day of creation. It actually MADE land appear in FORM, and water in FORM - each after its own FORM.

Response to this FORMING Ray, changes desire into ACTUAL FORM.
This is not mysterious for each energy produces results according to the nature of its own energy, and this ray produces form.

Egyptian mystics - who later designed the Pyramid of Gizeh - called this ray, the Mathonian Ray.
And it is not difficult for us to recognize that the first syllable of this word - math - is the root from which we have derived our word 'mathematics'.

While measurement is one basis of determining form on earth, this ray is much more than mathematical measurements.
All radiant rays have power to change the NATURE OF substance.

And the FORMING Ray has a PECULIAR power of its own!
Whenever it vibrates through a substance, it produces FORM.
This ray has PECULIAR power of drawing together, infinitely small particles - millions of times smaller than grains of flour - and assemblying them in definite FORM.
It can also trans-form energies into new forms of energy.

Crystal clear water flows down from mountains toward the sea; when it stops near the shore, this Forming Ray collects the chemicals dissolved in the water, and turns them into crystal FORMS - that is, crystallized sand.

This Forming Ray also builds up and gives FORM to things.
It also has power to give actual form to desires.

It is used by the Masters to give Form to their ideals.
It is used by mystics to produce forms at a distance.

As you increase your response to this power, you also <u>can</u> FORM your desires in spirit in such a way, that they will become real actual actualities for you.

I know that for many years, you have sincerely held 'thoughts' of things, for the purpose of giving form to what you wanted.
But thoughts alone do <u>NOT</u> produce actual <u>FORM</u>.
And by thought alone, many of your desires fail to take on actual form!

In many lines, man is miraculously efficient.

He makes machines of astounding power and phenomenal delicacy. By these, he can talk around the world; fly across oceans; and multiply the power of lightning a thousand times.

And man has sense enough to KNOW that to produce any such machine, he must first <u>conceive</u> it in some definite FORM.

YET, in his spiritual efforts, man <u>still</u> idealizes and desires in a vague will-o-the-wisp way, <u>without</u> spiritually, conceiving the definite FORM of what he <u>desires</u> to attain.

Even when most consecrated, he seeks and searches – tries this and that – and often even after years of effort, his life on earth fails to attain what he has most desired.

In his attempts to improve his own body, his methods are more wasteful than in any other effort he makes on earth.
He tries out one thing after another, and with the years, his body becomes older and stiffer, more bent and creaky.

In your own life, it is certain you HAVE thought and planned and tried to make the things you desired come true!
Yet lack of creating things in the ACTUAL FORM you desired, has been the greatest failure of your past efforts.

You have conceived greatly, but conception is not birth.
Remember, that even God's conceptions <u>in mind</u> were STILL "<u>formless and void</u>", UNTIL he used the FORMING Ray of Creation.

For results, you too must give FORM to what you conceive!
And now, with the definite power of the means of FORMING what you want, you can attain more in <u>four months</u> than you could otherwise attain in <u>forty years</u>.

Prepare now to become, a Divine Formist!

THE GREATER SPIRITUAL RESPONSIVENESS OF BODY

AND

AWAKENING THE BRAIN OF SPIRIT

by Brown Landone

THE DIVINE FORMIST - - - - - - - - - - - - - - - - - - LESSON XXIV

If your body is not responsive, less spirit comes through.
When it becomes more responsive, more spirit manifests.

And FORM has much to do with the degree of your body's
responsiveness, and the quality of power that does manifest.

So this lesson concerns form, and please at once free your
mind of all mistaken ideas of form as a fixed result!
And do not hold any mental picture of your body, possessing
a fixed form. If you do, your body will die more rapidly than it
is dying at present, and will not respond to the higher form - the
form of spiritual energy which can transform all outward forms.

Vision your body as a highly vibratory instrument - forever
being in-spired by spirit, with energies ever expanding and uplifting (1) to resurrect the body's cells; (2) to change its
form; (3) to make it more responsive to spirit; (4) to express
more of life for you.

This form is different from mind's ideal; this lifts form up
to spirit, so the Forming Ray can trans-form it!

Since before the time of the Greeks, man on earth has always
tried to improve the form of his body and increase his energy.
Hundreds of methods have been used; each praised by its user.
All faddish means have resulted in failure - usually in death
earlier than in case of people who do not use such methods.
And now our scientists are earnestly seeking means, not only
of increasing man's energy, but of lengthening his life.

But all results desired, can be accomplished only by greater
spiritual responsiveness, for only as spirit continues to manifest
in the body can it maintain its strength and youthfulness.

No scientist of the last century - excepting only one -
has studied the primal energies of nature or God.
Researches have dealt with the secondary energies, and
often only with the minor manifestations of secondary energies.

For example, scientists talk of affinity in chemistry.

24-103

Affinity is evidence of a power that draws particles together, and gives them new form, - either of substance or energy.

Yet not one great thinking chemist of all earth has sought to find out the power which activates affinity.

Affinity is merely the outer manifestation of a higher power. That higher power is the Forming Ray of God.
Not one scientist has as yet studied.

It is wise before we proceed to understand more clearly what we mean by form - what God meant by form - when he used Forming Ray, - to draw particles and energies together, so that each thing of earth would take on actuality in form.

There are four factors which are determinants of form: (1) shape, (2) direction of movement, (3) activity, (4) energy.

There is the form of an apple, form of a tree, form of a girl, form of a triangle, form of a building!
Such form is true form, but even the form of an apple can not be perceived except by direction of movement. That is, your fingers must move around it, or movement of your eye must follow the line that bounds it, to perceive its form. And this is true of any shape-form of triangle, of girl, statue, or building.

There are also forms of activity - some movements are in straight lines; others in waves or curves; others in spirals.
Then also scientists recognize different forms of energy.

The great Forming Ray of God, of the Third Day of Creation, can create all forms of all kinds, for actual manifestations.

Form in part determines quality and degree of manifestation.

Even the deadened forms of many things on earth - even of our bodies - hinder spiritual manifestation, in comparison with the great power of the uplifted spiritual forms.
And this is true of all other things on earth.

The Egyptians used the solid form, more than any other race.
They built forms that last, yet they themselves lost the spiritual concept of form, so that they themselves died out.
That is, their pyramids still exist, but the ancient Egyptians are themselves gone from the face of the earth.

The ancient holy Egyptian mystics understood the FORMING Ray.
But their spirituality was lost, before the pyramids were built!
Look at any picture of the Great Pyramid of Gizeh.
Much that has been written of it is true, and yet those who built the pyramid did not know of the higher forms of the Forming Ray.

Even the lesser mystics then directing the building, thought mostly of 'fixed' forms to carry a message to future ages.

Although mystic knowledge is revealed by the symbolism of its measurements, yet the pyramid itself is the LOWEST - the most deadened NON-living, NON-spiritual form on earth!

It is LIKE a PILE of EARTH!
It stands up because of mere dirt-form. Inclines of its sides are the same as would result if you took a shovel and piled up dirt, with the dirt rolling down the sides of your pile.

It IS the lowest FORM on earth!
There is NO spirit in its form - NO uplift to life!

It is an EARTH symbol! That is why most interpreters fail to find its true hidden meanings, which are revealed only by its cubic structure, and never by mere LENGTH measurements.
That is why the interpretations of meanings, based on its line measurements are completely mistaken!
Its real mystic truths are revealed one by the spiritual significance of its cubic structures.

This is NOT a Lesson on the Pyramid of Gizeh!
I write of it only to emphasize its lack of spiritual form, so different from the NEW PRYAMID now being built by mystic men of Tiayura who still live, and by those holiest of today, who forever abandoned Thibet as the great spiritual center in 1922 - now directing all higher brotherhoods from the new spiritual temple on inaccessible heights of the eastern side of the holy Andes.

But my primal purpose in this, is that you recognize relationship of spirit to form, and seek its application to your body.

Look at the squatty earth-like structural form of any pyramid; then look at photographs of the beautifully uplifted spiritual forms of our architecture of today - the spires of our cathedrals and the tower buildings - the Tribune Tower and Wrigley Tower in Chicago, State Capitol of Nebraska, University of Pittsburgh, Chrysler Building in New York, and Singing Tower in Florida.

Man advances first by producing the results IN the things about him. And often he dies and his civilization dies, because he is not able to do as much for himself, as he does for mere things.

Today we are the first civilization on earth in which man's spirit has risen to spiritual form in structural building, so that he produces inner form to hold up the weight, instead of merely piling up mass weight upon mass weight, from the base.
If you had x-ray eyes, to look through a modern skyscraper,

you would see all its weight hung upon an inner steel structure.

But in a pyramid, the weight is merely piled up - each section on a larger section below.

Now we come to the actual spiritual determinants of all the essentials of the higher form in practical manifestation - the powers of inspiration, expansion, resurrection, uplift, movement, activity, and the energy of spirit.

The above are the determinants of transforming life.

And it IS as possible to work miracles in changing form in our own manifestation of life, as it is for a mere grub worm to transform itself into a beautiful butterfly.

All perfect form is based on spirit; not on an earth-pile!

It gives man the opportunity of greater expansiveness of spirit, with the greatest manifestation of energy - transforming earth-man into the man of heaven on earth - a god on earth.

Perfect proportions of all such forms are 1, 4, 7, 13, 19, 31.

These are the perfect proportions of the human body, now proven by scientists even to a millimeter.

These are the perfected proportions of all newer spiritualized structures - such as buildings and towers previously mentioned.

These are proportions found in the great Taj Mahal.

These are the proportions found in completeness in the very ancient Temple of Heaven in pre-ancient Cathay, in the Temple of the Stars in Maya land, in the Temple of Eleusis, and in the Holy of Holies in the Temple of Solomon.

FORM on this basis is created by the Forming Ray of spirit.

Use this ideal of the uplifted and uplifting structural form, in your visioning of a transformed body, and of the physical attitude of your body, and in visualizing whatever you want, and transformation will result!

I presume you ask me now, - "How can one do this?"

How vision form, and yet prevent it from becoming 'fixed'.

How can one change the inner body form enough, so that it is responsive enough to the mighty power of the Forming Ray of God to create the new form of a new life here and now!

You do this by realizing form as movement in action, activated by energy. This is very different from mere fixed form; and also different from any 'thought' of any fixed shape of form.

Remember it is form-in-movement, activated by energy.

See that youth walking toward you down the street - head up, easily balanced, looking straight ahead, lithe of body, and so thrilled with life that you can almost imagine him ready at any step to break into running on tip toe, or flying through the air.

Then see that squatty fat woman waddling down the street, - no uplift in the back, the whole body weighted down merely by its own weight piled upon its own weight. So squatty, that if she wore skirts of the old type, she would look like a pyramid - a mere pile of the dirt-form of earth!

Yes, you can do much to change your form of movement, because all great powers are brought into manifestation, - first, by your ideal of it, and longing for it; and second, by action of your body expressed by the ideal in movement.

So now, - as the SEVENTH step of your sacred response, do this:
Slowly rise from a sitting position.
Stand erectly; head up slightly; eyes forward.
Let the arms hang easily at the sides.
Stand thou, like a god on a mountain top, looking out over thy kingdoms of earth, and up to the stars - symbols of the source of high spiritual power for thee!

Then easily extend your hands, outward at the sides - just a little - so that your arms form side lines of an upright tower; and feel your body up-held by spirit, within you.

Stand thus while you count seven, and feel the Forming Ray of God, giving an uplifted form to your body! Then relax easily, but do not let the body sag! Merely stand 'at ease' with weight on one leg, as a soldier stands when 'at rest'.
Count four while standing at rest in this way.
Then repeat the above, and repeat it seven times.
That is, stand erect, look forward and upward, arms easily at the sides, hands out a little away from the body.
Stand for seven counts, and then relax for four counts.
And repeat this seven times.

Then be seated and vision the FORM of whatever you want.

Your Body is a VIBRATORY form! While on earth, your soul manifests through it. Every movement which makes your body more responsive to spirit, gives form to your body, or form to whatsoever you desire. It also augments the spiritual power of each such form to become what you want it to be.

Do NOT be confused: I know that some teachers tell you never to visualize form, and to visualize nothing but spirit.

Such teaching is mistaken; it leaves the creations of your soul in exactly the same condition of God's creation of earth when He created it in thought only - that is, without form, and void!

Moreover, all such teachings - no matter who the teacher, book, or course - are mistaken in completely failing to realize the most primal law God ever gave to man - revealed four times even in the story of creation - that each thing creates after its own kind!

Every power of God creates after its own kind!
Therefore, if you do nothing but vision the form of what you want, you will rightly - by God's own law - obtain only visions of what you want, for visualizing creates after its own kind, - that is, it creates visions!

It is action which creates actuality - always after its own kind - and action changes the spirit of form into actual form.

I have asked you in this Lesson to create actual form of everything you desire or will desire in this life.
And the form I teach you, is MOVEMENT of the living vibrating power of spirit - the Mathonian Ray of Elohim - the Forming Ray which God used on the Third Day of Creation.

No matter what you desire, conceive (1) the purpose of your expression of it; (2) its uplifted form; (3) its freedom from limitation, and (4) its God power to expand into actuality.
No matter WHAT you desire, conceive it as the means of more complete expression of yourself.

For example, if you desire a suit of clothes, vision the suit as one of the means by which YOU can express yourself more fully - that is express your ideals of form, and fit and color, and your individuality as the equal of all others with whom you associate.
Desire whatsoever you want, as means of expressing your soul, and all power of God will work with you, to fulfill the desire.

And second, think of everything you desire in actual form, as standing-up by the power of spirit within itself!
This is the very truth of all matter, - for matter in any form can not stand up by itself, except by the atomic energy within it!
Such energy is but one phase of the Forming Ray of God.

Conceive each thing you desire, in the form, you want.
NOT as a squatty weighted-down-pile-of-dirt-form!
But as upright, uplifted form of spirit!

Always vision anything you desire in uplifted form - with solid base on earth, but with structure held up by the uplift of spirit within it!

And vision whatsoever you want, as alive with spirit; for only thus are you sincere in declaring that all is of spirit!

And third, give each of your desires, a limitless form!

Spirit never limits desire; it is always infinite in desire!

It is only your _mind_ that is always limiting your desires.
There are teachers who will treat you mentally to heal a pimple, or demonstrate a few measly dollars!
But such treatments are in opposition to spirit, for spirit is infinite and manifests infinitely!

Please, take no 'anxious thought' as of a pimple!
Instead, desire INFINITELY!
And Spirit - which _is_ infinite - will fulfill your desire!
The same law holds for ALL things you desire.

Please stop giving LITTLE 'forms' to your desires.
Dare to make the form of your desire as great as spirit!
Then it will be like the infinite power that creates it.
Then, "All these other things shall be added unto you!"

And fourth, hourly realize that your soul HAS the infinitely expanding power to ENFOLD what it wants.
In the past, your mind may have tried to draw or pull what you have desired, TO you, but this gives your desires a contracting or shrinking form, instead of an expanding actualizing form.

You attain as you become like spirit - actively expanding!
So instead of trying to 'draw' spirit into you, or to draw things to you, expand as spirit expands so that you shall enfold what you want, and in the form you want.

Become a divine in-spirationist and expansionist and formist!

Please note how SIMPLY - how PERFECTLY, how EASILY you can build up a Sacred Response to spirit.

FIRST, free the body for inspiration of spirit.
SECOND, expand out INTO spirit, out even to the stars.
THIRD, become conscious of infinity out AMONG the stars.
FOURTH, in this expansion, vision what you want.
FIFTH, use the Sacred Breath to Resurrect its life.
SIXTH, you give your desire the living _form_ you desire, so that it CAN become an actuality.

And always you desire what you want, with the hungering intensity of spiritual longing.

THE GREATER SPIRITUAL RESPONSIVENESS OF BODY

AND

AWAKENING THE BRAIN OF SPIRIT

by Brown Landone

THE GREAT IDEAL-REALIST - - - - - - - - - - - - - - - LESSON XXV

In FORMING what it wants, spirit always has a definite aim.
You also must have a definite purpose, if you are to give
form to your desires, so that they will come true.
This purpose must be in line with your greatest desire.

What DO you want MOST? Your answer can be clear if you forget small things and think of your soul and its expression!

When a beam of white light passes through a glass prism, the
white light is broken up into different colors - rainbow colors.
This proves that each color is but a PART of white light.
Then in laboratories, scientists can UNITE these same colors.
When they do, the united colors produce white light. This
proves that white light is the blend of ALL colors!

Both failures and the lacks in life, are due to partial
manifestation - that is, to lack of complete manifestation.

When you see green light, you see only a part of white light, -
because some green globe or shade is responsive only to green
rays, and lets ONLY the green rays shine through.
It is the globe or shade which holds back all the other rays.

WHEN you see a pure white light shining out in full glory,
it means that the substances through which the light comes to
your eye, are so responsive to light, that they LET practically
ALL of the rays of the white light pass through.
This is always evidence of complete manifestation.

Your body is a prism, for manifestation of your powers.
What then is your GREATEST desire?

Your soul is the holy light of spirit - perfect, complete!
Your GREATEST desire is to MANIFEST it FULLY and COMPLETELY!

All you want - health, vitality, abundance, love and illumination of spirit - are but parts. All will be included, if you
seek the COMPLETE expression of your soul! And that is heaven!

Become an ideal REALIST! Do not let desires dangle in air!

<u>Spirit ALWAYS</u> demands <u>a</u> <u>form</u> <u>for</u> <u>expression</u> <u>of</u> <u>each</u> <u>desire</u>.

There is nothing materialistic in this.
God himself - in beginning creation - knew that he needed a
body for his expression.
So God created one. All galazies of stars and all substance
and energy of earth and heaven <u>form</u> the body of God.

Every star, molecule, atom, electron, were used to create
the magnificent body for the glorious expression of God!

So also your soul - in its urge for infinite expression -
eternally needs a body. It will always need a body - either the
one you now have, or a body of another form in some other realm.
And all you do now to make this body more responsive to spirit,
makes all subsequent bodies still more spiritual.

To attain your ideal body here on earth you need NOT do anything to improve soul, for soul IS already perfect.
God made it perfect in the beginning, in his own likeness!

Your part is to make your <u>body</u> more responsive to it!

You have read: "The spirit is willing, but flesh is weak."
In the original, that is more clearly stated. It is -
"<u>Spirit is READY; but the body LACKS STANDING-UP POWER</u>."

This has been the trouble, with most of your past desires.
They did not have enough "stand-up" form, to become actual.

This is why, I teach you the <u>Forming Ray</u> of spirit - called
the Yadanian Ray by ancient Tiayurans - the Mathonian by the
Egyptians - The Qavahnian Ray by the Hebrew mystics - to give
power to man's desires, so that they will be able to stand-up,
and manifest as actual actualities!

You, yourself, do <u>NOT</u> need to prepare a house for your soul.

An <u>infinite</u> soul can <u>NOT</u> be housed-up inside of a little
body. Your body is only the focal point, through which your
soul expresses its glory of all power!

What your soul wants is a VIBRATORY INSTRUMENT for its
expression! And it cannot be atuned to express soul, unless it
is made responsive to spirit.

25-111

THE GREATER SPIRITUAL RESPONSIVENESS OF BODY

AND

AWAKENING THE BRAIN OF SPIRIT

by Brown Landone

THE "LORD GOD" of YOUR SOUL - - - - - - - - - - - - - - - LESSON XXVI

To create <u>form</u> which is an actuality, it is necessary that
you become a "lord-god" of the Forming Ray!

The word 'lord' in the Old Testament, is the translation of
a Hebrew word which means master!
This word was used both for men and for God.
And in the New Testament, the Greek word which is translated
'lord', also means <u>master</u>.
It also was used both for men and for God.

And you, created in the image and likeness of God, become
your true self, only when you combine the consciousness of <u>master-
ship</u> <u>and</u> <u>lordship</u> with certainty of your own divinity.

Become the great master-god - the lord - of your own desires!
Become 'lord-god' of infinitely expanding power of your soul!
Become a master-god in giving form to whatsoever you desire.

<u>Become</u> <u>the</u> <u>Lord-God</u> <u>of</u> <u>your</u> <u>body</u>!

Remember, there are only 2 billion people living on earth!
But 800,000 billion cells living in your body!

If any man should ever become absolute ruler of the two
billion people of earth, he would be the mighty Lord of Earth.
But already you are infinitely greater!
You <u>ARE</u> the lord-god of 800,000 billion individuals of your body!
You <u>are</u> the supreme god of all the universes of them!

They live IN the vibrations of every attitude of your soul.
You are their lord-master; lord also of all the expanding
powers of spirit which can transform these cells of your body.

By spirit in action, they become responsive to spirit.

As you become more responsive to spirit, the cells of your
body become more responsive to your soul. Then there is heaven.
That is the manifested truth of "the father in me and I in you,"
brought into actuality, every hour of your life.

26-112

THE GREATER SPIRITUAL RESPONSIVENESS OF BODY

AND

AWAKENING THE BRAIN OF SPIRIT

by Brown Landone

LIMITLESS FREEDOM IN ACTION - - - - - - - - - - - - - - LESSON XXVII

This is the beginning Lesson of the Holy Cathayan Ray.

This is the Ray whose power is symbolized by the creation of the Sun and the Moon on the Fourth Day of Creation.

Their creation was more than the creation of ordinary 'light'.
This is the power which in itself creates ordinary light - the power that transforms all things by purification.

This term should be understood clearly.
Purification means, each thing separate by itself.

Gold is pure; lead is pure! Mix the two, and you have both impure gold and impure lead.
Separate them, and you again have pure gold and pure lead.

It is in this true sense, that I use the word purification in all these Lessons.

This Cathayan power is symbolized by transformation of all things, as when the light of sun at dawn disperses the dark of the night; or the light of the moon transforms activity of earth into rest and calmness.

This Cathayan Ray is the power that both liberates and animates, and also purifies and transforms activities and substances.

It symbolizes everything that is done by the activating power of the light of the sun at day, and by the calming power of the light of moonlight at night.
It is the power by which the body is prepared for greater responsiveness, so it can begin creation of its own forms of life.

To understand its value more fully, it IS wise to repeat four truths: (1) spirit IS infinite; (2) nothing but lack of responsiveness causes the lacks of life; (3) the energy of spirit possesses limitless vitality, and hence all fatigue and illness and even death are due to the NON-responsiveness of mind and substances of the body; and (4) nothing but non-responsiveness hinders full response to and communion with all spirit.

You know from experience, that there are powers of the soul which purify and transform; that sometimes a mere moment of expectant joy, instantly cleans the body of fatigue poisons, and makes the body so spiritually responsive, that all fatigue vanishes in a second!

Such is the result of the Purifying Ray - the Cathayan Ray of Spirit.

This is the Ray used by God during the Fourth Day of Creation.

It is the great Ray which was dominant in the civilization of Pre-Cathay, which existed ages before Ancient Cathay, which in turn preceded Cathay, which preceded China.

Its mystics built the ancient Temple of Heaven.

This was, however, literally transformed - long ages before the later Ancient Cathayan Temple of Heaven was built.

<u>Energy</u> <u>CAN</u> <u>transform</u> substance: Even heat rays can so transform water, that it actually <u>disappears</u>! Vanishes in vapor!

Since a LOW powered heat ray can work such a change, imagine the miracles wrought by titanic Cathayan Ray!

This ray can transform the human body, as astoundingly as the change wrought in changing coal to diamonds.

Coal and diamonds are composed of the SAME chemical substances. Coal can <u>not</u> respond to light; light can not shine through it.

But diamonds are purified and made responsive to light!
Light shines through them, in glorious gorgeous colors!

The change from coal to diamonds is an astounding change, due to the Cathayan Ray which purifies lumps of coal deep down in earth, so that coal <u>does</u> become diamond!

I insert this short Lesson for faith and expectancy for you.
For it is very certain that, since coal <u>can</u> be changed to diamonds, miracles can be worked with your own body and your own life.

Even a soggy body can be transformed by the Cathayan Ray, so that spirit will flow through it, manifesting power and glory.

The first results of purification are great multiplication of energy, need of less sleep, an astounding uplift of the body; and this means unlimited freedom in action.

THE GREATER SPIRITUAL RESPONSIVENESS OF BODY

AND

AWAKENING THE BRAIN OF SPIRIT

by Brown Landone

LIBERATOR AND ANIMATING ENERGIZER - - - - - - - - - - LESSON XXVIII

There is also a vitalizing result, due to the Cathayan power.
Your lack of energy and deadness of body - due to its lack
of responsiveness to spirit - are often so great that you remain
UNCONSCIOUS (asleep) for at least one-third of your life on earth!

Sleep is not mysterious at all!
Sleep is temporary death, due to lack of purification sufficient
to let spirit flow through the body easily and continuously!

It is not difficult to understand that when the very spirit
of life flows through your body continuously, it first energizes
it, and then frees it of all fatigue, so that you do not need sleep.

Your greatest need is always more vitality and energy, - for
with more vital energy, your body will be healed; with more
spiritual energy, your personality will so change, that abundance
and success, happiness and love, cannot be kept from you.

Even physiological results of purification are astounding.

Consider Mr. Adams and Mr. Brown.

Adams and Brown are of approximately the same build, weight,
and structure; both eat the same foods and same amount of food.
They are approximately equal in intelligence and education;
do same kind of work for the same number of hours each day.

Both live, and have lived, IN the same universe of energy!

YET in manifestation, Adams and Brown are very different!

Adams is always tired; sleeps eight hours a day, rests a
lot; lacks vitality and health, and has no endurance.

Brown is vital, virile, strong, healthy; always filled with
energy; always active; sleeps five hours a day.

The brain of each is the dynamo of his respective body.

28-115

The muscles of each are his respective motors.

The nerves of each are the wires which carry energies from dynamo to motors - for all expression!

But the brain of Adams is NOT truly responsive to spiritual energy which surrounds and permeates all things.

It is so UN-responsive that only 1,000 units of God's energy flows INTO it each minute.
So at best, he has 1,000 units of power to use per minute!

Moreover, Adams nerves are not responsive. 300 units of his 1,000 units of energy are used up, just trying to get through the cells which form the nerve paths.

Then also his muscles are so blocked with wastes, that they do not respond easily to let the energy flow through them.
They are so UN-responsive that 400 units of energy are used up in friction, trying to get through his muscles into action.

Hence, 600 units of the 1,000 units of energy inspired into Adam's body, are used up, trying to get through his body.

So, he has ONLY 400 units of energy left for actual manifestation in strength and health, action and living!

He is always weak and tired; a colorless ambitionless man!

In contrast, the brain of Brown is so responsive to spirit, that 1800 units of spiritual energy flow into and through his brain every minute.

His nerves also are responsive; and less than 100 units of his 1800 units of energy are used from brain to muscles.

His muscles are so responsive, that they use up only 100 units more, in turning energy into action.

Brown has 1600 units of energy in actual USE, each minute!
FOR USE, Brown has four times the energy Adams has!
Yet all energy of the universe surrounds each of them!

The amount that comes through into use, depends on whether or not the body has or has not become consciously or unconsciously responsive to the Cathayan Ray of God's powers.

THE GREATER SPIRITUAL RESPONSIVENESS OF BODY

AND

AWAKENING THE BRAIN OF SPIRIT

by Brown Landone

CLEANER AND QUICKENING EMANCIPATOR - - - - - - - - - - - LESSON XXIX

I have said that the Cathayan Ray is a purifying ray.

The purifying processes taught here, are NOT materialistic.
When a glass is covered with black greasy dirt, - and then
washed to crystal clearness, so that light in its glory of colors
can shine through it, the change is material so far as the dirt is
concerned, but to the light the change is spiritual, for it lets
more of the spirit of light shine through!

So also with the body, purification fulfills the great purpose of making each cell more responsive to spirit, and hence - to
life, even to your life - it is a spiritual process!

Spirit and living blood purify the cells of your body!
The purifying activities of lungs, skin, kidneys and intestine,
are but helps to the blood's purifying processes.

Your blood does more than merely wash the cells!
It effects a holy INNER purification inside each cell.
ONLY spiritual purification makes the body more responsive!

There is a SPIRITUAL function of bodily organs!
And it is your duty to be their cleansing god - to clean them
spiritually, to use them, spiritually, to manifest more of spirit.
In ancient and holy Cathay four purifying processes were
worshipped as divinely spiritual processes taking place not only
in the body of man, but in all things throughout the universe.

For spirituality is spirit expressing through the body.

That is why, the four corners of the Temple of Heaven were
consecrated - one, to each process of purification.

We moderns have condemned and cursed and debased most things
that have been and are sweet and pure and holy in life.
We debase sex, prostitute love, ridicule brother-hood!

We have even condemned substances - the most beneficial substances God has made for man - and called their use sinful!

29-117

For a hundred years, men were hung without trial if caught
feeding carrots to their cattle, because the yellow in carrots was
condemned as a color of sin produced by witchcraft.

Now we know that the yellow substance is carrotine, vitamin A -
the actually essential substance for growth in all life!

Only a few years ago we condemned tomatoes, believing that
juice of even one tomato would make a young girl immoral for life.

We condemned tobacco, because of its niccotine. Yet now we
know that niccotine is the loving brother of vitamin B_1.

Scientists have kept this fact rather 'hidden', because they
know that prejudices of ignorance, might prevent its use.

And it is amusing, to see earnestly ignorant people, who
think it is a sin to smoke cigarettes, go to a drug store and pay
$2.00 for tablets of Vitamin B_1, which IS pure nicotinic acid!

Most of the things which the ancients spiritualized, we have
condemned as sinful, and we are suffering from our own condemnation!

Nevertheless, we are making progress!
All advances of men are FROM condemnation TO idealization.

Today we think only of the CRUDE physiological cleansing!
But in the holy days, the processes were spiritualized!

Cathay - sometimes spelled Cathar and Karthar, meant the
"response to the flow of the spirit which purifies".

Today we have only the crude remnant of the old meaning in
our word 'cathartic'. How debased our meaning is, is evident from
the fact that the word originally meant, chaste or pure.

Thousands of years after the Temple of Cathay, a little of
its spiritual idealism had come down to the holy men of early Judea,
for they wrote of the soul of man, in his reins or renes.

From root of this word we have ad-renals - the miracle glands
attached to the kidneys.

I write these truths only to awaken in you something of the
spiritual significance of the purification, needed to free the
body for greater manifestation of spirit.

FIRST, aid the purification work of the kidneys!
For this, use the substances in celery, which science has
found acts almost mystically.

Use celery broth, NOT RAW celery or raw celery juice!

Prepare it thus: Cut a quarter pound of celery stalks into
small chunks. Boil them 20 minutes. Salt to taste. Drain off the
water! The water is the broth for you to use.

OR buy canned celery juice at a food shop, and to one cup of such juice, add half a cup of water. Heat until it boils.

Every morning, use a cup of this cooked celery broth.
Drink it BEFORE you take anything else. Sweeten or salt, to taste.

NB: YES, I know that 'raw celery contains beneficial vitamins and salts; and that asparagus also increases flow of water from the kidneys, but our aim now is to aid them to help living blood to purify the cells of the body. For this, use the cooked broth.

SECOND: Every night - before you go to bed - help the purification process of the intestines!

NO, I am NOT writing of any mere cleaning of the intestines; I am NOT writing of flooding the intestines.
I am NOT interested in the intestine as a sewer.
But I AM interested in the PURITY of the billions of living cells of your body, and their responsiveness to spirit.

So I teach you purification which helps the living blood, to purify your entire body of cells, for greater flow of spirit.
To attain this result, do NOT depend on fruit juices.
The ACID fruit juices - of lemon, lime, grape fruit, orange or tomato - and all cathartics of oils or acids, tend to deplete the blood instead of helping it to purify the body.

NB: Of course, such juices cause 'freer movement' of intestine, because of their effect in flooding the intestine with water.

But WHERE does the water for such flooding, come from?
This is the important factor.
The process is this: all acids tend to eat-up animal cells; every tissue of your body is composed of animal cells, NOT plant cells. Delicate walls of your intestine ARE of animal cells.

When you take acid juices, or oils which free acids, to eat INTO the delicately thin tissue walls of the intestine, its intelligence knows that if its walls are eaten through, you will bleed to death internally. Consequently, its cells - to protect themselves and save you - DRAW quantities of water FROM the blood, and pour it into the intestine to dilute and weaken the acids.
This 'floods' the intestine enough to make it 'move', but weakens the blood so it is difficult for the blood perfectly to perform its work of purification of the cells of the body.

Certainly, mineral salts in fruits are good for the body, and we should eat them, but we can also obtain them from other foods without excessive use of acid fruit juices which - if sufficient to move the intestine - deplete the blood of its essential water.

Over-use of acid juices is THE worst food fad of these years.
(I consider these truths so important and so little understood today, that if there were nothing more than this in this entire course, it would be worth while to you.)

In contrast to all methods which take water from the blood and deplete it, I give you a method of purification which ADDS water to the blood, and HELPS it purify the cells of the body.
This is the only true purification help of which I know.

For this purpose, take one half cup of spinach juice (you can now buy it in cans), Add one half cup of sweet milk, and one full cup of distilled water!
Use distilled water. NO other water is valuable for this purpose.
If there is no commercial company selling distilled water in your locality, buy it at a drug store.

This makes two cups of this purification drink.
Within a week, you will feel a new lightness of the body.

During the fourth step of the SACRED RESPONSE, when your spirit is reaching out to the stars, vision the Great Cathayan Ray pouring into and through your body, cleansing and purifying it.
This purification makes your body more responsive to spirit.
In the Cathayan civilization - when purification was worshipped - it worked tremendous advancement in the lives of men, and in the race!

Although Chinese of today have long since lost knowledge of the spiritual significance of this Ray, yet results still persist.
The Chinese today possess greater continuance of life and youthfulness, than any other people on the face of the earth - greatest continuing vitality and virility.

The Egyptian civilization is but memory. Spiritual attainments of ancient Greece are passed. Atlantis and Mu, and all others, lost the power to continue to live.

But the Cathayan Ray gives such phenomenal continuance of life, that even Chinese of today - who have unconsciously inherited something of spiritual purification - continue their ancient race!
"This corruptible must put on incorruption!"

Nothing but the attitude of your mind, and the condition of your body, interfere with complete response to spirit.
And ALL the things you want - vitality, health, virility, endurance, success, illumination, communion, memories of the past, or certainty of the future, and the highest illumination - come only as you become more responsive to spirit.

THE GREATER SPIRITUAL RESPONSIVENESS OF BODY

AND

AWAKENING THE BRAIN OF SPIRIT

by Brown Landone

VIBRATORY HARMONY OF BODY - - - - - - - - - - - - - - - LESSON XXX

This teaches the Armonian Ray of Eleusia, the Psallonian Ray of Thibet, the Shamean of the mystic seers of the Hebrews.

To give harmony to each thing of his creation, God used this master ray of spirit - the Fifth Day of Creation.

This ray was lost to the Hebrew priests, but it was known to the ancient Hebrew mystics! They called it the Shamean Ray!
The mystics of Thibet, 4000 years later, called it 'penetrating music', or the Psallonian of the rising sun!

But no people worshipped this spirit power so devotedly, as the very holy souls who founded the early Eleusinian Mysteries!
They called it, the Ray of Eleos - the joy of freedom!
The result was armonia, from which we get our word harmony.

Jesus was initiated into the Mystery Powers of this Ray.

Christ used this word eleos and a derivative of it, in two of his great teachings, that have not yet been understood.

First, that God does not want 'sacrifices' from man, but that God wants man to feel (mercy) the joyousness of free life!

And second, that "those who gain joyous freedom for others, shall be blessed with joyously freedom themselves."

That is, the eleos and eleenom translated mercy in Matthew 9:13 and merciful in Matthew 5:7, - truly mean joyously free.

This ray IS the SYNCHRONIZING Ray of the universe, - for nothing but harmony brings joyous freedom in life.

There comes a period in the creation of anything, when creation cannot advance, unless all of its parts or energies work together in harmony, and they cannot work together harmoniously unless each part is free to manifest its own activity.

No matter how responsive you make your mind and nerves and brain centers, there is no transforming responsiveness, until ALL

30-121

tissues of your body are synchronized to vibrate to the higher unheard silent overtones, so that all cells work together in perfect
harmonic cooperation.

And remember, it is one thing to 'think' that you are freeing
your 'mind', so that spirit will flow more freely into your consciousness and lift it to super-consciousness.
It is quite another thing, actually to free your body, so
spirit does flow into and through it EASILY.

To free body activities, the muscles must respond to spirit!

Muscles may be strong, yet as non-responsive as bands of wood.
Or they may be weak, and as un-responsive as dish-rags.
Or they may be 'just muscles' - stiff, or soft and sloppy.

But no matter what their condition at present, you want them
to be responsive to spirit - as powerful as steel springs when you
need power, and as gentle as ripples of moonlight on quiet water,
when you wish them to be at ease, yet ready to be active.

The responsiveness of your muscles is vitally important!
First, because they form three-fourths of your entire body.
Second, because they are now so very non-responsive.
Third, because they are your one MEANS of expression.
Fourth, because they are the LAST BARRIER to the spiritual
responsiveness of your body, and all your expression on earth.

Yes, your muscles are your ONE basic means of expression.

You cannot produce even one tone, or speak, except by action
of the muscles of your torso, throat, cheeks, tongue and lips.
You cannot look at anything, unless muscles move the eye ball.
Every expression - face or body - is due to muscle movement.

It IS very important that you spiritualize their activity, so
that spirit in you can express fully and completely.

And yet your muscles are very non-responsive.
If a fly lights on the side of your torso, your muscles are
so deadened and un-responsive, that you can not even flip those
muscles, as a horse can, - to get rid of that fly.

Also you have almost killed normal responsive activity in
muscles, because of silly methods used to develop muscles.
You have TENSED muscles in exercises and BLOCK-UP energy;
then relaxed them to get relief from the fatigue of the tensing,
until you are so tired, you have no impulse to express anything.

So I teach you to tune up your muscles to perfect vibratory
harmony - to be responsive to the Synchronizing Ray - the ray that

harmonizes all spheres of creation, so that all substances of your body, even muscles - will move in harmony with spirit - with your activity wedded to activity of spirit, to manifest new life.

The Synchronizing or Shamean Ray dominated the civilization directed by the mystics of Thibet, and that of the super-holy men of very ancient Greece at the time when there was a truly spiritual understanding of Eleusinian Mysteries.

It is the ray of the Fifth Day of Creation - of harmonizing each 'living' thing or creature, for life of its own kind.
It also harmonizes the energies of man with the energy of stars, and hence increases man's power a thousand-fold.

To this point, I have used names, as previously translated.
But I myself shall change the translation, for the word Vitalizing more truly reveals the nature of this particular creative power which God used on the Fifth Day of Creation.

It is a harmonizing ray, and it manifests with mighty tone, vibrating-throughout all matter, but never-the-less, it is primarily the vitalizing which gives life to matter.

This is clear from what God DID the Fifth Day of Creation. There was the sea which not yet brought forth life, - for water is not life - nothing but two gases - hydrogen and oxygen.
So God used this Vitalizing Ray to impregnate water, and life was born out of that which had not previously been life.

This seems to be an impossible miracle.
Yet it is not impossible, even for man.
One of our own great biologists, whipped whapped mere soapy water by means of a laboratory machine operating at a tremendous speed, and created living cells out of infinitely tiny bubbles of soapy water.
Certainly the whipping-whapping itself did not create life.
But it did activate the vibration of the substances, so that the Vitalizing Rays of life could manifest through them.

This is the purpose of the power of the Vitalizing Ray - to bring forth life, out of substances that are not living.

Remember also that this Vitalizing Ray is a tonal ray - but of such high vibration, it can not be heard by the human ear.
Yet it vibrates through all the universe.
It is the harmonic tone - love - life tone of star to star!

This is the universal tone - the overtone of the universe.
This love-life vibration is essential for new life!
For "though I speak with tongues of men and of angels and

have not love, - I am become as sounding brass!"

I teach you the synchronizing tone of the stars - the Vitalizing Ray - the divine musician of your soul and body!

It can tune-up your body structure to the basal tone of the universe; and create life, where there has been no life!

It tunes-up every cell of your body - of brain and nerves and muscles, and all other inner organs - to its own sublime overtone.

The determination of this note is not based on a theoretical assumption, or poetic phrase - such as "music of the spheres".

This DOMINANT celestial overtone is NOW PROVEN!

Other great harmonic chords vibrate throughout the universe - through all stars and constellations of stars!

And the same harmonics vibrate through earth, and in earth, and in all things of earth - even in and through your body!

In their vibration, you live and move and have your being.

When you are not responsive to them, there is discordant hell both in your mind and in your body.

But when you are in tune, there is a heaven of activity.

There is however one BASIC overtone of these chords.
It is the key tone of the great Vitalizing Ray of heaven!

I heard it first in spirit. Later, I heard it here on earth - in wind in trees; in the murmur of brooks, in cooing of doves, and deep underneath and within the roar of waves of the sea!

Later I heard it in one great opera - Parsifal!

Then daily for years I heard it vibrating from one great temple gong of the Mystic Mountains of the East.

I write ONE gong, because even the Great Masters know of ONLY one gong on earth, which is tuned down to this basic tone.

The secret of making such a gong was discovered by the ancient Tihuanacans. They made one, and thousands of years later sent it to Psallo in Thibet.

And NOW, it is again sent back to our western continents, to tone the spiritualizing chants of the sacred shrine of this new age!

The tone of this gong is almost like A flat - below middle C of our piano of today - and is now revealed for you to use.

See the next Lesson.

THE GREATER SPIRITUAL RESPONSIVENESS OF BODY

AND

AWAKENING THE BRAIN OF SPIRIT

by Brown Landone

PERMEATING ACTIVIST AND UNIFIER - - - - - - - - - - - - - LESSON XXXI

Tune your body to the key tone of the universe, and you
harmonize all the vibrations of your actual physical body with
spirit, and open the way for harmony in all you create.

Such response augments your expectancy, expands thought;
uplifts emotions of peace and love and joy and power, so that you
are wholly - body, mind, heart, soul - holy in tune with harmonic
spirit.

First, learn to HEAR the tone - at least 'hints' of it - IN
all deep love tones of the human voice.

I used to teach a student to strike the key of A flat on a
piano - the A flat below Middle C - and to listen to the tone, so
that the student would try to tune his voice to it.

I do NOT teach anyone to do this, any more:

(1) because the great harmonic overtones of the universe differ
as they vibrate in every human body; and

(2) because many students - in spite of my caution not to
'think' much about this work - gave so much mental effort to trying
to produce a tone like the tone A flat of the piano, that they
hindered their higher spiritual response.

So NOW, I teach you the truer way of getting YOUR basic tonal
response to the great overtone.

Tones of different individuals vary, because of the different
structures of their bodies. And your tone should be your tone -
fitted to the structure of your body.

Before humming this tone, to make the body more responsive,
sit down quietly alone by yourself, vision the love of star for star.
love of plants for sunlight, love of electron for proton, so great
that it holds to the proton with such power that man finds it
difficult to separate one from the other, even with millions of
volts of energy.

31-125

Vision the love of mothers of all ages, and your love of the one you most love.

Next, vision yourself talking - with a great feeling of love - to the one person you love most on earth.
Then hum the tone you use to express your own deepest love.

It will be your tone, fitted at this moment to spiritualize your body - to vibrate in harmony with the great master harmonic tones of all the universe.

Now prepare to synchronize your entire body - every cell of it - WITH this harmonic tone of the universe - to let it vibrate through you - through every cell of your body!

In preparation, sit in an easy expectant position - in a position that is most restfully expectant for you!

And think of the stars, and of expanding out to the stars, and try to feel your spirit among them!

Then vision what you want; revive your body by the Holy Breath; FROM the concepts of what you desire, vision the cleansing power of the Cathayan Ray - and all the time, intensely and lovingly desire whatsoever you most want.

Then again expectantly reach out in spirit to the stars, and HUM easily, this mystic tone of love!

HUM it repeatedly for a few seconds at a time — about four minutes in all - each morning, each night - trying to FEEL it in your body!

Do NOT hum loudly! Hum very softly, and FEEL it vibrating!

And while you are humming this mystic tone, hold to the expectant attitude of body, head and eyes a little upward!
Hold to the expanding attitude of the soul - reaching out and up in spirit - to join with the peace and love and joy and power of the universe.

As you hum this tone, forget your body; just try to feel yourself expanding with its vibration, out into the infinite.
NO 'separate' time should be taken for this, BECAUSE it should be INCLUDED, as the SEVENTH step of the Sacred Response.
This opens all substance, including your body to become a CHANNEL for the symphonic ray of the universe.

THE GREATER SPIRITUAL RESPONSIVENESS OF BODY

AND

AWAKENING THE BRAIN OF SPIRIT

by Brown Landone

THE TELEOIC VIBRATIONIST - - - - - - - - - - - - - - - LESSON XXXII

There IS a music of the spheres. It is perfect in numbers and proportional relationship of tones - for spirit in all of its relationships and activities, is always perfect.

The DOMINANT note of the majestic Synchronizing Ray comes from the very center of the universe of stars.
It is known by its likeness to the Teleois number of perfect tones of the musical scale, and the Teleois numbers of the harmonic movements of universe.

The spiritual BASE of THESE perfect numbers is 1, 4, 7.
The KEY tone of the universe is perfect in these numbers.

There are FOUR base tones in the octave - do, mi, sol, do!

There are SEVEN intervals in the major scale!

There are THIRTEEN intervals in the perfected chromatic scale!

There are NINETEEN harmonics of each pure string note.

The DOMINANT tone of the universe is the mother love tone.
It is the tenth note of the thirteen intervals of the perfected chromatic scale!

Ten is the first super-perfect 1.
Thirteen is the first super-perfect 4!
See Lesson II and III for reduction on basic process.

Of course, 13 is so perfect, that ancient mystics taught common minds to be suspicious of it and to avoid it. They did not want the symbolism of its perfection, of energies known, except in their own priesthoods.

Since I do emphasize response to the synchronizing ray of the stars, you may wonder if I believe in astrology.
My answer - as previously stated - is, - NO and yes.
True astrology is the science of stars, for 'astro' means star, and 'ology' means science.

But today, the true science is debased - that is, it is off its base - for the emphasis is given to planets - such as Jupiter, Mars, Saturn, et cetera - and NOT to the stars.

I do not depend much on planet-ology, for all planets are dead. They have no energy of their own.

Each reflects only a tiny part of the light of sun and stars.

So I do NOT worry about the influence of any TINY part of such light - reflected from dead planets - when I can bathe in the whole living light - that is, the HOLY-light of the universe!

There are living stars - 100,000,000 times larger than our sun!

And there are star-suns so heavy that - if your brain substance were as heavy as their substance - your brain would then weigh 1,034,000,000,000 POUNDS!

Other stars are so THIN you could fly right through them; so thin that our air is a solid in comparison!

Then there are stars of black light; and other star-suns of gloriously gorgeous LIVING light!

All star-suns forever radiate titanic energies of God.

These energies, as cosmic spirit, do shoot through our bodies.

So I do believe in astronomy, and in the true astrology of energy of living stars manifesting as music of the spheres.

The music of the universe is silent to our ears!

But out of its infinite harmony comes the Ray of Power which vitalises all life, because it harmonizes it.

ALL the RESULTS you desire - whether of earth or heaven - are always attainable if the powers of spirit work together.

It IS this mystic Synchronizing Ray - and YOUR response TO it - which activates powers in you WITH the powers of heaven.

Responsiveness to spirit and to ALL its manifestations, is multiplied many-fold by this great harmonic TONE of the universe - which vitalises that which is not life, into that which is life!

It is an angel power from God; commune with it, and you commune with all angels of God.

Spirit IS infinite; hence there are angels!

The word translated angel in our New Testament, means "the good which is sent out" - a spiritual power sent out by God.

These Lessons will be read by students of different beliefs. I respect your beliefs, but nevertheless our mere mental beliefs are not important.

When any persons say, - "I don't believe in this," of "I

don't believe in that" - they do nothing but state their own limitations.

In contrast, spirit rises to super-consciousness and knows.

Many people ask, if I believe in spiritualism.

I answer, - NO or YES - for all life lives!
Life lives forever! And forever continues on.
But there are phases of spiritualism which are nothing but crude efforts to show off tiny LIMITED responses to spirit.

Since all life is intelligent and loving, it does not wish to be separated from that which it knows and loves!
And since it is intelligent and loving, it longs to continue communion with those it loves.

But certainly do not mistake the mere telephone receiver, (the medium) for the soul at the other end!

True spiritualism is the opposite of materialism.
Spirit is infinite in energy and capacity. Hence, all efforts to secure limited response, are outside the realm of true spirit.

To BE spiritual, you must be LIKE spirit.
To be like spirit, you must be able to respond to spirit, easily and fully in infinite manifestations.

True response is direct and conscious and intimate communion.
Direct intimate contact - with God, or the masters, or angels, or any soul that desires to help you - IS spiritual.

And the purification of the body given in this Course, opens YOU for true communion!
That IS neither fantastic, or twisted, or mistaken!

Now return with me to our Cosmic vibrator ray of harmony of the universe - the ray that Vitalizes substance matter.

Dwell IN it. Feel it vibrating through your body!
See Lesson XXX.

FEEL it vibrating so that it tunes up the substance of every cell of the millions of billions of brain cells, and of every nerve and muscle of your body.
So that ALL substance becomes responsive to the Vitalizing Ray which weds substance, so that new life is created out of that which is not yet manifesting as life; so that the very substance of your body gives birth to new life for you!

THE GREATER SPIRITUAL RESPONSIVENESS OF BODY

AND

AWAKENING THE BRAIN OF SPIRIT

by Brown Landone

THE INFUSING CREATION OF NEWNESS - - - - - - - - - - - LESSON XXXIII

This Lesson teaches the Godeshian Ray of the Masters - the sixth great Re-Creative Ray of God!

In this, we come to another phase of body responsiveness - rebuilding newness - re-creating tissues - creating youthfulness.

Many a man has so improved conditions of his body, that he feels like a new man. Such a person is sincere; he feels as though his body were made new!

But IF it were re-created, it would not continue slowly dying!

IF he built true newness, his body would be like those of the Masters - immortal!

Building ANEW comes from response to the Great Godeshian Ray - that is, the ray of the sixth day of God's creation.

On that day, God made MAN. It was the first formation of anything like that which had previously existed, - for God made man in his own image - like unto himself.

This ray is the Qodesh of Melchizedek; the Nephesian of holy Egyptians; the Tizonian Ray of ancient Tiayura and Thibet.

But, in terms of today, I call it - the RE-CREATIVE Ray!

Out in infinite space, - it creates new ATOMS, new STARS!
On earth, it creates new substances and new cells.

When you respond to it, it re-creates the CELLS in your body.

The power of this ray is astoundingly PECULIAR.
Its vibration is next to the highest of all SEVEN Rays.

It is the ONLY Ray which gives soul and every thing or substance, the power to re-create in these higher vibrations.

By it, animals can reproduce young; plants can reproduce plants; cells can reproduce themselves; and thus re-create a newness of the human body for man.

This sixth power of God is also able to re-create ideas and ideals and love, - even-re-create the very life of the soul.

But since it is of spirit, re-creation can not be effected by conscious mind, but be wrought by spirit after its own kind.

IF you do not accept the 'goodness' of spirit in ALL God has created, you cannot fully respond to it! For you must accept God's creation AS God's creation, to create as God Creates.

If you dislike many things or conditions or people, then your mind is in opposition to the very nature of the Godeshian Ray, which loves ALL because it re-creates all.

Dislikes prevent responsiveness to spirit, because dislikes are due to part knowledge.

Part knowledge is due to the mind which sees through a glass darkly; but holiness (wholeness) is of spirit, for spirit is whole and holy!

Each earnest soul in its aspiration, longs to be able to create as the Masters create, by use of the Fifth Ray, which vitalizes substance into life, and by use of the Sixth Ray which reproduces both substance and life.

In other words, many a soul wishes to create by what is called 'materialization'. This comes by use of these two rays, - but they are both of spirit and of God, and so long as conscious mind is prejudiced by part knowledge, you can not create the complete holy newness you desire.

Dislikes always prevent such re-creation, and I am writing now of your persisting prejudices against many of the things God himself created, and your condemnation of them.

Although sincere, they ARE in opposition to spirit.
They indicate lack of agreement with God's own pronouncement, that all he created IS very good!

To build your body anew, to impregnate it with the mystic Vitalizing Ray - the Re-creative Ray - RISE ABOVE all your old dislikes and prejudices - renew your mind - and, LIKE spirit, conceive the goodness of ALL things, as God does!

THE GREATER SPIRITUAL RESPONSIVENESS OF BODY

AND

AWAKENING THE BRAIN OF SPIRIT

by Brown Landone

INFINITE LOVER AND JUDGE - - - - - - - - - - - - - - - - LESSON XXXIV

In origin, HOLY and WHOLLY come from similar root-words!

To become holy, man must rise to the love of ALL THINGS, - for the truth IS definite - "God saw EVERYTHING that he had made, and behold, IT WAS VERY GOOD."

It is only man's misuse of things that produces ill results; and ill use of emotions and impulses which produces evil.
Note well: God idealizes all things; but man condemns!
It is condemnation which produces the evil.

God created an ideal world for man.
And God gave his creation into your hands, and gave you spiritual rule and dominion over ALL things he made!

God did not tell you to condemn and SHUN any of them, but he did tell you to USE ALL of them for your good! The greatest factor that keeps you from all you desire, are your dislikes, which BAR you from the spiritual use of things already created for you.

God knows that all he made IS good.
But unless you accept God's truth, your attitude makes you NON-responsive to spirit, and keeps you FROM God.

What hinders you is condemnation. It is due to part knowledge, - for "Knowledge of the holy (whole) is UNDERSTANDING!"

It is lack of whole (holy) knowledge - and condemnation due to that lack - that has hindered man in all the ages.

Let me give you a few illustrations of such condemnation:

Take a few foods, as examples.

Carrots, first: A few hundred years ago in England, even scientific men believed the yellow color of carrots was PROOF of the presence of evil spirits.

So if a farmer fed carrots to his cows, he could be hanged by the neck until dead - and without trial!

Then potatoes: 262 years ago in Europe, scientists knew that potatoes were deadly poisonous.

Yes, the scientists knew it - no doubt about it. For forty years potatoes in Europe were used only by military forces, to be fed to prisoners, hoping to kill them off.

And tomatoes: Only 90 years ago, physicians in our country believed that tomatoes were POISONOUSLY detrimental to morals.

No mother would let a young daughter eat a tomato, because all scientists knew that even one tomato would make a young maid IMMORAL for life!

Scores of other things that are good, have been condemned; and the condemnation has spread to soul emotions and desires.

And man suffers because of his condemnation of them.

In the past, whenever a new product was first imported from a foreign country, it was condemned as evil!

This was the attitude, when carrots were first taken from Italy to England; when potatoes and tobacco were taken from America to Europe; when coffee was first brought from Java; et cetera.

All dislikes and fears are due to LACK of knowledge!

But with new knowledge, old condemnations pass.
Things we once thought were evil, are now KNOWN to be GOOD!

Ultimately man will realize that ALL IS GOOD!
So why not get ahead of the race? Accept God's truth NOW.
Then with love and use of all things, you can rise to heights attained by the Masters, and create as they create!
Idealize and use all things - each after its own kind!

There are still people who believe that spirituality is attained, by what one does not do! And such people try to become spiritual, by avoiding the use of many things which God has provided for them to use.

They 'assume' that The Masters are transcendingly great, because they do NOT do this, or do NOT eat that.

But one becomes a Master, by attuning oneself to God's creation!
Great Masters integrate their lives WITH ALL things!
That is why they are WHOLLY (HOLY) in tune with spirit!
Hence they transcend age, and actually build NEW bodies!

To build your body anew, integrate your life WITH the life of all things, and USE all things.
For example, no matter what kind of food you eat, INTEGRATE your spirit with the spirit of its SUBSTANCE, and thus FREE its

life, - by recognizing that its substance is created OF SPIRIT!

All true life is integrated with Spirit and is continuous.
Scientists as well as mystics know that life in every form IS
conscious. Each manifestation is conscious.
The plant IS as conscious as the animal.

And any spiritual ray, which has already attained power of
producing a form for itself here, can produce another new form, -
for the very power which gives it consciousness to create one form
is the same power which CAN create OTHER forms for continuing
manifestations.
When one form disappears, life is freed from that form!
It then moves on, in accord with God's law, from life to life.

These Lessons will be studied by many people - by some who
eat meat, and by some who are strict vegetarians.

I am NOT a propagandist, one way or the other!
I do NOT ask you to eat meat foods, or NOT to eat them.

But I do urge you to integrate yourself with ALL life and all
changes, as the Great Masters have done and do.
Never let part knowledge and its prejudices block your advance
to the highest spiritual responsiveness!

I present spiritual truth. All 'forms' of anything you eat,
are but forms of manifestations of life; NOT life itself!

FREE your soul of prejudices, and hence of all fear of things.
Free your body, to respond to ALL that is spiritually limitless!
God IS love! Of love, he created all things.
Lift yourself UP to love of all things and become like God!

Love impregnates and transforms ALL things - even foods.
Love foods, and all their lower vibrations vanish, - for love
TRANSFIGURES all things!
Choose THE substances which make the body MOST responsive to
spirit - those which are MOST responsive to Godeshian Ray, which
creates newness!

Ancient priests of Judea - even though they had lost most of
the spirituality of their holy men - worshipped this ray.

The Inner Temple was the Qodesh haq Qodeshim - Holy of Holies.

In it, man worshipped the Ray of Creativeness - the Elohim
Power used by God during the Sixth Day of Creation - the ONLY ray
which re-creates like God - with power to RE-CREATE ANEW!

THE GREATER SPIRITUAL RESPONSIVENESS OF BODY

AND

AWAKENING THE BRAIN OF SPIRIT

by Brown Landone

THE RE-FORMING ARCHITECT - - - - - - - - - - - - - - - LESSON XXXV

Come now to actual response to the ray of re-creation, and choice of responsive substances for the cells of a NEW body.

It is NOT so important to fuss over starches or sugars or fats or proteins, - for they always build a body that slowly dies after its first 21 years.

They build a squatty body - built like the old Pyramid of Gizeh - heavy on itself - with weight built upon weight.

In contrast, I teach you to build a NEW body like the NEW pyramid - thrilled by spirit, upheld by spirit, and reaching upward!

"Are not cereals and all starch foods good for the body?"
Certainly, starch foods are good for solidity, but they are of little value as materials responsive to spirit.

For myself, I do NOT want a concrete house for my soul!

I want an infinitely responsive instrument for spirit!

Starch food builds up a "good" SOLID, STUPID body, which always tires out so quickly, that it needs much sleep!
It ages quickly because it is NOT able to respond fully enough to the finer vibration of spirit to create new youthfulness.

The starch foods are:

(1) underground vegetables - potatoes, turnips, beets, et cetera;

(2) grains - wheat, rice, corn, barley, rye, and all products made from grains - white and whole wheat flours, breads, cakes, breakfast cereals, et cetera;

(3) legumes - peas, beans, lentils, soy beans, et cetera;

(4) most nuts, and two fruits - bread fruit and bananas.

NB: During childhood, starch food is needed for substance.

35-135

to increase the size of the body.

Eat MORE protein foods. A diet high in protein is NOT detrimental to any organ of the body. The proteins DO make the body more responsive to spirit. Such foods are: fish, eggs, cheese, red meats, lentils, gelatines, et cetera.

Eat FAT foods, for responsiveness of nerve and brain tissues.

NB: Fat foods will NOT make you stout, UNLESS you also overeat starches and sugars.

Now we come to the mystical creators - two of the greatest mysteries of spirit and substance!

Just as God directed man to make glass to be responsive to light to manifest its glory of color, so God created two substances to be responsive to the Godeshian Ray, to manifest NEWNESS!

The first is mystic chlorophyl - the living GREEN substance in leaves; the second are those mysterious new growing substances called auxinons which have power to activate new growth.

Chlorophyl is still THE mystery substance of this earth.

In all green plant leaves, this substance IN-SPIRES (that is, takes-in) the rays of radiant energy of sunlight, and works a transformation with non-living substances of soil, producing living substances.

In food substances for man, it seems to be MOST responsive, in taking-in (in-spiring) the spiritually cosmic energy of the universe, into man's body.

In other words, chlorophyl as food apparently makes your body so responsive, that the cosmic energy of spirit flows into and through it freely and abundantly.

This mystic substance - so mysterious that it still confounds all scientists - IS responsive to the Vitalizing Ray which creates structure of the body, ANEW!

Remember that spirit energy IS limitless; it NEVER tires!

So when the body is fed this mysterious substance, and becomes more responsive to spirit, its fatigue is lessened and its aging processes delayed.

If I myself should live on the ordinary diet - or on diets of food fadists - my body would become so UN-responsive to spirit - so NON-responsive to the Vitalizing Ray, that my body would have to suspend consciousness for many hours each day.

That is, I would have to remain unconscious (sleep as you call it) for seven or more hours each day.

It is evident that so long as spirit flows easily into and through the body, the body does not tire, and there is abundant and vitally impulsive energy.

And so long as there is no fatigue and no lack of energy - then certainly, there is NO need of sleep.

When I use foods which contain chlorophyl - a couple of glasses daily of green leaf juice, for instance - and do NOT load my body down with starches, but instead eat plenty of responsive protein foods - then my body responds more fully to spirit!

Oh, become responsive to spirit.
It is criminally IN-efficient to live so that you need to spend one-third of your life (7 or 8 hours daily) in bed, UN-conscious.

Some say, - "But sleep is NATURAL." So is a pig, - natural!

It is the UN-responsive condition of the body which makes it necessary for most people to spend one-third of their lives in the temporary death, which we call sleep.
And all because, they live so earthily, that the body cannot respond enough to spirit, to live spiritually and vitally.

NOW, consider the second group of mystic substance, which tends to make the body very responsive to the spiritually Vitalizing Re-creating Ray of creation.

It is not enough merely to make your body responsive enough to take-in the creative energy of spirit.
It must be made so responsive within, that the inspired creative energy of the Godeshian Ray WILL in turn create NEW and youthful CELLS each hour!

For this, the second group of substance mentioned is created by God - responsive to the Re-Creative Ray of Creation.

Infinite intelligence in nature works in mysterious ways.

It produces AUXINS in all things when they are NEWLY growing.
And auxins IN plant or animal, impel new growth of new cells.

These are exceptionally responsive to spirit, for new growth takes place whenever they are present.
They are the substances which are responsive to the RE-Creative power of the Vitalizing Ray of creation.

Scientists who have investigated this subject for several

years, have written of these substances as 'immature' foods.

Immature foods are the young sprouts of seeds or plants, used as foods before the sprouting stems or leaves reach maturity.

Nature loads these new growing sprouts - with AUXINONS for NEW GROWTH and Auxinons used as foods, apparently impel new growth of new cells and youthful tissues.

New growing structure IS super-responsive to life!
Hence, auxinons are substances for VIRIL manifestation of life!
By their use as foods, organs and tissues are changed!

One helping, at least twice a week, of half a handful of new growing sprouts of seeds, or very tender young leaves, works miracles in new growth.

Supply your body, NOT with substances which are said to produce a 'good solid' body; NOT with substances which weigh it down; NOT with substances which make it a drag on the energy of spirit; NOT with substances which will leave a lot of wastes in your body.

Instead, make your body spiritually responsive to life, and to the Godeshian Ray of Spirit which impels all new life.

This IS the mysterious secret sought for ages.
This is the secret of the mystic alchemists!

And yet there is nothing mysterious about it.

With use of more responsive substances as foods, the body becomes more responsive.

When more responsive, spirit flows more freely through it, with less friction, less wear and tear, less fatigue!

Spirit can TRANSFORM your body into actual NEWNESS, and your body will respond to all energies about you; and you will respond to the consciousness of others; to the souls surrounding you; to the spirit of the infinite itself!

Then the body - as it responds to the Godeshian Ray - becomes spiritualized, and actually creates new cells - the mystic creation of "being born again."

THE GREATER SPIRITUAL RESPONSIVENESS OF BODY

AND

AWAKENING THE BRAIN OF SPIRIT

by Brown Landone

HOLDING YOUR CREATION - - - - - - - - - - - - - - - - - LESSON XXXVI

The ACTUALIZING RAY of our age was once called the mystic
COSMICIZING RAY, which actually FULFILLS the prayer of Christ, -
"Thy will be done IN earth as it is in heaven."

As you respond to it, your heaven of desire becomes an actuality on earth, - for this is the ray - back of all cruder rays which
scientists call cosmic rays; the highest of all rays.
It can UNITE movement of vibration with movement of matter.
It is THE power of consummation - last step in creation.

I have translated its basic meaning by several names.
But to make it clearer to you, I call it the HOLDING RAY!
That is its nature. It has the power to hold what has been
created, so you can continue to use it. I shall reveal later that
this, is the meaning of God "sabbathized the Seventh Day".

There is divine sequence in the sacred response to spirit,
because the seven rays are used in the same order in which God
used them in the Seven Days of Creation!

First, before you can create any actual thing or condition,
spiritual energy must be in-spired into the creation you want.

Second, you must expand desire and effort, and continually
resurrect your primal urge to keep it vitally alive!

Third, you must use the power which gives your ideal or desire,
actuality; that is, gives it identy and a form of its own.

Fourth, you must clarify the ideal or purify the substance, so
it will not be a messy mixture of what you want, and do not want.

Fifth, to give it life, you must vitalize it; even create
life out of that which had no life, and unify all parts to work
together in harmony. Otherwise it will wear itself out, or be of
little use because of the friction within itself.

Sixth, you must prevent fixity and stagnation, by giving it
power to recreate itself, to continue producing what you desire.

36-139

And seventh, since its actuality may still be separated from you, you complete your work by the power of the Holding Ray - power to keep and use what you have created.

This Lesson brings us to the last barrier, which hinders full response of both mind and body to spirit.
That barrier is the NON-responsive condition of your MUSCLES!

Perhaps the last thing you have thought of doing is making your muscles spiritual in action.
They seem so UN-spiritual, that it seems impossible.

YET, to make body responsive to spirit, you must tune up your muscles, because they form THREE-FOURTHS of your body!

And no matter how responsive you make brain and nerves, you will not attain full responsiveness, UNTIL you do learn how to make your muscles respond to spirit, so that they can act without fatigue and with a continuous thrill of energy!

Without doubt, you have tried to improve your muscles!
At some time, you have probably taken some kind of exercises to make them healthier and stronger.

All such exercises alternately CONTRACT and RELAX muscles.
Some systems teach psycho-tensing; other special relaxation. Oh, there are MANY systems, but none of them do anything more than tense and relax, in one way or another.

And what is the RESULT of TENSING? It is FATIGUE!
And the more you tense your muscles, the greater the fatigue.

And WHY do you study systems of relaxing your muscles?
To try to give them a little rest from the fatigue due to the tensing.
That is, you relax them, so you can tense them again and cause more fatigue! At least this is SILLY, for an intelligent human being, and very silly for a spiritual being, who knows that ALL your energy is of spirit, and that spirit NEVER tires.

And how does tensing affect your energy?
It HOLDS energy IN your muscles.
Stops its easy flow THROUGH them.
BLOCKS-up energy so much, it soon exhausts you.

And since the very impulse of energy is to flow continuously, stopping its flow, works HAVOC!
THAT is WHY our strong men ALWAYS DIE SO YOUNG!

Next consider what relaxation foes to your energy.

It makes muscles slack and inactive - so slack they are not active enough to receive more energy.

Hence, relaxation prevents more energy from flowing into your muscles, and this produces a constant feeling of lack of energy; a continuous tired-out feeling.

And now YOU are thinking, - "Well, what can I do with my muscles, except contract and tense them, and release and relax them?"
And probably, your muscles have NEVER done anything else!

Yet, certainly what you have been doing is NOT in line with spirit - for spirit is the urge to continue a constant flow of tireless energy! And yet WHEN you are actually longing for more energy, you block-up energy and stop its flow into the body, and that is rather stupid.

NEITHER tensing nor relaxing make muscles responsive to spirit, - for relaxed muscles are too inactive to take in more energy; and tensed muscles block-up and hinder energy from flowing THROUGH them.

Yet your muscles CAN respond to spirit, - for even what you call muscle-power, IS spirit energy!

The PROOF is this: No matter how strong you think your arm muscles are, IF you cut the nerve which carried energy from your brain to those muscles, the energy you thought was muscle energy disappears instantly, and your arm muscles are paralyzed!

What you call muscle-energy or nerve-energy or even brain-energy, VANISHES, the minute you cut off spirit energy.
Even physical strength is the spirit energy which is first inspired into the brain and then sent to the muscles.

There IS something you CAN do, besides tensing and relaxing,
There is a WAY of using your muscles, which give you complete freedom of movement; continuous and abundant energy; with never a feeling of nervous exhaustion of tensity on the one hand; or the let-down of slackness on the other!

Such a heaven of activity, is attained by free flow of energy INTO your muscles; unhindered flow THROUGH them INTO actual ACTION: and then EXTENDED flow OUT to something BEYOND yourself.

ONLY a few Great Masters have attained this full use of the extended flow of muscle energy OUT BEYOND the self.
It is this, which spiritualizes the activity of your muscles, by making their activity LIKE spirit's expanding activity.

What I now write of 'selfishness' is not merely my own thought

I have learned it from the centuries, and from the inspiring help of mystic Masters still active in consciousness and body.

THE TRUTH IS THIS: There IS physical and physiological and even chemical selfishness, just as there is personal selfishness. And all great transformation depends on unselfish action.

All effort which blocks up energy IS selfish!
All effort to HOLD it IN the muscles is selfish!
All effort to use it only IN the muscles is selfish.
And selfish action always destroys any structure!

BUT, when energy flows out beyond the muscles, that is UNSELFISH, and makes even muscle action like spirit activity.

This is the sacred secret of the Seventh Day of Creation!

With such action even the spiritual energy of muscles reaches out BEYOND the body, out into the cosmic, and even the muscles of your body become SPIRITUALIZED.

And when your muscles - like spirit in action - reach out into all intelligence and love and power of spirit - it is then that your body becomes a PERFECT channel of spirit!

And the blind receive their sight, and the lame walk; the lepers are cleansed; the deaf hear; the dead are raised up!

This cosmicizing activity is not so impossible as it seems.
In fact, the little muscles of your EYES, already do it!
That is, you have SEEN stars, many stars in your life time!

Yet you could never have seen even one star, IF the MUSCLES around your eye ball had not adjusted your eye to the position and distance of the star, far out BEYOND those little muscles of your eyes.

COSMICIZING a muscle activity means, letting it reach out into the cosmic, out beyond the muscles. Stars are trillions of miles away! So you have already cosmicized the activities of the little eye ball muscles - making them reach out beyond themselves every time you have seen a star trillions of miles away.

This is spiritualized activity of muscles! Do you now begin to understand why walking beneath the stars, seeing them, always brings you celestial power and peace!

Give your muscles this power, by the work of the next and last lesson - the ultimate in spiritual response - resulting in the power to hold for use whatsoever you create in fulfillment of desire!

THE GREATER SPIRITUAL RESPONSIVENESS OF BODY

AND

AWAKENING THE BRAIN OF SPIRIT

by Brown Landone

THE TRANSFORMATION AND HEAVENLY COMMUNION - - - - - - LESSON XXXVII

Sit easily in an upright chair - like a dining room chair!
Reach out with your arms - free, easily - in front of you.
Vision yourself - freely, softly - playing a piano.
Or let us say - an organ, for its tones are richer, fuller!

Move your arms and hands and fingers - using both hands -
just as a child does when pretending to play a piano or organ.
Run your hands and fingers up and down the keyboard.
Imagine playing, any tune you like; hum it if you wish.

THIS IS REAL! NOT imaginary! It is real ACTUAL movement!
The only thing that is imaginary, is the organ!
All else - movement of playing - are real actual movements!

Now next, vision the keyboard six or seven or eight inches
away from you - out beyond the reach of your finger tips.
But KEEP ON playing - moving your arms, hands and fingers!
And vision yourself sending energy OUT FROM your finger tips,
through the few inches of space, out TO the keys.
That is, EXTEND your activity OUT BEYOND your physical self!

Then vision the keyboard of your organ, THREE FEET away!
And keep on playing this imaginary organ!

Next vision the organ across the room; and continue playing!
    Lift your arms a little higher; move your hands in a wider
range from side to side - as you vision the organ to be larger -
with keyboard extending from one side of your room to the other.

Now with infinity of spirit, see beyond walls of your room.
    Let the walls disappear; and vision a much greater organ
half way down the block with a keyboard 200 feet long.

Also vision infinite spirit in you - manifesting through the
muscles of your arms, active in your wrists and hands, but moving
out beyond your finger tips - actually reaching out to the keys
of that gigantic organ half way down the block.

And continue playing on that keyboard - a half block away.
Make it real, and actually hum the tune you are playing.

37-143

In actuality your soul IS doing this, your arms are doing it; your fingers are doing it - it IS real!

The only imaginary thing in all of this is the organ.
Actually express your soul infinitely in actual action - reaching out and out with energy EXTENDED BEYOND the physical self!

NOW vision the STARS as KEYS of a majestic KEYBOARD of a spiritual organ of the universe - billions of miles away!
Lift your arms and hands higher!
Vision your finger tips sending out energy in movement to the keys of that celestial organ, and keep on playing on the keyboard of the stars - producing the silent music of the universe.

Oh, friend - expanded soul - realize what you are doing!
Your soul is expanding out INTO the infinite, and in action!
Your very muscles actually are ACTING in harmony WITH spiritual expansion.
That is, even your muscle activity is UNIFIED with spirit's expanding activity.
And it is probable that this is the first time in all your life, that you have even done this, except perhaps in dreams.

Often in the past, you have attempted to attain a greater consciousness of the infinity of yourself, but you have limited the efforts your mind, reaching far out beyond itself in 'thought'. Such attainment, in mind only, was 'without form and void'.
What I have just taught you to do is the one means of attaining actuality in action - out in infinity!
It makes even muscle action like unto the activity of spirit.

This is the greatest attainment any soul can make on earth.
No matter how simple the exercise of playing an imaginary organ, it is the extension of ACTIVITY OUT INTO THE INFINITE, which is the greatest thing you have ever done.
To extend action, so that it becomes infinite, is like unto the activity of infinite spirit - like unto the activity of God!

This makes it possible for MORE spirit energy to flow INTO your muscles and THROUGH them, because you do not LIMIT the action of spirit to the mere size or extent of your muscles!
Thus your body - even its muscle structure - becomes responsive and vitalized and transformed, like to spirit action!
Now cosmicize muscle activity of your torso and lower limbs.

Stand up easily; lift head a little; and LEAN a little forward.
And while standing, repeat the organ playing - on the magnificent organ of the universe - with stars for keys - far, far away.
As you reach out - lean forward a little - to play on the key-

board of the stars, so that the action of ALL your torso and even
your leg muscles join in the action of the arm muscles.

Thus the activity of ALL muscles - from head to toes - respond.
This is the heaven of wedding spirit to matter IN action!

This carrying of action out into the infinite is the process
which completes actuality in attaining things you desire.
With it, things you want no longer remain formless and void.

It establishes a habitual tendency of your mind and heart and
soul to do more than merely create what you want in mind.
It establishes the habits of all energies of the soul whenever
you desire anything to move out into action beyond yourself - both
to create and also to enfold what you want and hold it as your own.
Please note this phrase 'hold it as your own!
I shall write more of this later in this lesson.

NOW be seated once more; again play your magnificent organ!
And "Lift thine eyes to the hills" - to mountains of the stars!
FEEL the energy in your muscles moving out and up, even to stars!

You can now attain the glory of the power of freedom in action!
For your body is NEITHER tensed nor relaxed.
Yet its muscles are thrilled with energy and are active!

As you make this habitual, it will not take more than 4 minutes for this entire STEP of playing the organ - near you, farther
away, then even far far out - with stars for keys!
But never let one night pass, without thus spiritualizing
your muscles. They are the last barrier, hindering full response
to spirit!

Thus, all tensity of 'holding' energy in muscles, disappears!
And all of the slack all-gone feeling of relaxation vanishes.
And yet abundant energy flows INTO and THROUGH your muscles.

Probably, this is the first time in your life, you have actually UNIFIED activity of all body WITH the activity of spirit.
By such unity of responsiveness, you are spiritually ready,
for all intelligence and love of spirit - past, present, future -
to flow INTO and THROUGH you, so that you will be constantly unified
with spirit and always intimately communing with it.

I INCLUDE 'the past' for you, for life IS infinite!
Life always has lived, and always will live!
Your memories may be blocked now, by an un-responsive body.
But as body responds, you will awaken infinite memory!
Soul is perfect - with past memories, present expanded con-
sciousness, and prevision and even knowledge of the future.

The soul being free to manifest, CAN respond to consciousness of continued and continuing life, and to all its manifestations!

The marvel of these uses of these Seven Elohim Rays is that all of them are always constructive!
They are the only rays of the universe which are creative!
God used them to give form and actuality to ALL creation.

When responsive you can commune with spirit, for then your deepest emotions are in harmony with all higher spirit.
And again I emphasize the law that like responds to like. You cannot even see blue color, unless something in the retina of your eye, and also in your soul, is LIKE blue and responds to blue.

So also, your soul cannot become at-one with that which you wish to commune, unless your own soul attitudes are LIKE those of spirit and its manifestations.

Spirit always lives in attitudes of peace and love and joy.
So to attain greatest spiritual response to spirit, you must attune your emotions to the same attitudes - of peace, love, joy.
By such likeness of attitude, you can feel oneness with, and commune with, consciousness of all things of earth and heaven.

Full responsive communion, depends on unity of LIKENESS!

This is true of all communion and all communication. Even on earth, communication of ideas is possible only by likeness of the language used, or gestures used.
If a friend speaks only Greek, and you ONLY English, you can NOT communicate, except by like meanings of gestures you use.

So also in spirit, communion depends on LIKENESS!
Spirit never feels sad or separated!
Hence so long as you are sorrowful, and feel that you feel 'separated from one whom you love' - JUST SO LONG will you remain separated in consciousness from the spirit of that soul.

Feelings of sorrow differ from those of spirit.
You can NOT become one with anything unless you respond in LIKENESS - love responds to love; peach to peace; joy to joy!

God is joyous, and the angels of God live in realms of joy! Those who have passed on live in joy infinitely greater joy than that which we know and just as beautiful music can not harmonize itself without discordant clanging noises, so you can not be constantly responsive to their joy, except by joy in you.
Let thy soul be joyful, and "sorrow shall be turned to joy."
"Your heart shall rejoice - your joy no man taketh from you."

For perfect communion, free yourself of all self-centeredness.

Let your soul reach out in feelings of love of grass and trees
and hills; to the infinite peace and harmony of stars; and to all
time - all the past and a million years hence.

With such expansion, there will come greater LOVE for you!
Love of souls you love; love of all - growing grass, trees
and ferns; the rush of waters; winds of mountains; angels; God!

Sit NOT in the silence of the response, with mere 'thoughts'
expanding out among the stars. That is NOT enough!
Let your soul feel the peace and love of all things of
heaven and earth, to consciously, continuously commune with all.

I digress here to give you the actual proof of what God DID
the Seventh Day of Creation.
It was quite different from the usual interpretation, which
is mistaken in thinking that God was inactive - did nothing on
the Sabbeth.

Certainly you now realize that something was needed to be done
that day. After use of the first six powers of God - the first
six days of creation - all that was created was not in condition
to be held as a recreating process for all time.
Permanency of creation had not yet been established.

So God used the Sabbathizing Ray on the Seventh Day.

This ray captivated what had been created, and held it - NOT
in inactivity, but in limitless activity!

I have previously written that often in the ancient Hebrew,
the same root word is used repeatedly in the same sentence.
For example, the meaning of activity was used several times
in the sentence, - "God created man in his own image."
It really means, "Infinite activity activated the activity of
man, in the activity of God, to be like the activity of God."

So also in telling of God's action of the Sabbath one word
is translated by three words; in the original texts, - one meaning but three different in the English translation.

The Hebrew words which are translated 'finished' and 'ended',
are translations of the same word, kala. In this verse kala is
a verb. It means, - all activity and limitless activity.
Consequently, it does NOT mean stopped activity at all, but
rather activity that is limitlessly active.

The word translated 'work', is melakah! It is spelled with
an aleph which signifies the greatest strength.
It is derived from the root melek which means - king, to reign,
to radiate power forever.

The word translated 'rested', differs from all other Hebrew
words in the Bible which mean - to stop work or to be inactive,
or to be idle, or to take a rest.
In this verse, the word used, does NOT mean inactive rest.

Rested and seventh and sabbath, are each and ALL translations
from the SAME root word.
In many Bible verses this word IS translated by words which
mean - HELD; CAPTURED; HELD CAPTIVE; ACTUALLY ACQUIRED!
That is, the 'rest' of the Sabbath, was making spiritual
creation actual, so it could be HELD as an actuality.

Lastly, the word 'sanctified' is a translation of Qadesh,
which means - set apart for a particular purpose.
Hence in this verse, the power was set apart for actualiza-
tion; that is to be HELD captive in continuous activity for use!

This reveals, that on the Seventh Day, God used the seventh
great Creative Ray, to make all processes permanent.
That is, he HELD them in captivity for limitless action!

In our words this means the power to HOLD what we idealize
and create - hold it for our own use and for the good of others.

Vision this true ideal of the Sabbath, to understand the
Sabbathizing Ray or Holding Ray of Creation.

All fulfillment of ALL you desire, comes ONLY by response!

All you desire - vitality, energy, freedom from fatigue, endurance, calm nerves, healing - come ONLY as more spirit manifests in and through your body.
More vivacity and less dullness and sleepiness; more charm,
and youthfulness; companion winning power; more virility and
strength - come ONLY, when MORE life of spirit manifests.
Initiative, success, and abundance are due to more power
of spirit becoming ACTUAL in your life, and taking FORM.

Illumination and the super-consciousness of soul, and
alchemic changes and transformation are wrought by response.
Clearer memories; consciousness of the presence of Masters;
entering in spirit into the temples of the past, come only by
response to spirit.
All true guidance and true communion-un-tainted and intimate -
come only by spiritual response to spirit.

Remember, my friend, also you are now making the most astounding change man can ever make on earth - CHANGING from dependence
on energies which always tend to destroy, to use of the seven
spiritual energies which are always constructive.

AND it is VERY SIMPLE - and soon it will become ONE unified process of response for you - beginning by quietly inspiring spirit, then expanding to the stars; giving form, clarifying, vitalizing, re-creating, and ending with your spiritualization even of muscle energy - at-one with spirit - so that you hold what you have created - with LIMITLESS freedom of power!

In closing, again summarize these Seven Great Rays of Creation!

Often clarify in your own mind, the Seven Hold Powers of God of the Seven Days of Creation!
There is nothing else like these powers in all heaven and earth.
They never destroy; they are always constructive.
And each always produces a result after its own kind.

For the First Day of the process of creation, there is the In-spiring Ray - the radiation of energy into the ideal of what you desire, or into the substance of thing or condition you wish to create.

For the Second Day of the process, there is the Expanding Ray; which starts the creating of something different from that which was inspired by the First Power.

For the Third Day, there is the Forming Ray which begins to give form to what is expanding, to actualize the ideal of what you desire.

For the Fourth Day, there is the Clarifying Power. You may also call it the Purification or Differentiating Power - each part taking its own place, being harmonized so that each part works together harmoniously to produce what you most desire.

For the Fifth Day of our process of creation, there is the Vitalizing Ray to be used.
It is mystic and mysterious in its power; it gives life even to that which does not have life - just as God on the Fifth Day brought forth life out of water which in itself is not living.

For on the Sixth Day, the Re-Creative Power - the power of each thing to reproduce itself, like to its own kind - the source of all abundance of earth - whether abundance of energies, or life, or of things of material wealth.

And for the Seventh Day, the Holding Ray - that is, the power that keeps what you have created for use for yourself and for others, and also keeps what you have created in the form or condition in which you created it, so it does not lessen, or deteriorate, or disappear.

PUBLISHER'S NOTE:

Before putting up the five lessons of "Mysterious Catalytic Foods" in this permanent form, Dr. Landone tried out 1000 preliminary copies, in order to find out in advance, if possible, what parts needed further elucidation.

The present edition contains all the explanations and revisions that were found necessary as a result of those preliminary trials.

IN ADDITION, the following letter from Dr. Landone gives the answers to the questions most frequently asked by his first thousand students.

Printed by courtesy of and arrangement with, "Writings of Brown Landone, Incorporated."

MYSTERIOUS CATALYTIC FOODS

A Course in Five Lessons with Ten Charts

by

BROWN LANDONE

The ONLY simple and practical course on LECITHINS and NEWLY discovered youth growing food AUXINONS.

Since this Course is sent you as a FREE GIFT, Dr. Landone has no connection with its distribution and cannot, of course, afford to answer any questions or correspondence in connection with it. It is our FREE GIFT to you.

Dear Student of Youthfulness:

Greetings – AND vital GLORIOUS new youthfulness, to YOU!

I want you to USE my new Course on Catalytic Foods.

I did not write this Course MERELY to have it sold!

I wrote it to start you on the way to NEW YOUTHFULNESS!

Whatever can be done freely to help you on that way, I shall willingly do – for I hope you will CHANGE your body, to ENJOY increased vitality, energy AND youthfulness.

I can NOT, of course, answer questions which require long answers, without charge. If I did, I'd have no time for anything else.

Here are the answers to questions asked by the first 1,000 students of "Mysterious Catalytic Foods:"

1 – ACID FRUITS: These should not be eaten with starchy foods. They do have an alkaline base, but they remain acid in the stomach for hours. Eat them by themselves – either as the ONLY thing you eat for a breakfast or luncheon; or late at night.

2 – ALMONDS: No! No! You do NOT need to roast almonds before eating them.

3 – AMOUNT OF FOOD DAILY: No one can tell you, how much to eat daily of any one food, or of all foods you eat. Moreover, your own needs change from day to day. Trust instinct within you.

4 – AUXINONS OF MUNG BEANS: See "Auxinons from Sprouts", – following the item "Yeast".

5 - BAKON YEAST: A pulverized yeast with a bacon flavor. It is the nearest perfect product of this kind of which I know. It is <u>non-fermentative</u>; and its content of vitamins is guaranteed in International and Sherman-Bourquin units.

6 - BLUEBERRIES: Yes, CANNED blueberries ARE good.

7 - BRAN BROTH: Soak a cupful of any bran breakfast food for 4 hours in a quart of cold water; drain off the liquid; drink a glass or two each day.

8 - BREWERS' YEAST. Fleischman's Yeast is satisfactory as a substitute.

9 - CANNED FOODS: Foods canned by standard companies are now often better than similar products cooked in your kitchen, because canneries cook with steam, and much oxygen of the air is excluded during cooking. And since some water is eliminated, many canned products contain larger percentage of minerals than when fresh.

10 - CAPSULE CONCENTRATED FOODS: Yes, enough concentrated foods "can" be put up in capsules - so small that a vest pocketful will last a month. BUT there is DANGER in using ALL concentrated foods. They tend to stop normal activity of the digestive system - particularly large intestine - and ITS activity is VERY important in maintaining balanced distribution of blood in the body.

11 - CAPSULED CATALYSTS: Do NOT try to obtain the "catalytic" lecithins and auxinons in capsules! NO good, if in capsules. (But, see VITAMINS.)

12 - CAVIAR: Any kind of fish roe is satisfactory as a substitute. (See FISH ROE.)

13 - CHOLESTEROL: No matter what one faddist has lately written, there is NO danger in eating foods containing cholesterols; they are ESSENTIAL in order to live.

14 - COMBINATIONS: Proteins CAN be eaten WITH starches. (For your soul's sake - as well as your body's - forget the faddists.) Nature ALWAYS COMBINES proteins AND starches in every nut and cereal food on earth!

15 - COW PEAS: Cow Peas are large, ripe, dried peas.

16 - CURES by FOODS: No particular food "cures" any disease. God and nature cure. Use all the foods suggested in the Master Chart; then the body will become more responsive to Vital Energy and healing will be helped.

17 - DEHYDRATED LIVER and BRAIN FOODS: I do not know of any such product on the market.

18 - DIETS FOR CURE OF DISEASES: See also, - Cures by Food. With the exception of deficiency diseases, it is probable that no particular diet will cure any particular disease. But a complete and composite diet, - see, Chart H - maintains such health of body, that God and nature effect the cure of the particular disease.

19 - EGGS: Prepare them any way you desire; do not worry about faddish advice.

20 - EXPENSE: Foods recommended in this course are not more expensive than those of an ordinary diet.

21 - FADDISH? NO: I have never been a faddist. But in my search for vitality and youthfulness, I have sincerely 'tried out" all the fads. THIS Course is NOT faddish; it presents a COMPOSITE diet, including ALL well-known good foods, AND also the catalytic aminos, enzymes, lecithins and auxinons.

22 - FISH ROE: Any kind of fish roe is satisfactory. Roe are eggs. Only female fish lay eggs. So do not ask your grocer for "male" fish roe! FISH roe can be OBTAINED in cans, put up by Gorton's, sold by A & P Stores.

23 - FLAX-O-LIN: This contains the highest percentage of properly balanced minerals found in cereals. It is NOT sold separately. It is included in DR. JACKSON'S MEAL and other Jackson products.

24 - FRIED FOODS: Fried foods are not easily digested, unless you masticate them thoroughly.

25 - FRUIT: Yes, fruit IS good for the body; BUT - BUT - some fruits are NOT acid, but most fruits we eat ARE ACID. (See ACID FRUITS.)

26 - GELATINE: Knox Gelatine is one of the 'perfect' proteins. It has been proven by university test greatly to increase vitality and endurance.

27 - GREENS: Any green leaf product can be used as a substitute for another.

28 - GUARANTEES: Any statement in a printed folder about a food product is NOT necessarily a legal guarantee that the statement is true. But statements on the food package are guarantees. Also, any statement that a food is made "from" natural products which contain certain elements, is NOT proof that the product you buy contains those elements.

29 - HONEY: Honey has a drugging effect. As a food, it is not so good as our brown sugars, molasses, maple sugar and syrup. Bees never live on honey, except when they wish to be drugged into inactivity, to sleep unconsciously for months. When active in the summer time, they live on sugars found in pollens of flowers.

30 - LECITHIN: There is lecithin in wheat germ oil and soy bean oil. BUT, the body may NOT be able to use such lecithins, just as the copper in a penny is NOT the kind of copper which your body needs. For best sources of THE lecithins which your body can use, see Chart F.

31 - LETTUCE JUICE: If you have no "liquefier", grind a head of lettuce in an ordinary meat grinder; then add a kitchen quart of water; let it stand three hours; drain off water for use.

32 - MEAT FOODS: Meat foods are not forbidden in the Bible. The forbidden meat foods were those of animals - like the pig, - which were diseased in those days. Meat foods were the sacred foods of the Hebrews, used at all of the holy sacrifices and feasts. See, - Vegetarian Diet.

33 - MEAT PEPTONE: For this, eat beef bouillon, red meats, gelatines (not Jello).

34 - MILK: When the word "milk" is used, ordinary sweet milk is meant. This means COW'S sweet milk - not sour milk, or goat's milk, unless designated. Milk as the MAIN factor of a diet is NOT beneficial to the adult. BUT USE a LITTLE milk - a pint each day - for milk does contain calcium, and other foods do not contain enough calcium for maintenance of vital red blood cells. Hence, it is better to use a little milk and get calcium, than to use no milk and not get enough calcium. Pasteurizing does NOT destroy the calcium value.

35 - MOLASSES: Raw sugar may NOT be comparable to molasses in mineral value.

36 - NERVES: Bran Broth is valuable in re-invigorating nerves. (See BRAN BROTH.)

37 - OYSTERS: Shrimp, clams and lobster can be substituted for oysters.

38 - PROTEINS: No! No harmful effect from liberal use of proteins. (See COMBINATIONS.)

39 - RED MEAT: BEEF is our one important red meat; other red meats are veal and lamb; they differ from the white

meat of fish, pork chops, chicken and turkey. But the DARK
meat of fowls and wild game is red meat.

40 - SALMON: Canned salmon can well be substituted
for fresh salmon.

45 - SPECIAL DIETS: Any special food, may work wonders
for a time. Every special product, - vitamin, mineral, yeast,
acid-fruit-juices, is a specific. Each should be used in
exceptional quantities, only to remedy deficiencies. Many
people are led to make unwise continuous use of exceptional
amounts of these specifics, because such products are commer-
cialized, and advertized excessively to create continuous
profits for those who produce and sell the products.

42 - SPROUTS, CANNED: We use sprouts for their auxinons. Auxinons are live chemical impulses to grow. Cooking
kills the impulses to grow. Boil a seed and you can not make it
sprout. Hence, I do NOT advise sprouts which have been canned.

43 - VEGETARIAN DIET: Free choice, I lived on vegetarian foods for several years, - hoping to make my body more
spiritual. But it is now proven that we get a higher spiritual
responsiveness of body by a mixed diet. Those who object to
the use of meat, from the ethical standpoint, do not fully
realize that science has now proven that plants also have consciousness. Individuals and races who live on vegetable foods
only, tend to become hermit people or hermit races. To maintain youthful vitality on vegetable foods alone, one must take
a great deal of exercise, and waste a lot of time in extra
breathing and sleeping, to get rid of extra waste poisons of
such foods.

44 - VITAMINS: Of all the vitamins, cooking destroys
only Vitamin C. Hence we advise lettuce and orange and tomato
juice for Vitamin C. If you need extra vitamins, use CATALYN
-- a product of the Milwaukee Vitamin Company, sold in all
drug stores and many health food shops.

45 - WHEAT GERM OIL: See, - Wheat Germ Cereals.

46 - WHEAT GERM CEREAL: Bemax, Embo, and DR. JACKSON'S
MEAL are good sources of germ cereals. Wheat germ oil is
found in these products.

47 - WHITE FLOUR: White flours do not contain as large
amounts of the essential minerals as do whole wheat and other
brown flour products.

48 - WHITE SUGAR: White sugar does not contain some
of the minerals found in brown sugars and molasses.

49 - YEAST: See above, - Bakon Yeast and Brewers' Yeast.

50 - AUXINONS from SPROUTS has brought many OTHER questions about MUNG BEANS, and the growing and use of SPROUTS. These sprouts provide the AUXINONS, which are so valuable in maintaining YOUTHFULNESS.

(a) "Sprouts" can be grown from several kinds of seeds - beans, peas, etc. BUT for the MOST VITAL AUXINONS, sprouts of Mung Beans ARE the BEST.

(b) Do NOT expect your Mung Beans to sprout more than once, for whenever any seed sprouts, it destroys itself to produce the plant that grows from it. This is true of ALL seeds.

(c) When the sprouts (stems) are 4 or more inches high, CUT them off and eat the sprouts, NOT the bean seeds.

(d) Eat the sprouts uncooked, as advised in this Course.

(e) Eat a small handful of these chopped sprouts every other day, or two or three tablespoonfuls of the chopped sprouts daily.

(f) If used with salads, use any salad dressing you desire.

(g) NOT ADVERTISING: I am NOT advertising any product, but to save myself answering many, many letters, I am telling you NOW that you can obtain the Auxinon Mung Bean Seeds and "SPROUT-GRO", which makes your sprouts grow very rapidly, from Rapid Growth Products Company, Newton, New Jersey.

Now for answers to a few miscellaneous questions:

LANDONE'S DIET: Please don't ask me for "my" special diet. I use the foods as given in "Mysterious Catalytic Foods." See Master Chart.

LANDONE'S SPECIAL ADVICE: My heart would like to give "Special" dietetic help to each of you. But time is limited. I can NOT meet all the demands.

HOW PREPARE FOODS: It is so long since many of our really vital foods have been used, that some people today do not even know how to prepare them. Prepare KIDNEYS as kidney stew, just as you prepare beef stew. Prepare BRAINS and SWEETBREADS by broiling or gently frying; OR scramble them with scrambled eggs.

RESULTS for YOU: Just as science has proven that small

young SPROUTS, called "immature foods", work actual miracles in transforming animals under test, so I am certain that EVERYONE who USES the foods suggested in THIS Course, CAN work a TRANSFORMATION for himself.

PHOTOGRAPHS of MIRACLES of YOUTHFULNESS: I wish I could send you photographs of some youthful people - 79 to 89 years old - who are not only young in appearance but also youthfully active. (But the photos are personal; I can't send them.)

This IS a new age. Scientists, testing lower forms of life, have proven that transformation can take place. And Dr. Carrel states, in effect, that science now gives man the means of transforming human life.

I have written this course with the expectation that you will USE it!

And MY wish for NEW youthfulness goes out TO YOU, from one who HAS attained it.

Faithfully,

Brown Landone.

THE MYSTERIOUS CATALYTIC FOODS

by

Brown Landone, F.R.E.S.

PREVIEW

This Course is NOT a substitute for any book on foods
or diet, whether it is written by the highest scientific au-
thorities or by natural food specialists.

Moreover, this Course is NOT a substitute for ANY
other food COURSE, - no matter what its nature or scope.

Each book or course previously written has a value
of its own in meeting a particular need of a particular field.

Such books and courses should be kept - some for reference, some for study - and for use of whatever is scienti-
fically proven.

THIS Course does NOT treat of foods as MATERIALS,
because there are a thousand good books and perhaps a hundred
courses already written on that phase of food science.

This Course IS devoted wholly to foods of CATALYTIC
energy - the MIRACLE WORKERS of foods.

This Course is now the ONLY simple and practical presentation of this subject.

It IS the FIRST SIMPLE and PRACTICAL presentation of
the value and use of enzymes, aminos, auxinons, lecithins,
chlorophyl, cholesterol, ergosterol, et cetera.

This Course deals exclusively - NOT with the material
substance of foods, but - with the particular foods which
act as MIRACLE WORKERS of astounding energy.

THE MYSTERIOUS CATALYTIC FOODS

by

Brown Landone, F.R.E.S.

A Course of Five Lessons
With Ten Simplified Charts

------ o ------

LESSON I — MIRACLE CATALYSTS and INNER FOODS

Let's waste no time in getting down to the brass tacks of practical facts.

First, you LACK either the energy, or vitality, or virility, or youthfulness you want, - OTHERWISE you would not even be reading this course.

Secondly, since you DO lack these results, you are NOT getting what you want from foods. EVEN with ALL the minerals and vitamins, balanced foods, and proper combinations of natural foods grown in sunshine, - YET your body still BEGINS DYING before you are 24 years old, and continues slowly to die all the rest of your life.

This need NOT be. So again, let's get down to brass tacks, to learn: HOW the newly discovered foods DIFFER from those you now eat; what CATALYTIC foods are, and WHERE found in sufficient quantity to TRANSFORM your body and your life.

SEVEN RESULTS YOU WANT

If you are like I am, you want SEVEN definite results from the foods you eat.

First, you want ENERGY that is abundant, and does not tire you out in getting it.

Second, you want a RADIANCY of energy that augments PERSONALITY.

Third, you want BEAUTY OF SKIN, not only for its appearance, but because beauty is the only proof that your skin is healthy enough to activate the mystic adrenal glands with which the skin is neurally connected.

Fourth, you want a body - NOT solid - but RESPONSIVE like a 140 HP engine.

Fifth, you want the continuing ENDURANCE of the energy of catalytic foods.

Sixth, you want maintained VITALITY and strengthened VIRILITY.

Seventh, you want continued youthfulness and INCREASING YOUTHFULNESS.

If you are like I am, THESE are the seven results you want from foods.
But, you are NOT getting these results from the foods you NOW eat.

My first step is to teach you not only of the value and amazing power, but also of the absolute necessity, of the INNER foods which we call hormones.

They are the secretions of the magical endocrine glands. Every scientist now knows that they CONTROL ALL bodily activities, and that when they are balanced they CAN TRANSFORM not only the body itself but the very character of the individual.

BUT in the PAST, when partly depleted, only TWO remedial means have been used.

One means is the monkey or goat gland operation. But this helps only one gland; and it is very costly; and the good results seldom last more than 11 months.

The OTHER means is injecting artificial hormones into your blood. This also is costly; effects do NOT last; and it is VERY DANGEROUS unless done by a specialist who makes no mistake in knowing conditions of your body. Injecting too much of one hormone, may make you unconscious; too much of another, might rip your muscles into shreds.

BUT NOW let us recognize the normal way: hormones ARE inner foods; they can be built-up by substances of which they are composed, and by activating the endocrines.

So, let me first give you a very brief vision of hormones as inner foods.

Each inner food is about 80,000,000 times as powerful as foods you eat.

Nature knows how to send them throughout the body, at tremendous SPEED — faster than blood flows, faster even than nerve messages. HOW this is done, we do not yet know, but we DO know they can be INSTANTLY fed to ANY part or organ of the body.

These inner foods are the SUPREME foods - DOMINANT in ALL body functioning.

Too much or too little of them stimulate or fatigue, restore or atrophy, muscle cells; astoundingly increase or decrease muscle energy; increase or decrease heart beat, blood flow, blood pressure, and circulation of all fluids in the body; they also determine all processes of breathing, elimination, digestion - even the use of vitamins.

They produce astounding effects on energies of sex and all related conditions. Increase or decrease activity of adrenals; stimulate sex impulse; absolutely essential for all primary and secondary sex characteristics of both male and female; change male characteristics to female and visa versa. Vitalize sex organs. Increase size and activity of degenerated organs.

They can banish fatigue in a second, and so affect structure that a lack of them produces fear and cowardice; while a plentiful supply changes shyness to boldness and transforms a coward into a courageous hero. They also so affect brain structure, that lack of one of them causes idiocy, while a plentiful supply causes genius.

HEIGHT and structure growth are controlled by these inner foods, — determining giants or dwarfs. Remedial results attained are almost miraculous; many cases; one adolescent UNDERSIZED youth, for example, grew 8¼ inches in 21 months.

ALL TRANSFORMING changes are controlled by them. As fantastic examples, note that tadpoles deprived of one inner food, never change into frogs; with the same inner food without growth food, they change so quickly the frogs are no larger than flies. White rats made to grow so rapidly they cut their teeth in one day after birth, instead of eight.

ORGANS TRANSFORMED, — shrunken tissues restored to normal size and activity.

There seems to be no limit to transforming changes due to these inner foods!

One scientist says, "results are almost beyond belief", and then he adds that IF we desired to do it, we might produce "college graduates at 12 years of age".

WEIGHT is controlled - increased or decreased - by the inner foods - reduced even 23 pounds in 29 days, and with great improvement of health and WITHOUT dieting.

Bodily ENERGY increased in an instant - giving one man the strength of ten.

NEW and youthful SKIN cells grown; rather amazingly, different amounts of one inner food, makes the skin muddy and dull, or gives it tints of peaches and cream.

YET THIS list of results is NOT EVEN ONE TENTH of those NOW PROVEN by scientists.

These inner foods are the MIRACLE working foods of the body. And we NOW know the aminos (of which they are built-up) and which foods give us the best aminos.

Hence THIS course STARTS with these INNER foods; then proceeds to the mystic builders, and the AMINOS or amino-acids of which the inner foods are composed; then to the other food catalysts necessary for use of all food substances; and for increased consciousness of power, and for youthful growth of NEW cell structure.

So always keep this in mind: The ONE basic purpose of THIS course is to reveal WHAT feeds the endocrines, and what other miracle-working foods should be used to produce the conditions which will make the endocrines produce more of the mysterious inner foods.

Before we proceed, remember that I am NOT writing of fats, proteins, vitamins, et cetera - for they ARE already adequately presented in scores of books.

Remember that the foods you have been eating, are used as MATERIALS for the body building materials, heating materials, balancing materials, and protective materials.

Remember too, that all these are MATERIALS, like the lumber and brick you may use in building a house. But that the materials will be of NO value in building, UNLESS you have efficient WORKERS to do the building.

Knowledge of the common MATERIAL foods has been widespread for 40 years.

Hence, there is NO reason for me to write a course on the use of such foods.

So THIS Course IS devoted to the NEWLY DISCOVERED foods and their use, for in the last ten years - yes, in the last SEVEN years - we have obtained more knowledge of the MYSTERIOUS WORKER foods than in all preceding centuries.

NOTE WELL, THESE SEVEN GROUPS

Under SEVEN headings, I give you the NEW knowledge of mineral elements, of chlorophyl, cholesterol, enzymes, amino-acids, hormones, lecithins, auxinons.

And ALL this Course is devoted to SEVEN groups of MIRACLE WORKERS.

FIRST, I write of the MYSTIC BUILDERS, - the mineral elements, now so lacking in your food. They act as CATALYSTS and can actually USE all the foods of building materials, and BUILD them into your body as LIVING tissues. And they can make use of the vitamins, and of the fuel foods, and MULTIPLY their energy many times.

SECOND, the SUBSTANCE TRANSFORMERS - the miracle working enzymes, of power TITANIC.

One enzyme unit can transform 40,000 times its own weight of food in 30 minutes.

THIRD, the mysterious ENERGY TRANSFORMERS and HORMONE BUILDERS - the amino-acids. These form a very special class of workers. You know that a carpenter, with an electric motored saw, can multiply his work, eight or ten times. BUT these catalytic transformers can multiply energy and work from two million to four million times.

FOURTH, the WIRELESS POWER RECEIVERS and COSMIC ENERGY TRANSFORMERS - chlorophyl and its associates, which actually respond to and take-in energy from the sun and perhaps from interstellar spaces! Cholesterol and ergosterol act as COSMIC energy transformers.

Not only do these food substances TAKE-IN cosmic energy, but they actually CREATE other mystic substances in your body, of mysterious power - essential to your life.

FIFTH, the CONTROLLERS of FORM and POWER and CHARACTER - hormones - 'INNER' foods.

SIXTH, the LECITHINS - which you might call SOUL CON-TACT foods, for that IS what they really are. WITHOUT lecithin there is NO consciousness. No matter how healthy your brain, if lecithin is greatly lessened, you lose consci-ousness. Lecithin IS the INTERMEDIARY between matter and mind. Hence, I call it, the soul-contact food.

And SEVENTH, the YOUTH CREATING foods - the AUXINONS. These are CREATIVE in so true a sense, that we might even call them "Lord-God" foods for they ACTUALLY CREATE new and YOUTH-FUL CELLS and TISSUES. They actually impel growth of NEW CELL substances.

Perhaps they will initiate the discovery, which will lead to the continued youthfulness which man has sought since the beginning of the world.

Re-read the above several times. The common MATERIAL foods are NOT so important.

If one or more of them is lacking, the worker foods will substitute others.

It is the CATALYTIC MIRACLE WORKERS - the wireless power receivers, transformers, energy multipliers, actual creators - which are VITALLY ESSENTIAL.

Please get a clear PRE-VIEW now - of THIS COURSE on amino-acids, minerals, enzymes, vitamins, hormones, chloro-phyl, cholesterol and associates, lecithins and auxinons.

In this Lesson I, I teach you the POWER of INNER foods and CATALYTIC foods.

In the next Lesson II, I teach you the MIRACLE BUILDERS and TRANSFORMERS — particularly of the catalytic minerals and enzymes and amino-acids.

In Lesson III, I teach you the CONTROLLERS of form and power and the COSMIC ENERGY TRANSFORMERS —the foods which make your body RESPONSIVE to the SUPER ENERGIES. That is, cholesterol, ergosterol, phytosterol and chlorophyl — which respond to the higher energies which come from the sun, and by augmented action of the endocrine glands, increase the INNER foods — the miraculous hormones.

In Lesson IV, I give you knowledge of LECITHINS which make consciousness possible and which INCREASE your consciousness of power and maintain virility.

And in Lesson V, I teach you of the miracle growing auxinons. These are found in NEWLY GROWING substances and only in such substances. When such substances are eaten as food, they actually restore the feeling of youthfulness to old organic structure.

This statement is carefully considered; it is based on results of scientific experiments which have proven that "immature" foods — that is, young growing leaves and stems - fed to animals under test, have resulted in actual new youthfulness. And more than one human individual using such foods, HAVE possessed remarkable vitality and amazing activity even though from 80 to 90 years old in years.

I GIVE YOU TEN CHARTS

ALL my CHARTS of this Course are very simple, yet complete. For the FIRST time, they bring the NEW knowledge together, and make it so SIMPLE, that you CAN USE it.

Books on mineral foods give tens of pages of mineral contents of foods, BUT there are so MANY and so MANY figures that you do not know which foods to choose.

But in my Chart A, you have all the 11 mineral foods — in PERFECT BALANCE.

This "balance" IS important, - for you may need 3,390,000 infinitesimal units of one mineral and 17,300 of another; or 730,000 of a third, and only 16 of a fourth.

This balance factor gives REMARKABLE value to this Chart — CHART A.

But you need NOT bother with figures of balance. The chart solves it for you.

My Chart A of CATALYTIC mineral foods — is so simple, that IF you choose BUT TWO different foods each day of the week — you have ALL the minerals needed.

And my other CHARTS, for amino-acids, lecithins, et cetera, are just as simple.

The NEW discoveries of POWER foods have NEVER BEFORE been presented in this way.

And never BEFORE has any of the knowledge been presented in USEABLE form by CHARTS.

To understand something of POWER of CATALYSTS, read the following carefully.

WHAT IS A CATALYST?

And please note that this word catalytic is different from the word cataleptic. Cata-LEPTIC, as used in cataleptic fit - means a stiffened STOPPING of action!

But cata-LYTIC designates the GREATEST chemical ACTIVITY known on earth!

Now, let me help you to understand something of the POWER of a catalyst.

Consider first, a chemical catalyst in action, OUTSIDE the body.

Think of three chemicals: potassium chlorate, manganese dioxide, and oxygen.

Now, if potassium chlorate is heated even to a temperature almost twice that of boiling point, it will give off VERY LITTLE oxygen, and VERY VERY SLOWLY.

But, manganese dioxide acts as a catalyst in the presence of potassium chlorate.

SO, IF you drop just a pinch of pulverized manganese dioxide into the heated potassium chlorate, oxygen is given off at a TREMENDOUS RATE and in TITANIC TORRENTS!

Yet, from the residue, you can GET BACK ALL of your manganese dioxide, UNCHANGED!

That is, a catalyst not only astoundingly increases the energy or activity of other substances, but it practically NEVER uses up its own energy or substance.

CATALYSTS IN and OUTSIDE the BODY

Now let us consider an example of catalytic action in the HUMAN BODY.

To illustrate, let me tell you of one of the catalysts which acts to break up starch during digestion. This is the result of a test outside the body.

One such catalyst was highly purified by modern methods.

Then ONE tiny part was diluted with 100,000,000 parts of water.

Now certainly, you will naturally think that adding 100,000,000 parts of water, ought to dilute and weaken it so much, that it would have little power left.

But note what that ONE unit of that very diluted solution did.

It attacked an amount of starch food, — 4,000,000 TIMES its own weight.

And it broke up and split up ALL of it!

And while it was doing that job, it did something else, also!

It actually BUILT UP another substance, equal to 2,800,000 times its own weight.

Let us try to get some concrete idea of what such power actually means.

Suppose we could find in New York City, ONE man — NO larger and seemingly no more powerful than any other man — who was able actually to subdue 4,000,000 other men, and handle them as he pleased — and ALL of them AT THE SAME TIME!

Such a super-man would be a sort of CATALYTIC MAN.

And if, WHILE he was subduing those 4,000,000 men; he could also CREATE 2,800,000 other men full grown in a few moments — what a God-man he would be to us!

Yet catalytic substances in your body can perform just such miracles.

Moreover, such catalysts have TRANSFORMING power, actually to change SUBSTANCES!

Imagine a brick wall, 4 inches through, 4 FEET high and 21 MILES long.

And now comes along another brick, which looks just like the bricks in the wall!

BUT it IS different; it possesses catalytic power. And WHAT does it DO?

It tears down and breaks up every brick in that 21 mile wall, and at the same time, it creates out of their dirt, 2,800,000 beautiful porcelain vases!

THE ASTOUNDING CONTRAST

The above gives you some idea of the astounding POWER of CATALYTIC foods.

In CONTRAST, the common foods — fats, proteins, et cetera — have little energy.

They are often mere LOADS and wastes to your body, UNLESS your food also contains ENOUGH of the catalytic minerals with power to TRANSFORM the common foods.

FIVE words in this Lesson will be worth more than the cost of the entire course to you, IF you think ENOUGH of them to CHANGE your choice of foods.

These five words are, — "MATERIAL Foods and WORKER Foods!"

This is the most significant distinction ever made of foods.

Think about it enough to change your foods, and it can CHANGE YOUR LIFE.

In this lesson, you HAVE learned THE four MOST IMPORTANT facts of food values.

First, that the material foods — starches, sugars, proteins and fats, — are NOT important by themselves; that they are of NO use at all WITHOUT the worker foods.

Second, that the worker foods ARE CATALYSTS, and NOT at all like material foods.

Third, you HAVE learned WHAT a CATALYST is, and something of its astounding energy.

Fourth, you have learned that these catalyst foods give mighty power to your body, and that INNER foods CAN actually TRANSFORM both substance and energy in your body.

Of course, I can not crowd my entire Course into this first Lesson.

But I have ALREADY taught you enough, so that you should STOP RIGHT NOW, bothering about starches and fats and sugars. Never worry about them again.

And STOP WORRYING about food combinations!

WITHOUT catalysts, ANY combination of foods may cause trouble.

BUT WITH catalytic foods, combinations are easily adjusted.

The reason you have eaten so much of the material foods in the past, is that you've wanted more energy. So you've kept on eating more, TRYING to get more energy.

BUT it IS the CATALYTIC foods which MULTIPLY ENERGY a HUNDRED TIMES!

There are practically NO important catalytic foods in starches or sugars.

There is ONE very valuable catalytic - lecithin - in a FEW phosphorized fats.

IN SOME of the proteins — the COMPLETE proteins - we find the essential aminos which help to build-up all the mighty hormones, the inner foods of your body.

Other special foods contain chlorophyl, cholesterol, ergosterol and auxinons.

Each works after its own kind, to produce a definite effect of its own in your body.

Each is found in a particular group of foods; ALL are SIMPLY grouped in my CHARTS.

FROM WHAT, TO WHAT

Do you see, WHERE I am leading you?

It's AWAY FROM 'material' foods which load your body and give you little energy.

It's TOWARD the amazing catalytic foods of astounding power.

Make a comparison based on scientific facts: Imagine taking ONE ounce of one of these catalytic substances, and dividing it into 100,000,000 tiny tiny parts.

46 of those hundred-millionth parts WILL give you 100 units of power!

IF you COULD get similar energy out of meat and potatoes, you would have to eat 843 pounds of meat and potatoes to get the same 100 units of power.

My purpose IS to lead you AWAY FROM a body loaded with dead weight of foods of little energy — a body, slowly dying year by year!

To lead you, TO a body thrilled with energy of tremendous power.

Now you are ready for Lesson II with its Mystic Builders of catalytic power; Enzymes as transformers of substance, and Aminos of which hormones are built-up.

Also Chart A of Mystic Builders; Chart B of Balancers; and Chart C of Enzymes and Aminos — with these, you are on your way, to a new body thrilled with energy.

THE MYSTERIOUS CATALYTIC FOODS

by

Brown Landone, F.R.E.S.

------ o ------

LESSON II — MYSTIC BUILDERS and SUBSTANCE and ENERGY TRANSFORMERS

In Lesson I, you have already learned WHAT a catalyst IS; and that hormones ARE 'inner' foods; and that food science of the past has been concerned with food materials; while this course is devoted to foods of titanic catalytic energies.

In this Lesson, I give you the MYSTIC BUILDERS and AMAZING TRANSFORMERS.

  I — The Mystic Builders are Mineral Catalysts, which USE the vitamins.

  II — The Substance Transformers are Enzymes, mighty in power.

  III — The Energy Transformers are Aminos of which hormones are made.

GROUP I — THE MYSTIC BUILDERS

There are ELEVEN of these ESSENTIAL Mystic Builders: calcium, chlorine, copper, iodine, iron, magnesium, manganese, potassium, phosphorus, sodium and sulphur.

Oh yes, I know that you already know of these, BUT the thing you have been taught in the past is that they are SUBSTANCES needed for parts of the body — iron for the blood, calcium for teeth, et cetera. That is only a TINY part of the truth.

First, they ARE actual WORKING CATALYSTS, — that is their SUPER function.

Second, WHEN they are present in your body, tissues are NOT torn down rapidly.

Third, they miraculously MULTIPLY other energies by catalytic action.

Fourth, they can change NON-living substance, and build it into LIVING tissue.

Fifth, they also affect CHARACTER! Hundreds of tests prove that reducing the calcium needed by animals, makes them irritable and even viciously antagonistic.

And school children, without sufficient calcium, become troublesome and quarrelsome.

And YOUR PERSONALITY is affected by lack of these minerals. If your body is not well fed with them, you are all-on-edge, unreasonably irritable, and often disagreeable.

Sixth, these mystic minerals are also the DICTATORS of the building activity of all tissues. They even MOVE the blood; three of them are essential for the heart to work.

If the right proportions of these three are long unbalanced, the heart STOPS.

And seventh, these mineral catalysts also activate ENDOCRINE and SEX glands!

And yes, I also know that other minerals have been 'found' in the body — such as arsenic and silicon — but only in tiny parts of approximately a 100,000,000th each.

And these are NOT natural in the body. The amounts found in the body have been taken in with foods. Arsenic with fruits which have been sprayed with arsenic insecticide; silicon as tiny flakes of sand taken in with the green leaf foods.

YOUR FIRST STEP

I ask you now to make your FIRST great change in choice of foods YOU eat.

From now on, do NOT choose fats, starches, et cetera, as the important foods.

Instead, choose your foods MAINLY FOR these MINERAL ELEMENTS, and later we will add the choice of other mystic-powered foods.

Study CHART A. It is simple, yet complete; and it is VERY VERY EASY to USE.

The FOURTEEN foods listed on CHART A, supply ALL the 11 essential minerals.

If you choose ANY TWO of these 14 foods for one day, two others for the next day, and continue with two different foods each day for a week, you will obtain each week, ALL of the ESSENTIAL mineral CATALYSTS needed by your body. These are THE important foods.

They ARE the MIRACLE BUILDERS. They CAN make USE of all the building material foods and the heating fuel foods. WITHOUT them, all other foods are USELESS.

And WITHOUT these minerals, ALL vitamins are USELESS in the body. REMEMBER THAT!

YOUR SECOND STEP

Since vitamins are USED by the mineral catalysts, and since the vitamin tables you find in books are so elaborate that they are confusing, I give you ANOTHER CHART — the result of many years' work — of foods for ALL vitamins in ONE simple CHART.

Under vitamins, on CHART C, you will find only THREE groups of foods!

This list does not contain all foods which are rich in vitamins, yet, it is the ONLY PRACTICAL grouping of foods which DO supply ALL the vitamins and in BALANCE.

I give seven foods in each group. So you need not eat the SAME foods each day.

Note the marvel of this CHART C. IF, each day, you eat but ONE of the foods of EACH group, your body will have a plentiful supply of ALL vitamins you need.

ANY one food of Group I, will provide vitamins A and G (B2).

ANY one food of Group II, will provide what you need of vitamins B1 and C.

ANY one of the foods of Group III, will give you vitamins D and E, — providing you also eat a reasonable amount of butter each day and use a little brewers' yeast.

The yeast can be used in salad dressing or as a tasty addition to many foods.

If Brewers' Yeast is not easily obtainable, do not worry about it. ALL yeasts which you can buy on the market, are about equally valuable. Bakon yeast is the most valuable.

In the past, your dominant use of common MATERIAL foods has been like using IRON wire to wire your house for electricity. It takes days to do it; yet when you turn on the electricity, the wires are burned out in an hour. So you rewire it again, and burn out the wires again; and rewire it, and again burn out the wires.

I, for one, do NOT want to spend my life — wearing out and repairing, wearing out and repairing my body. I do NOT want to WASTE my life in that way.

But, IF you wire your house with COPPER wire, you need not rewire and rewire.

So also, if you use more of these miracle builder foods, there will be little need of repairing your body and hence you will have MORE abundant energy to USE.

Make this change first — choose more and more of the catalytic mineral foods.

Now a still GREATER change: Not only improvement, but actual TRANSFORMATION of tissues by enzymes - as mysterious as the long sought secret of turning LEAD to GOLD.

Nothing you have seen a magician do on any stage — and nothing you have ever read of mystic occult phenomena — equals the miraculous transformation effected by enzymes.

GROUP II — SUBSTANCE TRANSFORMERS

ENZYMES are energy multipliers, but they also TRANSFORM SUBSTANCES.

ENZYMES are commonly defined as "CATALYSTS formed in plant or animal cells."

They act as catalysts in the body; multiply energy, often a million times; also multiply work done; and then multiply and TRANSFORM substances themselves.

We now know there are several KINDS of enzymes. Each has astounding power.

Some of them — miracle of miracles — seemingly make SOMETHING OUT OF NOTHING!

For example, one CAN produce carbon-dioxide WITHOUT using any free oxygen.

This IS a miracle, for carbon-dioxide is made by uniting carbon and oxygen.

As we know in chemistry, carbon-dioxide can be made ONLY by the union of ONE atomic part of carbon and TWO atomic parts of oxygen.

That is, to form carbon-dioxide, two parts of oxygen ARE NECESSARY.

BUT what CAN these mystic enzymes do? They work MIRACLES in transformation!

They can make carbon-dioxide without using any free oxygen! It is like building a brick house of actual brick, without using any bricks — a true miracle!

YOUR THIRD STEP

This is the THIRD step I ask you to take in choice of new foods.

Make wise choice of foods for enzymes, see second column of CHART C.

Choose at least ONE of these foods, for EACH day of each week.

With a greater use of the catalytic minerals and their vitamin associates, and with TRANSFORMING enzymes, your body BECOMES REFINED — with INCREASED vibrant energy.

GROUP III — ENERGY TRANSFORMERS

And now we come to those miraculous energy multipliers, the AMINO-ACIDS.

All I teach you about use of amino-acid foods is linked up with PROTEINS.

First, because amino-acids are found ONLY in protein foods and in NO other foods.

Second, because it is the amino-acids which determine whether each particular protein food is of exceptional value to the body, or whether it is a deficient food.

Protein is protein, just as carbon is carbon. BUT in VALUE, carbon of diamonds differ from carbon of coal. So also, different proteins DIFFER in VALUE as foods.

SOME proteins are excellent foods; because they contain ALL the amino-acids needed.

Others are VERY DEFICIENT because they do NOT contain all essential amino-acids.

The matter of choice of proteins is vitally important to you, for their amino-acids ARE linked up with HORMONES — the MOST POWERFUL substances in your body.

MANY HARMFUL IDEAS ARE TAUGHT OF SUBSTITUTING ONE KIND OF PROTEIN FOR ANOTHER.

Although there are many amino-acids, several of them can be made IN the body!

BUT there are TEN which MUST be taken INTO the body in foods.

So you should choose THE proteins which DO contain all THESE TEN.

These ten are ESSENTIAL to life! UNLESS your protein foods contain ALL of them, there is a DECREASE of hormone production and activity in your body.

THESE are the ten amino-acids which ARE ESSENTIAL to the life of your body:

Arginine   Isoleucine Lysine   Phenylalanine Tryptophane
Histidine Leucine   Methionine Theeonine   Valine

DON'T bother with these names; it's NOT necessary for you to remember them.

The ONE important thing is, — WHICH proteins YOU are to CHOOSE for YOUR food.

Some protein foods we call complete proteins; others we call 'incomplete'.

Complete proteins contain ALL ten essential amino-acids. The incomplete, DO NOT.

These are THE foods which contain the COMPLETE proteins, which in turn contain ALL the amino-acids, which in turn ARE ESSENTIAL to life and HORMONE production.

Almonds; but no other nuts   Eggs of all fowls   Milk
Cheese of all kinds   All lean red meats

Remember that proteins of meats, cheese, eggs and milk are ALWAYS complete!

But NOW note these 'OTHER' protein foods. They ARE NOT complete! The proteins of nuts, gelatines, beans, peas and lentils, and gliadin of wheat are NOT complete!

Nuts and beans and peas can NOT be wisely substituted for complete proteins.

You should also know that there is something peculiar about CORN and SOY BEANS!

Each has one complete, but each also has one INCOMPLETE protein.

Use them for other values, but NEVER depend on them for all complete proteins.

The use of complete proteins is of TREMENDOUS importance to your body!

BECAUSE they contain ALL the amino-acids necessary for production of HORMONES!

Don't try to substitute incomplete proteins for complete amino-acid proteins.

YOUR FOURTH STEP

Choose AMINO-ACID foods wisely, from CHART C. These foods are THE foods which contain the BEST COMPLETE proteins, which contain ALL the essential amino-acids.

And it IS the amino-acids which ARE important, not only for their own catalytic powers, but also because they are linked with the creation of HORMONES.

The AMINO-ACIDS work in specific ways as precursors of the HORMONES.

ADRENALIN is related in its chemical structure to tyrosine, an amino-acid.

INSULIN also may be "accounted for by nine of the amino-acids".

And THYROXINE, the absolute dictator of the increase or decrease of the energy of your body, is closely related to one of the amino-acids.

I AM persistent — often repeating — your NEED of eating COMPLETE proteins.

It is because they contain the amino-acids out of which HORMONES are built.

Hormones are the MOST POWERFUL body substances, and also controllers of power — of character, of sex, of virility. They also activate and CONTINUE these powers.

Their production depends on THE aminos contained in the COMPLETE proteins!

This requires a link-up with the subjects of the next Lesson, and consequently I tell you MORE of HORMONES in Lesson III in connection with chlorophyl and cholesterol.

You are now ready to proceed to Lesson III — the foods which increase VITALITY and VIRILITY — by making the body responsive to the cosmic energies of the sun.

LANDONE ACTIVATING FOODS — CHART A

	Calcium	Chlorine	Copper	Iodine*	Iron	Magnesium	Manganese	Phosphorus	Potassium	Sodium	Sulphur
Almonds	240	40	1.2	20	3.9	250	1.0	465	740		160
Blueberries	20		.1	206	.4		4.4	10	50	15	10
Chard	150	40	.1	980	2.5	70	.8	40	315	85	125
Cheese, Am.	930	880			1.3	35		680	90	600	260
Cocoa	110	50	3.3	80	2.7	420	3.5	700	900	60	200
Cowpeas	100	40				210		460	1400	160	240
Fish Roe, Average	110	530		615	3.0	130		1150	1670	370	1120
Haddock				5630							
Shad				4100							
Lentils	110	50			8.6	100		440	880	60	280
Meat Peptone	25	560				125		1130	2440	640	220
Molasses	210	320	1.9		7.3	70		45	1350	20	130
Oatmeal	70	70	.5	150	3.8	110	2.8	390	340	60	200
Oysters	50	590	3.0	1160	4.5	40	.2	155	90	460	190
Parsley			.2	9600(1)	19.2		.9				
Turnip Greens	350	170		2300	3.5	30	1.4	50	300	70	70

* Iodine, in parts per billion
(1) Oyster Juice, canned

Blank spaces mean only lack of 'richest' mineral content. For use of this Chart, see page 9.

Figures on this Chart are NOT given for you to fuss about. They are given only for reference — for proof that if you use the 14 foods listed, as directed on page 19, you will secure all the eleven mineral catalysts your body needs.

LANDONE ACTIVATING FOODS - CHART B
OTHER FOODS RICH IN MINERALS
(Additional to Chart A) (1)

CALCIUM: Kale, legumes,* milk, nuts, olives, watercress, wheat bran.

CHLORINE: Bananas, butter, caviar, celery, clams, cornmeal, dandelion greens, dates, egg-white, endive, milk, raisins.

COPPER: Beets, calves' liver, dried fruits, legumes,* mushrooms.

IODINE: Cabbage, cucumbers, seaweed, all shellfish, watercress.

IRON: Apricots, dried bacon, beets, chard, dried fruits, egg-yolk, meat juices.

MAGNESIUM: Beans dry, chard, dates, figs, peas dried, spinach.

MANGANESE: Beans dry, beet greens, beets, chard, lettuce, peas dried, pineapple fresh.

PHOSPHORUS: Egg-yolk, legumes,* lean red meats, milk, pumpkin, whole cereal products.

POTASSIUM: Apricots dry, beans dry, dates, figs, mushrooms, prunes, spinach.

SODIUM: Apricots dry, butter, egg-yolk, crackers, endive, meat extracts, and all brined and salted foods.

SULPHUR: Bacon, cauliflower, dates, egg-yolk, legumes,* onions, watercress.

  * Legumes, as here designated, means DRIED beans, lentils and peas.
  (1) These are not the foods which are rich in the minerals listed. These are in ADDITION to the 14 best foods listed in Chart A.

HIGHEST DEGREE (COMMON) ACIDIC ASH FOODS

Bread (W Wheat)	7	Eggs	11	Haddock	16
Crackers	8	Wheat Flour	12	Venison	16
Rice	8	Pork	12	Chicken	17
Fish, average	10	Oatmeal	13	Egg-Yolk	27
Wheat, entire	10	Beef	14	Oysters	30

HIGHEST DEGREE (COMMON) ALKALINE ASH FOODS

Lettuce	7	Dates	11	Raisins	24
Celery	8	Parsnips	12	Spinach	27
Potatoes	8	Almonds	13	Beans	
Beets	11	Chard	16	(Lima Dry)	42
Carrots	11	Beans, Dry	18	Olives	47

MEMO: No special instruction is given for use of this Chart, because it is merely supplementary to Chart A.

LANDONE ACTIVATING FOODS - CHART C

	AMINO ACIDS	ENZYMES
Almonds	Ex	
Cheese (Am)*	Ex	
Cheese (Camembert)*		Ex
Eggs, whole	Gd	Ex
Egg, white	Ex	
Egg-Yolk	Ex	Ex
Fat of	Ex	
Protein of	Ex	
Glutenin (of corn)	Ex	
Kidney		Ex
Liver		Ex
Meat (Red Lean)	Ex	Ex
Milk	Ex	Ex
Pancreas (Sweetbread)		Ex
Thymus (Sweetbread)		Ex
Tripe, broiled		Ex

FOR VITAMINS A and (G) (B$_2$)

	A	(G)(B$_2$)
Beet Top Greens	1010	50
Carrots	1300	15
Cheese, Am.	600	55
Eggs	650	40
Escarole	6100*	60
Kale	5900	70
Liver	2800	310

FOR VITAMINS B$_1$(F) and C

	B$_1$(F)	C
Green Peas	60*	15
Spinach	20	25
Cabbage, new	Gd	20
Orange Juice	10	15
Grape Fruit	10	15
Sweet Potato	Gd	Ex
Tomato Juice	10	20

FOR VITAMINS D and E

	D	E
Beef, Lean		Gd
Butter	F	Ex
Lettuce		Ex
Oysters	Ex	Ex
Salmon	Ex	Ex
Wheat-germ		Ex
Sardines	Ex	

THEN DAILY — Brewers' Yeast Ex for B, and 710 G(B$_2$)

Ex — Excellent
Gd — Good
F — Fair

* Amino-Acids in cheeses increase with age of cheese.

A cheese 18 months old has approximately 200% more than the same cheese 6 weeks old.

Ex — Excellent
Gd — Good

* Units in any one group should NOT be compared with units in another group.
    Different vitamins are not found in the same proportions in foods.
    Hence, 6000 for vitamin A is not better than 60 for vitamin B.

Use the complete proteins for AMINO-acids to increase HORMONES.

THE MYSTERIOUS CATALYTIC FOODS

by

Brown Landone, F.R.E.S.

------ o ------

LESSON III – COSMIC ENERGY RECEIVERS and TRANSFORMERS

Again, get a clear vision of WHERE I am leading you, and where YOU are going!

I am leading you AWAY FROM a body loaded with HEAVY substance materials which have NO power in themselves. I am leading you away from the use of foods which WEAR OUT almost as soon as you build them into your body, so that they have to be replaced and replaced so often, that your body is continually TIRED OUT by the process.

I am leading you to attain a body, – RESPONSIVE to energy, and THRILLED with it.

You have already taken four steps in the choice of foods for these NEW uses:

First, choosing foods that ARE catalytic miracle builders of tremendous power.

Second, choosing vitamins for these workers to USE to protect their own activity.

Third, choosing enzyme foods, able almost instantly to transform substances in body.

Fourth, choosing COMPLETE proteins – to give you aminos – occult creators of HORMONES – the MOST powerful substances on earth – either inside or outside man's body.

Now, I lead you to the use of THREE other groups of mighty catalytic foods:

First, the WIRELESS POWER RECEIVERS – the chlorophyls, found in green leaves.

Second, the COSMIC ENERGY TRANSFORMERS – cholesterols, ergosterols and phytosterols – which act with the vitamins, hormones, minerals and aminos.

Third, the CONTROLLERS of Form and Power and Character – the INNER foods – HORMONES.

In addition to keeping up the youthful FORM of your body, you want energy, and more energy, – because with abundant energy, there can be no ill health in any organ, and with such energy you can CONTINUE activity without fatigue, and that means joy in living.

Then also, as previously suggested, more energy means augmented personality.

WHERE ENERGY COMES FROM

All your energy comes first from without. Later it becomes active within your body.

All energy of all things on earth comes from without first, whether it is the sun energy in plants or animals, or the energy embodied in any substance of earth.

If you are a religionist, you accept the truth that all energy comes from God, and that in it you live and move and have your being.

If not a religionist, you accept the SAME fact in different words, — for whether you are running a machine or your own body, the energy must first come from without.

ALL your energy is taken INTO your body in TWO ways: (1) either IN the food you eat, or (2) it is INSPIRED into your body by its response to higher vibratory energies.

So, religionist or non-religionist, you know that ALL your energies first come from without; then later they are integrated within you; and lastly, they are expressed by you.

And the AMOUNT of energy you have to use, does NOT depend so much on the 'heat' or calorie-energy which you get out of the fats and starches and sugars you eat, as it does on your response to the cosmic energies surrounding you at all times.

Scientists KNOW that there ARE certain substances which make the tissues of both plant and animals more responsive to energies of the cosmos. These substances are so responsive that they actually absorb, or take energy INTO their own substance.

IN PLANTS, this substance is chlorophyl, — and perhaps also phytosterol.

IN ANIMALS, the substances which take in energy are made by chlorophyl when it unites with the cholesterol and ergosterol and vitamin D, in animal tissues.

In the plant, this inspiration of energy takes place in its LEAVES.

In man, it takes place in the SKIN of the body.

Since man's skin is not covered with fur or scales, and is delicately developed, it takes-in energies which LIFT man far above other forms of animal life.

We now know that skin-cells are KIN to brain cells. They are of the same origin.

They respond to energies, even higher than those to which ear and eye respond.

Your skin is the place, where sterols unite with the higher energies, and actually produce mysterious NEW substances for your body.

You know that two persons may eat seemingly the same quantity and quality of foods, and YET DIFFER greatly in energy, vitality, virility, youthfulness and personality.

Perhaps a little dramatically, I might say that the person with the greater vitality is a "SON of the SUN". His body IS more responsive to the cosmic energies.

Science says that his remarkable energy is due to hormones. That is true, BUT the hormones produced within him are determined by the condition of his endocrine glands.

And the HEALTHY activity of his glands IS determined by the cosmic ENERGIES to which his body responds, activating the COMPLETE proteins he eats.

There are just two means of changing from a DUMB-BODIED man to a SUN-BODIED man!

One, is your attitude — you must, of course, want to become super-energized.

The other is to eat more foods which ARE responsive to cosmic energies.

To become more responsive to such energies, TWO processes are necessary.

First, you must become more RESPONSIVE and take-in more energy.

Second, you must transform the energies so that they can be used in your body.

For responsiveness, chlorophyl is THE exceptional food substance.

For the transformation, cholesterol and ergosterol with Vitamin D, are necessary.

If all this seems a little difficult to understand, don't worry about it.

Just read it again and again; and THEN for practical use, DEPEND on the Charts.

There is also, another phase of this responsiveness to cosmic energy. It is the effect of two substances which impel growth of NEW CELL structure to take the place of old cell structure and thus change the inheritance of aging cells to YOUTHFUL cells.

These two substances — lecithins and auxinons — I take up in succeeding Lessons.

IV — SUBSTANCES WHICH INSPIRE and TRANSFORM COSMIC ENERGY

The only means of securing CONTINUOUSLY abundant energy, is to make the structure of your body MORE RESPONSIVE, so that energy will flow through it more freely.

This means responsiveness to energies IN the body, AND to energies from outside.

WE NOW KNOW that — with proper feeding and conditioning of the skin — the body will respond to energies from cosmic space — particularly to sunlight from the sun.

There is a complicated mathematical formula of this chemical reaction, which is to man the most important on earth. It simply means that when rays of the sun, from 93,000,000 miles away, are INSPIRED into the GREEN substance in plant leaves, they CREATE actual LIVING substance OUT of NON-living water and NON-living gas.

CHLOROPHYL is THE GREAT MYSTERY! It SCREENS the rays of the sun; keeps OUT perhaps 99% of them; takes in only a mysterious vital 1%; and at the same time appears to work WITH sunlight to CREATE ITSELF. We can extract it from green leaves, also keep it in solution, so that it RETAINS its miraculous catalytic power for a considerable time.

When you eat chlorophyl as food in green leaves, it alone is of no value in your body.

It must be associated with ergosterol, and phytosterol and cholesterol, before your skin becomes RESPONSIVE ENOUGH to take-in vibrant cosmic energy.

Since chlorophyl, to be of value to you, must work with three sterols — ergo-sterol, phyto-sterol, and chole-sterol — let us now turn to them.

COSMIC ENERGY TRANSFORMERS

CHOLESTEROL is VERY essential to the life of your body; it is so essential that is is believed to be "universally distributed among ANIMAL cells". It seems to be a COSMIC Co-WORKER. In some way, it makes it possible for the cells of your body to USE the radiant rays of the sun, and probably other rays of the universe.

When you eat foods which contain cholesterol, it IS very readily absorbed.

BUT, it needs the help of OTHER sterols, and will not work by itself, ALONE.

MOST of the sterols in vegetables are so foreign to animal life, that IF taken into the human body as foods, they are NOT readily absorbed, and are of little use.

But TWO plant sterols ARE linked to animal sterols, in producing vitamin D.

Sun rays, acting on your skin, will readily produce vitamin D, IF there are minute quantities of these two other sterols. ONE is ergosterol; and the other phytosterol.

ERGOSTEROL is most abundant in ergot and in YEAST.

When light waves act on pure irradiated ergosterol, it produces a vitamin D activity about 500,000 TIMES the vitamin D activity of cod liver oil.

PHYTOSTEROL is found in the OILS of seeds of grain, in olive oil, and in cotton seed oil. It is closely related to cholesterol in animal fats.

Again I repeat, if this seems difficult to understand, don't worry about it now.

Later study this again. In the meantime, for PRACTICAL USE, depend on CHART D.

Anyway you now have the trinity of sterols, which make it possible for your body to become a light impregnated body, — a SUN BODY responding to cosmic energy.

This is energy you want. But you can NOT get it from PLANT foods ALONE, because this entire mysterious process is linked up with vitamin D.

And since the higher plants do NOT require vitamin D, they do NOT produce it.

Hence, it is NEVER possible to get sufficient vitamin D from any vegetable food.

Then also, you can NOT get the cholesterol your body needs, from PLANT food.

The plant sterols are essential co-workers. BUT cholesterol is THE dominantly important sterol as a receiver of cosmic energy. It is THE sterol which makes your body so responsive, that it WILL take-in the higher energies INTO your body.

These sterols are actual "INSPIRING" substances.

They DO take-in energy which comes to you from the
universe, just as chlorophyl in plant leaves takes-in sun-rays.
The high light rays your eye perceives, vibrate 700,-
000,000,000,000 TIMES a second!

But these sterols take-in sun energy, and other
energies of MUCH HIGHER vibration.

This gives your body a kind of energy, you can never
get from ordinary foods.

In other words, it gives your body something of the
energy-quality of the cosmos.

We used to think that foods which supply cholesterol
and the two other sterols, were all that were necessary for
the responsiveness, but now we know that unless you eat foods
containing the chlorophyl of green leaves the sterols will
NOT work well.

YOUR FIFTH STEP

I now ask you to take the FIFTH step in changing your
choice of foods.

To transform your body to TAKE-IN more of the higher
cosmic energies — choose foods which contain chlorophyl
and cholesterol and associated sterols. (Sheet Chart D.)

Study carefully, Chart D to learn WHICH foods to
choose, and how to do it SIMPLY and with certainty to make your
body change — that is, to TRANSFORM your body from a body of
tallow and protein to a living vibrating energy body.

The results will be astounding vitality, greatly
strengthened virility and continued youthfulness.

All these powers must be controlled and regulated.
So we come again to the subject of the Controllers of Power, -
most of which are INNER foods — hormones.

V — THE CONTROLLERS OF FORM and POWER and CHARACTER

ALL functions of your body — and of your mind and
emotions also — and yes, even the difference between idiocy
and genius — DEPEND on HORMONES.

Hormones are products of the magical endocrine glands.
They seem to CONTROL every bodily activity and form a supreme
'messenger system' surpassing even the nerves.

Some scientific investigators have called them the
chemical nervous system.

They TRANSMIT energy and power in INSTANTANEOUS FLASHES
and — because of their mysterious nature - they seem ALSO to
BE the very powers which they themselves transmit.

Their POWER is TITANIC — one ounce of a pure hormone is so powerful that for use, it must be diluted with all the water, which can be held by a line of modern street sprinkler tanks — a line of tanks TWENTY MILES long, 200 tanks to the mile!

These hormones CONTROL (1) the life processes and FORM of the body; (2) the nature of SEX and its activity, and even (3) the actual CHARACTER of the individual.

They also particularly affect the SKIN and the SEX organs.

If there is not enough of one hormone, the body may be DWARFED in HEIGHT; and the individual will not attain normal height until such hormone is increased.

Other hormones completely control the ENERGY of the body.

And also, if one hormone is lacking there may be idiocy. But, when it is present in abundant quantity, there is exceptional INTELLIGENCE, and oftentimes GENIUS.

Other hormones control other CHARACTER qualities. By stopping the production of but one hormone, the most heroic and courageous man can actually be changed into a cowardly weakling, and he cannot help himself until that hormone is again increased.

Now of course, I do not mean that such a hormone IS courage itself.

But, it is the MEANS by which courage manifests — just as a copper wire is the means by which you can get a manifestation of electric current.

INCREASE of hormones is PERMANENTLY beneficial to your body, ONLY if the increase is due to the NORMAL process of increasing endocrine gland activity.

Hormones increase with increased health and activity of the endocrine glands.

And the health and activity of these glands depends mainly on the mysterious foods — amino-acids, enzymes, auxinons, and other complex food substances produced by cholesterol in animal foods and chlorophyl and ergosterol in plants.

There is also a very close relationship between the CATALYTIC action of amino-acids and cholesterol and ergosterol, and the hormones and the production of vitamin D, which is active only in association with calcium and other mineral foods.

Hence there is a link-up of the activity of hormones, with the particular proteins which contain the ESSENTIAL amino-acids, with mysterious FAT substances which contain the sterols; and then both of these are linked up with MINERALS, ENZYMES, CHLOROPHYL, and AUXINONS.

So, to increase the activity of the endocrine glands, and consequently to increase their hormones, you should eat a sufficient amount of the essential mineral foods and the best foods for enzymes, amino-acids, cholesterol and chlorophyl.

The number of hormones from endocrine glands and tissues producing hormones is 48 according to the latest data of scientists. But many of these, more than one-half of them, are listed as different hormones produced by one endocrine gland, the pituitary.

That gland is NOT the master hormone gland, but it is the master assembly-plant, producing hormones which can be substituted for hormones of other glands.

The SIX important hormones - from the standpoint of foods which help to increase endocrine gland activity, and thus augment the production of hormones — are:

THYROXIN of the thyroid is the great pace-setter of the energy of your body. It speeds up all digestive and assimilative processes, and increases nerve activity.

ADRENALIN of the medulla of the adrenal is the great MOBILIZER of all energies of the body, whenever exceptional energy is needed in emergencies.

CORTIN from the cortex of the adrenal is necessary for all VIRILE functioning of SEX. It is especially active in cooperation with vitamin C, B_1 and B_2.

INSULIN, of islets of the pancreas, controls the body's use of starches and sugar.

PARATHORMONE of the parathyroids regulates the use of CALCIUM in the body.

Both calcium and vitamin D in food are essential for its abundant production.

PROLAN A and B, from the pituitary — discoveries are being made at an astounding rate - cause development of mature sex organs in immature animals, and cause INCREASE in both SIZE and ACTIVITY of depleted and atrophied sex organs in senile animals.

YOUR SIXTH STEP

The NATURE of hormones helps to determine WHAT FOODS you should eat to increase the activity of the endocrine gland. Such glands secrete a PART of THEMSELVES AS HORMONES.

Therefore similar glands of animals ARE of VALUE as FOODS. See CHART E.

In activating and restoring endocrine glands to increased production of hormones, all complete proteins containing all the animal proteins, are exceptionally valuable as foods, combined with calcium and iodine and iron and phosphorus and all the vitamins.

This Lesson helps you to change your body from a DUMB-body to a SUN-ENERGY body.

First, by choice of foods which do TAKE-IN radiant energies of the universe.

Second, by choice of foods which TRANSFORM these energies and produce new substances.

And third, by choice of foods which activate the endocrine glands to produce more hormones — the mightiest powers which God and nature have given to the human body.

In the next two Lessons, I take up LECITHIN which increases consciousness of power; and AUXINONS, which impel growth of NEW and youthful structure.

LANDONE ACTIVATING FOODS — CHART D

CHOLESTEROL	
Almonds*	54
Brains, beef	3200
Brains, calf	1900
Brains, mutton	960
Butter	148
Chestnuts, fresh*	194
Chicken, young	281
Corn, sweet*	100
Cottonseed Oil*	Gd
Egg, whole	375
Egg, yolk	1745
Herring Roe	310
Kidney, lamb	1800
Kidney, veal	311
Liver, calf	1850
Liver, pork	128
Olive Oil*	120
Peanut Oil*	82
Salmon Roe	2200
Sweetbreads, (Pancreas, Calf)	3100
Sweetbreads, (Thymus, Calf)	2300
Wheat Germ Oil*	Gd(1)
Yeast, Brewers'*	Gd

* — Associated Vegetable
   Sterols — Ergosterol
   and Phytosterol, et
   cetera.
Gd — Not high in content,
   but important.
(1) Available in commer-
   cial products, such as
   Bemax, Embo, et cetera.

CHLOROPHYL

CHLOROPHYL is found in the GREEN substance of all plant life.

It is most plentiful in green leaves.

THICK leaves have developed cellulose; and they are NOT good as sources of chlorophyl.

The THINNEST, most delicate green leaves of the following plants are the BEST sources of CHLOROPHYL for food for the human being.

The foods below are listed in order of their value as sources of chlorophyl, — the best, first.

Parsley leaves
Watercress
Turnip Tops
Chard
Spinach
Dandelion Greens
Kale
Lettuce (Romaine)
Broccoli
Borage
Onion Tops
Cabbage Greens
Escarole
Collards

For sufficient mystic catalysts — of aminos and enzymes (Chart C) and mysterious sterols (this Chart) you MUST eat foods which we have neglected for half a century — brains, kidneys, sweetbreads, testes, tripe, et cetera.

Also yolks of eggs. But hens' eggs are not so valuable as years ago, because the hens are now fed on depleted foods. In some catalytic factors ducks' eggs are 900% more potent than hen's eggs, which suggests an opportunity for a very profitable new business for someone.

40

LANDONE ACTIVATING FOODS — CHART E

ENDOCRINE GLANDS AND TISSUES WHICH PRODUCE HORMONES	NUMBER OF HORMONES NOW REPORTED BY SCIENTISTS*

IN HEAD:
    1 - Pineal
    2 - Pituitary

Adrenals 5
    4 - Cortex
    1 - Medulla

IN NECK AND UPPER CHEST:
    3 - Thyroid
    4 - Parathyroid
    5 - Thymus

Ovaries 3

Pancreas 2

Parathyroids 1

IN MID AND LOWER TORSO:
    6 - Stomach Walls
    7 - Adrenals
    8 - Islets of Langerhans
    9 - Placenta
    10 - Intestines

Pineal 1

Pituitary 25
    22 - from anterior lobe
    3 - from posterior lobe

Intestines 1
Placenta 1
Stomach Walls 3

IN PELVIC REGION:
    11 - Testes
    12 - Ovaries

Sympathetic Nerves 1

Testes 2

GENERAL:
    13 - Ends of sympa-
        thetic nerves in
        involuntary
        muscles

Thymus 1

Thyroid 2

        TOTAL 48

* New hormones are being discovered, as one scientist states, at such "a bewildering rate" that data here given relates only to number reported at date of this writing.
NB: Some scientists hold that the 22 reported hormones of the anterior lobe of the pituitary, are but variations of four or five basic hormones.

TO YOU, the important thing is to know which foods improve health and activity of the endocrine glands and hence increase hormone secretion.

Hormones are chemically related to the amino-acids, contained in the complete proteins of milk, white of egg, red lean meat, and ovovitellin of yolk of egg.

Hormones may also be obtained from foods of organs of animals producing similar hormones — thymus (sweetbreads), pancreas (sweetbreads), testes. Also from associated glands — kidneys and liver foods; and from calf and beef brains.

For ADRENALS, - choose foods containing iron, calcium and vitamins C, D_1 and D_2.

For PARATHYROIDS, — choose calcium and vitamin D foods.

For PITUITARY, producing the Prolan A and B, — phosphorus, iodine, and vitamin E.

For THYROID, producing thyroxine, iodine, calcium and vitamin D.

But MOST important, choose BEST amino-acid foods, see Chart C.

THE MYSTERIOUS CATALYTIC FOODS

by

Brown Landone, F.R.E.S.

------ o ------

LESSON IV — FOODS FOR INCREASED "CONSCIOUSNESS"

This is the Fourth Lesson. With the next and Fifth Lesson, I complete my presentation of the NEW knowledge of the seven groups of NEWLY DISCOVERED CATALYTIC foods.

But, before I take up the subject of LECITHINS — the subject of this Lesson, — there are two or three miscellaneous subjects, I wish to make clear.

I am certain that I am giving you the most complete knowledge yet brought together on the value and use of these NEWLY discovered catalytic foods.

BUT in spite of such knowledge, I can NOT guarantee the quality of foods you are able to obtain for use, — either from your grocer or from your own garden.

The reason is this: Our soils are now so depleted — that even when fertilized — SOME vegetables are NOT much better than PAPER and WATER. This is NOT an exaggeration. Paper contains cellulose and a gelatinous protein. So if you soak paper in nine parts of water, you get something about as good as SOME vegetables from depleted soils.

If there were enough data I would advise you on selecting vegetables, according to regions in which they are raised. But we have too little data on this now.

I hope scientists will soon make other tests and give us more information.

1000 UNITS or ONLY 8 UNITS — WHICH?

Already we know that vegetables from some states, Pennsylvania for instance, contain MORE calcium and iron than the same vegetables raised in several other states.

We also know that some green vegetables raised in Pacific states may contain LESS than 8 units of iodine; while the same vegetables grown in Florida contain 1000 units!

This difference in content is not only important from the standpoint of vitality, but also of costs. If, in six months you buy $10 worth of fresh asparagus, you want to know if you are getting 1000 cents' worth of iodine, or only 8 cents' worth.

I wish I could do something about these depleted foods, but I am NOT SOIL DICTATOR of these United States. So the best I can do is to tell you, and beg for your help.

I pray that all of you who read this Course will awake to this new problem.

Working together, we CAN bring about a change. We can at least induce local truck farmers, to raise vegetables which WILL contain a FULL amount of ALL essential minerals.

It IS now possible, with Rapid Growth chemicals which we now know how to use, to raise vegetables equal to those of 60 or 70 years ago, and EVEN BETTER.

We can, AT HOME, and with almost no trouble, now raise vegetables which contain ALL the minerals they should contain, and perhaps with an INCREASED content of vitamins and chlorophyl.

A GREAT OPPORTUNITY FOR SOMEONE

Or we CAN induce 'truck farmers' to raise vegetables, containing all essential minerals, because such farmers are not making fortunes, and each one wants more profit.

And all of us would SAVE money by paying a little more for REAL vegetables.

During a season you may now be paying $10 for some one vegetable, and instead of getting 1000 cents of elemental catalysts, you may be getting only 8 cents worth.

This means that in paying $10 for such vegetables, you are losing $9.92 of what you should get.

So you and I would willingly pay $11, to get 1100 cents worth of the real food.

If we all work together we CAN make truck farmers so PROFIT conscious, that they WILL raise vegetables, worth many times as much as our present vegetables.

And as soon as truck farmers — or anyone else — make such vegetables available, hospitals everywhere will insist on buying such vegetables — even at an increased price.

And we have 6,242 hospitals, treating 8,646,000 patients every year.

IN THIS, I see a marvelous opportunity for NEW WEALTH for a lot of people!

New wealth always comes by doing some thing new, to meet a NEW NEED.

I am not wasting the space of even one line in what I have written above.

Your health, vitality, virility and endurance depend on real vegetables.

The life-vitality of your children, also depends on securing such vegetables.

Ten million people now have weak hearts, because the heart slows down, flutters and then stops, whenever there is a lack of three essential minerals in the body -- potassium, phosphorus and calcium.

This is BUT ONE result of our depleted foods.

There are, of course, "special" foods on the market. I give two charts of these with the next Lesson. But after all, they can NOT compare with REAL products grown on perfectly fed soil, - fed with all the catalysts the vegetables need.

From the last Lesson, you got a clear idea that your problem is to RESPOND to energy, to TAKE-IN MORE energy; and to use as food, substances which help in this.

THIS LESSON is concerned with another substance. It IS necessary for consciousness.

As previously stated, - IF you are a religionist, you accept the fact that your energy comes from God and that in him you live and move and have your being.

If NOT a religionist, you accept the fact that every living thing as well as every machine, first gets its energy from outside, and then reactivates it and uses it.

This leads us to the SIXTH group of my seven groups of catalytic foods.

GROUP VI - LECITHIN

Previously, I have written that chlorophyl is THE mysterious substance of PLANT life.

But LECITHIN is THE most - yes, the MOST - mysterious substance of human LIFE.

It seems to be the 'intermediary' between material substance and mind or soul.

"Lecithin helps the cell to connect with its environment". It makes it possible for each cell to relate its activities with outside conditions.

In some mysterious way, lecithin makes the CONTACT - between the material body and the soul. That is why consciousness is NEVER possible, WITHOUT lecithin.

Pure lecithin is found IN the brain and throughout the body.

Lecithin coats all cells with a coating so thin we cannot conceive such extreme thinness, yet no cell could live without this coating.

It seems to be deposited ON the thin outer-walls of all cells — particularly brain and nerve cells — in just about the same way, that gold or silver is deposited by electrolysis when we gold-plate or silver-plate an object.

Moreover, lecithin is the MEANS by which mysterious ENERGIES are FLASHED through the body at astounding speed. Reduce the amount of lecithin a little bit and the speed of nerve messages is greatly reduced. A little less, and there are no messages!

Still a little less, and there is unconsciousness and ultimately death.

Scientific tests show the results of the increase or decrease of lecithin.

Energy and vitality of body — and of mind and emotion — increase or decrease, hour by hour, with the change in the amount of lecithin covering brain and nerve cells.

Lecithin also seems to give off a pure WHITE LIGHT. Perhaps this is what spiritual seers of the past have called the "holy light" within. At any rate this light increases when lecithin is plentiful, and decreases when there is less lecithin.

Without lecithin, not even the life of a single cell would be possible.

When CHLOROFORM or ether or ALCOHOL is used, this mysterious lecithin covering of brain cells begins to disappear quickly. So much of it is dissolved by any one of these substances, that the person becomes unconscious — as when under an anaesthetic or dead drunk. If the lessening of lecithin continues, there is death.

YOUR SEVENTH STEP

Daily, eat a PLENTIFUL supply of lecithin foods. See Chart F.

LECITHIN is associated with PHOSPHORUS and phosphorized fats and some proteins.

This gives great importance to MILK as food, because 10% of the phosphorus in milk, "Is in the form of phosphatids or phospholipids" which contain lecithin.

YOLK OF EGGS contain fat finely emulsified. And a large portion of this fat of the yolk consists of phosphorized fats, which contain lecithin.

Another substance in egg yolk contains lecithin. It is the peculiar and mysterious protein of egg yolk, which scientists call ovovitellin.

Lecithin, as an available catalytic food of exceptional value to MAN, has NOT yet been proven to exist in vegetables. In its available form — that is, in THE form in which our bodies can use it and attain remarkable results from its use — it is found ONLY in ANIMAL food. I well know that lecithin as a chemical product is found in Wheat Germ Oil, Soy Bean Oil and other vegetable oils. But there is NO proof that such lecithin is of value in the human body. We have NO evidence of re- markable changes being effected by its use. ONLY the lecithin, found in animal foods, HAS wrought amazing changes.

Such lecithins can be obtained from all of the glands eaten as food — liver, sweetbreads, kidneys, testes. Calves brains are also a good source of lecithin.

And a caution: Certain capsule foods are being adver- tised as containing the extraordinary catalytic foods needed by man. If by such statements, it is suggested that they con- tain the catalytic lecithin, auxinons, cholesterols and chlorophyl, the suggestions ARE FALSE.

There are many capsule and tablet foods which contain minerals of great value to man; such mineral foods have been known for 40 years. BUT they are NOT what we call the newly discovered catalytic lecithin and auxinon foods.

Since these lecithins make contact of brain and mind possible, they are THE substances which make the matter of your body responsive to the HIGHEST ENERGIES.

I have already given you five different CHARTS. With this Lesson I add THREE more.

One is CHART G — prepared only to simplify your choice of material foods.

It gives at least 14 in each group. With 14 foods listed in each group, you have a variation from which to choose, so there need be no monotony in your diet.

YOUR EIGHTH STEP — USE MY MASTER CHART

With this Lesson, I am giving you my MASTER CHART, — CHART H.

It IS the MOST COMPLETE, and yet the SIMPLEST chart of its kind ever prepared.

Many many years of work were necessary, before I could make this Chart.

It LOOKS SIMPLE, and it IS simple to USE, but it is a MIRACLE of COMPLETENESS.

And it is the COMPLETENESS of this Master Chart, which I first emphasize.

At the TOP, I have listed SEVEN foods, which you are to use EVERY day.

DO eat a little of EACH every day, to maintain the BALANCE of elemental mineral catalysts and vitamins as well as the other vital elements.

Certainly you are already using four of these — milk, butter, eggs and lettuce.

Let the amount you eat of each of these, DEPEND on your daily desire for it.

Three other foods for daily use are Wheat Germ Cereal, Bakon Yeast and Fish Roe. A little of each of these is necessary every day to balance the supply of any possible vitamin lack in other foods. I ask you to use these each day to balance possible vitamin lacks. Two of the best Wheat Germ Cereals are Bemax and Embo. See Chart K Next Lesson.

BAKON YEAST (or any good yeast) should be used EVERY day — either in salad dressings, or as a relish with other foods — an amount equal to one-fourth a cake.

And FISH ROE — don't fail to eat at least half a tea-spoonful each day in salad dressing or as relish. Caviar or shad roe can be obtained in glass jars or cans now.

NOW study the BALANCE of the CHART. It is not only complete, but VERY SIMPLE.

All substances containing activating catalysts, can be stored up in the body for a few days at a time.

So the value of this Chart is due to the fact that, IF EACH DAY, you eat BUT TWO of these 28 foods, your body will be provided with ALL the minerals, amino-acids, enzymes, cholesterol, chlorophyl, and lecithin you need. (Choose auxinon foods from Chart F).

For SIMPLICITY, only a few of the foods which contain the essentials, are listed.

Too many would make it too CONFUSING. Hence, "xs" indicate ONLY the BEST foods.

Each of the 28 foods contains one or more of the worker catalysts — 11 elementals, 6 vitamins, 10 essential amino-acids, 6 enzymes, and ergosterol, cholesterol, lecithin.

These particular 28 foods can be obtained practically anywhere.

Use the Master Chart in this way: EACH day, choose ANY TWO of the foods listed.

And choose TWO DIFFERENT foods each day. Thus you will have a variety of foods for two weeks, never repeating the same foods, and still obtain ALL the eleven essential minerals, the ten ESSENTIAL amino-acids, and ALL the vitamins, enzymes, cholesterol, chlorophyl, lecithin, your body needs for GENERAL health and vitality.

BUT, for PARTICULAR RESULTS, to meet YOUR needs, use ALL my OTHER Charts also.

WHAT a CHANGE, you are now bringing about in your body!

You are eating less of heavy material foods, and more of the mighty catalysts!

You are changing from wearing out and repairing, wearing out and repairing your body, to building a body that is SO RESPONSIVE that it is constantly thrilled with energy.

You are using enzymes to TRANSFORM the substances of your body and REFINE them.

Using amino-acids — the very essence of hormones — to multiply energy.

Awakening your body to RESPOND to the COSMIC ENERGIES of the universe by use of food substances which ARE responsive to such energies — becoming SUN-bodied!

And, in this Lesson, you have learned to use lecithin foods, to increase the contact between consciousness and body, and greatly increase your power of consciousness.

In the next Lesson, you learn of auxinon foods, — actual creators which impel re-growth of structure, creation of NEW CELLS, new organic tissues, continued youthfulness.

LANDONE ACTIVATING FOODS — CHART F

LECITHINS

Brains, beef	Ex
Brains, calf	Ex
Brains, mutton	Gd
Egg-Yolk	Ex(1)
Roe, Herring	Ex
Roe, Salmon	VEx
Roe, Shad	Ex
Kidney, lamb	Ex
Kidney, veal	Gd
Liver, calf	Gd
Milk	Gd(2)
Sweetbreads (Pancreas)	Ex
Sweetbreads (Thymus)	Gd
Testes	VEx
WHEAT GERM OIL	VEX(3)
Yeast (Bakon)	Ex

VEx — Very exceptional
Ex — Excellent
Gd — Good

(1) In the phosphorized fats of egg-yolk and in its protein, ovovitellin.
(2) In the phospholipids of milk and cream.
(3) Available in commercial products such as Bemax, Embo, et cetera.

AUXINONS

AUXINONS are miraculous catalytic substances, which produce NEW GROWING YOUTHFUL cell structure.

Auxinons are found in NO substances EXCEPT those which are are themselves NEWLY GROWING.

NO food in the list below will be of value in providing these YOUTH growing auxinons for your body, if they are half grown or matured.

For example, to choose asparagus for its youth growing auxinons, secure asparagus which has grown not more than two or three inches out of the ground, JUST BEGINNING TO GROW. But if you are using Mung Bean sprouts — they are BEST source of auxinons — they can be eaten whether 3" or 12" high.

To obtain auxinon value, the sprouts must NOT be cooked.

They should be eaten within two hours after being cut from the living plant.

TINY YOUNG SPROUTS OF:

Asparagus	Navy Beans*
Beet Tops	Soy Beans*
Broccoli	Kale
Brussell Sprouts	Lettuce
Cabbage	Parsley
Celery	Spinach
Barley Seeds*	Turnip Tops
Peas*	Watercress

* Not the seeds, BUT the tiny sprouts grown 2 or 3 inches from the seeds.

And Mung Bean sprouts 3" to 12" high.

The sprouts, which are RICHEST in auxinons, are grown from sprouting Auxinon Mung Beans.

You can sometimes secure these beans at seed stores; or you can always secure them from Rapid Growth Products Incorporated, Newton, N. J.

LANDONE ACTIVATING FOODS – CHART G

PERCENTAGES

of

Water, Protein, Fat, and Starch

in Edible Portion of Foods.

WATER FOODS

Cottage Cheese	72	Melons	93	Cabbage	95
Potatoes		Tomatoes	95	Celery	95
(boiled)	80	Asparagus	95	Cucumbers	97
Berries	90	String Beans	95	Green	
Oranges,		Lettuce	95	Vegetables	98
Grapefruit	90				
Greens, cooked	90				

PROTEIN FOODS

Eggs	13	Baked Beans	18	Cheese	24
Gluten Flour	15	Fish	18	Peas, dried	25
Lentils, dry	15	Meats, Lean	20	Ham, fresh	25
Soy Beans,		Fish Roe	20	Gelatine	91*
baked	15	Almond	21		
Oatmeal	16				

FAT FOODS

Milk	9	Cheese	34	Bacon	65
Avocados	20	Chocolate	49	Brazil Nuts	69
Olives	25	Pistachio Nuts	54	Pecan Nuts	70
Cream	30	Almonds	55	Butter	81
Egg-Yolk	33	Butter Nuts	61		

STARCH FOODS

Bananas	23	Beans,		Corn Meal	75
Bread, wheat	50	Lima dry	66	Shredded Wheat	78
Bread, white	53	Oatmeal	67	Buckwheat	
Cowpeas, Dry	61	Crackers, soda	73	Flour	78
Peas, Dry	62	Macaroni	74	Hominy	79
		Crackers, Graham	74		

SOURCES OF SUGAR FOODS

Beet Sugars	Dates	Maple Syrup
Cane Syrup	Figs, dried	Raisins
Currants, dried	Sorghum Syrup	Honey

* Please note that Gelatine is different from Jell-O.
Jell-O is 86% carbohydrates and only 11% protein. Gelatine
contains 91.4% protein and NO carbohydrates.

LANDONE ACTIVATING FOODS – MASTER CHART – H

These are the seven BASE foods, of each of which you should eat a little every day.

Butter, eggs, lettuce, milk, fish roe, wheat germ, yeast. (See Lesson IV p. 45).

Then of the list below, choose two different foods, each day for 14 days.

	Min-erals	Amino Acids	En-zymes	Chole-sterol*	Chloro-phyl	Leci-thin	Vita-mins
Almonds	X	X		X			X
Beef, lean	X	X	X				
Beet Tops or Turnip Greens	X				X		X
Blueberries	X						X
Brains, Beef	X	X		X		X	X
Cabbage	X				X		X
Carrots	X						X
Chard	X						X
Cheese, Camembert	X	X	X				X
Chicken	X	X		X			
Corn, sweet	X	X		X			X
Cowpeas	X						X
Escarole	X				X		X
Kale	X				X		X
Kidney, Lamb	X	X	X	X		X	X
Lentils	X						X
Liver	X	X	X	X		X	X
Molasses	X						X
Oatmeal	X						X
Orange Juice	X						X
Oysters	X					X	X
Parsley	X				X		X
Salmon Fish	X					X	X
Sweetbreads	X	X	X	X		X	X
Sweet Potatoes	X						X
Testes	X	X				X	X
Tomatoes	X						X
Tripe	X		X				

* Or Associated Sterols.

NB: This IS a Master Chart, very simple yet very complete. The BASE foods are listed in the THIRD LINE, beginning with 'butter'.

The other foods, grouped under the headings, will give your body a sufficient supply of the Miracle Workers, IF you eat at least two of them each day; and two different foods each day; every two weeks.

THE MYSTERIOUS CATALYTIC FOODS

by

Brown Landone, F.R.E.S.

------ o ------

LESSON V - AUXINONS - TISSUE CREATORS of NEW YOUTHFULNESS

I have added to this Lesson, two additional Charts - J and K.

They list certain foods which I call "special" foods - foods produced by scientists and manufacturers to meet special needs.

Naturally, I can not guarantee the mineral or vitamin content of any one of these.

I can give only the data of scientific investigations which have been made.

Many other products, not listed, are without doubt very good!

But some products on the market are NOT what they are claimed to be.

Of course, I list NO product, IF its advertising states: "This product is made 'FROM' pure so-and-so WHICH contains 'such-and-such' vitamins and minerals."

Carrots contain Vitamin C. But anyone might prepare a juice FROM fresh carrots which would NOT contain any vitamin C. All of it can be destroyed by the PROCESS of preparation. It's the content of the product you BUY that is important, NOT what the vegetables originally contained.

Another matter: I call attention to the fourth group on Chart J - "Special Carbohydrate Foods". Often times you, as a buyer, see the word "gluten" in the name of a food, and conclude that it does not contain carbohydrates. This may or may not be true. For example, some gluten flours contain no carbohydrates, while others do!

As adults, we want foods of a SMALL amount of carbohydrates. To meet this need, many foods have been put on the market, containing little starch or sugar, but a comparatively high content of protein and fats. See second and third groups, CHART J.

And now one other subject about which I feel I must be very definite.

FADISTS and FADISTS

Please do NOT be mis-led by EXTREME fadists. There are fadists and fadists.

Some are sincere students of scientific facts. Others are merely prejudiced.

From the latter, I have heard much strange advice in the last fifty years.

I have heard some advise you to eat apples, BECAUSE they contain PHOSPHORUS.

Yet, you would have to eat 99 good sized apples, to get as much phosphorous as you can get from one pound of oatmeal!

Others advise you to eat the skins of potatoes to get CALCIUM for your body.

But there's MORE calcium in two glasses of milk, than in the skins of 20 potatoes.

And I've seen printed instructions, to drink MILK for its IRON! But you would have to drink 56 glasses of milk to get as much iron as is found in one pound of beans.

And some conscientious mothers, make their children eat SPINACH, to get VITAMIN D.

But, to get enough Vitamin D from spinach to meet bodily needs for even ONE day, your child would have to eat FOUR BUSHELS of spinach every 24 hours!

I do not cite these facts to ridicule, BUT to help you avoid PART-truths.

And now, before we proceed to the subject of AUXINONS, I want to sum up for you something of the work of the entire course in relation to the seven particular results you wish to gain from foods; that summary of suggestions, I include here.

What follows in the next Seven Groups is largely for REFERENCE!

FIRST, ENERGY: For INCREASED energy, it is essential to build up the blood, keep the thyroid gland active, and increase oxidation in the body.

For this, the ELEMENTAL mineral foods most essential are calcium, copper, iron, sodium, sulphur and magnesium. Iodine foods to activate the thyroid and speed up the energy control. Potassium foods to counteract fatigue. Use also the natural sugars, lecithin, complete proteins, and a plentiful supply of foods containing vitamins B_1, C and D.

SECOND, INCREASED RADIANCY of energy: Such increase depends on augmented responsiveness of muscles and nerves. For this, foods containing potassium, copper, calcium and iron are essential. Use magnesium to keep nerves in smooth working condition; and manganese for increased heart activity. Iodine, phosphorus and sodium to prevent nervousness. Iodine and sodium foods to prevent (or relieve or remedy) neuritis and neuralgia. Use also foods containing lecithin, cholesterol, and phosphorized fats with foods containing Vitamins A, B_1, C and D.

THIRD, SKIN: For increased activity, renewed YOUTHFULNESS and BEAUTY of SKIN, it is necessary to activate rapid growth of NEW skin cells. To aid this, a healthy condition of the blood and perfect action of the intestine are essential. Hence, choose special foods containing calcium, iodine, potassium, sulphur, sodium and magnesium. Calcium and potassium to increase activity of skin. And foods containing vitamins A, B_1, C, D, and a very plentiful supply of B_2 and of G. And more than the usual amount of cholesterol and lecithin foods.

FOURTH, INCREASED RESPONSIVENESS of body: For this, brain and endocrine glands must be awakened to greater activity, heart lifted up to freer and untired action; and arterial walls kept free of hard deposits. For this purpose complete proteins containing all essential amino-acids, with chlorophyl, cholesterol and lecithin foods-are essential. Of the elemental minerals, those which are most valuable are iodine and manganese, with a very liberal supply of potassium, phosphorus, and calcium to keep the heart buoyantly active; iron, iodine and potassium to prevent or remedy hardening of the arteries. The same elemental minerals to increase circulation; with manganese and phosphorus and calcium particularly for nerve and brain cell activity; manganese, sodium and copper foods for the glands; and plenty of foods containing vitamins A, B_1, C, D, and E.

FIFTH, ENDURANCE: Endurance is CONTINUED energy. Much depends upon activating a new healthy growing condition of the marrow of the bones, so the bones will constantly produce an abundance of new red blood cells. Then the nerves must be sustained in activity without undue fatigue. For these results, choose foods of iodine, phosphorus, potassium and sodium, calcium and magnesium and manganese. Also fat foods, complete proteins containing all the amino-acids, and foods containing all the vitamins A, B_1, C, D, E, G.

SIXTH, VITALITY and VIRILITY: For continued or restored VIRILITY, it is not enough merely to reactivate glands. The glands must be impelled to regrow, by increased flow of vital blood, sustained by increased heart action and augmented activity of the thyroid gland, and by hormones of the other glands necessary for vitalization and virility – that is, increased amounts of hormones from the pituitary and the adrenal glands.

So first of all, a predominance of the foods containing cholesterol and chlorophyl, lecithin and the amino-acids of the complete proteins, are essential.

And for the purpose here desired, the phosphorized fats and proteins of the yolks of duck and goose eggs are even better than the yolks of hens' eggs; and red meats much better than white meats, or fish.

The elemental foods most necessary are calcium, iron, potassium and sodium.

Then copper is essential, with manganese, to increase the nerve activity.

Iodine to reactivate the thyroid. Also foods containing liberal amounts of vitamins A, E, G, B_1, and D; and lecithin foods of brain, liver, testes and sweetbreads.

SEVENTH, CONTINUED YOUTHFULNESS: For maintenance or return to a more youthful condition and the growing of NEW TISSUE, all that is written above about foods necessary for increase of vitality and virility, is applicable here.

For youthfulness, iron foods should be used with potassium and iodine foods to help dissolve old hardened deposits in the body, particularly the arteries.

Calcium and phosphorus and potassium to keep the heart YOUTHFULLY vital.

Vitamin G foods to activate the processes for NEW GROWTH.

And of course, vitamins A, C, and E, for growth and REPRODUCTION of NEW CELLS.

Then there MUST be additional use of AUXINON foods and then MORE auxinons and then STILL MORE auxinon foods -- together with lecithin and chlorophyl and cholesterol foods, with complete proteins containing the amino-acids to augment regenerating hormones.

I now come to my seventh and last group of catalytic foods, the AUXINONS.

GROUP VII — AUXINONS

Auxinons are found in IMMATURE foods! Their amazing value has been proven by experiments for at least 18 years!

Yet nothing publicly has been written about them for the use of any of us.

They have, not only an astounding effect on the GROWTH OF NEW cell structure, but they are also POWERFUL in the activation of depleted and even atrophied organs.

They ARE effective in increasing VITALITY and maintaining VIRILITY and YOUTHFULNESS.

AUXINONS are THE miracle substances produced by GROWING PROCESSES. They in turn PRODUCE new growing structure. They are found ONLY in substances, NEWLY GROWING.

Note how nature works, miraculously. In winter when a cow is fed DRY food, her milk contains NO vitamiin C. But vitamin C is necessary for vital health of a new born calf.

So, as soon as a cow is to have a calf, a miracle is wrought.

WITHOUT any change of food, vitamin C MYSTERIOUSLY appears in the cow's milk.

SO ALSO seeds of plants, when STARTING TO GROW, miraculously produce a substance which in turn mysteriously promotes NEW and YOUTHFUL cell growth!

Scientific tests prove that the catalytic power of such substances is TRANSFERRED to animal life, when such immature foods are eaten by the animal or human being.

Results of use of the IMMATURE foods, containing auxinons, seem incredible.

In one test, in which worn out old animals were fed for a few months on IMMATURE foods, the shrunken vital organs WERE restored not only to activity and virility, but their form and structure were increased to normal size.

Remember that catalysts are much more than mere substances. They are activating powers; and I want you to understand not only WHERE you can find the highest content of these marvelous catalytic foods, but also WHY you find them where they are.

Each life begins to manifest a structure of its own, from a seed or a germ.

In plant life, this germ is found inside the seed — a TINY PART of the seed.

In this part, most of the catalysts needed to impel life and new growth, are locked up in mysterious OIL, — such as wheat germ oil, corn germ oil, et cetera.

Then also, vitamin E is necessary for reproduction and new growth. It is found in the oil of GERMS of seeds. Hence, we have wheat germ foods on the market.

And the yolk of egg contains the germ which produces new life of its kind!

Now note what HAPPENS when growth begins. Take a common garden pea, for example. Inside that pea seed, is the germ out of which a new plant will grow.

In the germ there are most of the substances needed for the new plant life.

BUT, IF some are lacking, nature and divine intelligence works a miracle.

The dried pea seed, for instance, contains very little if any vitamin C.

Yet vitamin C is needed for a young plant's growth.

SO, mysteriously — and seemingly out of nothing — as soon as that pea seed begins to sprout, it CREATES an ABUNDANCE of vitamin C.

All other vital elements which it does not already have within itself, it MYSTERIOUSLY creates WHILE SPROUTING.

Then it SHOOTS all of them out into its first tiny stems and leaves!

THE substances from which new life comes ARE actually LOADED by nature within the seed — whether in plant or animal. Then they are poured forth into stem or leaf or other new tissue, to cause the first spurt of new growth.

Hence, these NEW tissues are loaded with substances for rapid youthful growth.

That is why we find these marvelous new growing auxinons IN the SPROUTS of plants.

When seeds sprout, they shoot these substances INTO their young growing plants.

That is why, foods — containing lecithin, cholesterol, auxinons; and foods containing vitamins — A and E — are such astounding helps in maintaining buoyant health, and in increasing vitality and maintaining continued virility and youthfulness.

YOUR NINTH STEP — USE AUXINON FOODS

But please remember these auxinons are found ONLY in NEWLY GROWING food products.

That is, if you — in selecting foods from the list given in CHART F — choose asparagus for example, it will be of little value in providing auxinons for your body, if it is full grown or even half grown asparagus.

For auxinon value, asparagus must be eaten, when very young — when it has grown NOT MORE than 2 or 3 inches out of the ground — when JUST BEGINNING TO GROW.

And to obtain the auxinon value, it must NOT be cooked, and it must be FRESH. This applies to auxinons in beet tops, brussels sprouts, chard, spinach, turnip tops, et cetera.

ALL must be NEW SPROUTING LEAVES — to give you the new youth growing auxinons. If the sprouts are of Mung Beans, they can be eaten whether 3'' or 12'' high.

To illustrate the power of auxinons, let me tell you of a newly discovered plant auxin. If we extract a little of a root growing auxin, mix it with a little wax and paste it on the TIP of a leaf, it will make roots grow ON THE TIP of the leaf!

For you, of course, the root auxinons of plants are of NO value.

You want YOUTH GROWING AUXINONS of value to human beings — See my CHART F.

You may think, "Oh, it's just too difficult" to get ALL the auxinons you need.

But I consider them so important for myself, that I even raise them.

Sprouts from Auxinon Mung Beans can be grown in four days, and such sprouts — tiny young stems growing from seeds — provide an ABUNDANCE of AUXINONS for the body.

Years ago I recognized there was "something" which gave the Chinese, their astounding VIRILITY and CONTINUED YOUTHFULNESS. In north China, you often find not one but thousands of men, youthful and virile, even though 80 or 90 years old.

The virility of our races begins to play out in the 5th generation, — in 120 years.

But the Chinese, even after 272 generations, are STILL VIRILE!

For generations — yes, for centuries — Chinese HAVE used SPROUTED FOODS!

Do not be discouraged! If you can not at once secure fresh growing sprouts, you can at least buy the SMALLEST YOUNGEST vegetables you can get.

If carrots, for example, get the tiniest young carrots you can find. Don't buy old matured carrots. This applies to all vegetables which you need for auxinons.

You will find the best food sources for auxinons — together WITH a list of the best foods for lecithin and chlorophyl — designated in my CHART F.

THE TENTH STEP — GROW THEM, IF NECESSARY

Of course, my attitude may be different from yours.

I VALUE myself, and my continued youthfulness, and my vitality and virility of life ENOUGH, to make sufficient effort to GET the auxinons I need.

With a little Sprout-Gro and a hand full of Mung Beans, I can grow ENOUGH of these Auxinon sprouts - twice a week - even in a couple of flower pots - to meet my needs.

It is very easy to do it, when a pot of soil or sand is given all the minerals needed by plants. It is also easy to keep two or three Romaine lettuce plants growing, anywhere, any month — indoor or outdoor — so that you CAN continually pick the little fresh green leaves BEFORE they mature.

And the more you pick, the more leaves they produce — and you HAVE sufficient auxinons.

Nature and science help amazingly, WHEN WE have desire enough to make use of them.

I have now given you ALL that is necessary to help you to attain ALL the SEVEN results we definitely designated at the beginning of Lesson I.

This information has never before been brought together in one place.

It has never before been SIMPLY presented with charts, EASY for you to USE.

I have given you the seven GROUPS of mysterious

catalytic WORKER foods — and told you which ones build-up the mighty hormones.

I have given you TEN STEPS of WHAT TO DO.

I have given you many paragraphs of scientific explanation for STUDY and REFERENCE.

I have given you TEN CHARTS.

These CHARTS make the USE of the mysterious catalysts EASY and SIMPLE for you, EVEN IF you do not at first fully understand the scientific knowledge of them.

And now, student of mine, your transformation is up to you. Study of these Lessons will be of little value, unless YOU choose the foods necessary to bring the results.

You can increase ENERGY, attain a RESPONSIVE body with CONTINUING ENDURANCE, maintain VITALITY and VIRILITY, increase BEAUTY of Skin, and augment PERSONALITY.

You CAN change the tissues of organs. In scientific experiments, organic tissues have been grown, even outside of the body. Within the body, amazing changes have been wrought. You CAN change the rate of the dying process of the body. Instead of letting organs slowly die, you can change the tendency of the tissues to increased vitality, and maintained virility and youthfulness.

To attain such results is man's greatest desire, and that is the attainment I wish for you.

LANDONE ACTIVATING FOODS – CHART J
SPECIAL FOODS OF HIGH CONTENT of CARBOHYDRATES AND PROTEINS

(13)	Akrelac	Dried Soy Beans	Green Seed Mung Beans
(8)	Dietetic Gluten Rusks	Green Soy Beans (1)	Gluten Flour

SPECIAL FOODS of HIGH CONTENT of PROTEIN AND FATS

(6)	Cheese, Kraft	Cheddar Cheese	(8) Almond Casein Maca-
	American Pale Cheese	Point l'Eveque	roons Nutrivoid Bread
	American Red Cheese	Vendome Cheese	(4) Soy Flakes
	Brick Cheese	(1) Soy Flour	

SPECIAL FOODS of HIGH PROTEIN CONTENT,
with LITTLE OR NO STARCH OR FAT

(11)	Casec	(5) Sparkling Gelatine*	(10) Soy Beans and Tomatoes
(1)	Gluten Biscuit	(7) Dietetic Flour	(10) Soy Cheese
(1)	Soy Bean Biscuit	(19) Meat Juice	

SPECIAL CARBOHYDRATE FOODS

(Figures not in brackets indicate the respective
percentage of carbohydrates)

(1)	All-Bran	65		Force	79	(18)	Patented Barley	78
(12)	Banana Powder	84	(1)	Gluten Flour	43	(1)	Pep	77
(16)	Bran Flakes	74	(1)	Malt Breakfast	75	(17)	Puffed Wheat	76
(11)	Dextri-Maltrose	92	(11)	Pablum	70	(20)	Rice Flakes	81

(These are good foods WHEN and IF you need starch in
EASILY digestable form.)

SPECIAL FOODS, EACH CONTAINING
CARBOHYDRATES AND PROTEINS AND FATS
(Very few foods contain liberal amounts of all three
of these food substances)
(Figures indicate percentages of
carbohydrates, proteins, fats – in order given)

(8)	Boscotten Karlsbader	18	32	40	(13)	Milk Protein Powd'd	23	27	27
(8)	Bran & Gluten Cereal	21	34	20	(3)	Mushroom Soup	9	4	6
(6)	Cheese, Velveeta	6	18	25	(9)	Peanut Cheese Sand.	58	19	23
(2)	Klim Milk Powder	38	27	28	(11)	Recolac	53	16	27
(15)	Lactogen	53	16	25	(10)	Soy Beans with Tom.	7	11	5
	Milk Larosan	2	3	2	(1)	Soy Wonder Beans	6	9	9

*Gelatines are different from Jell-0. They look alike, but
that's all. Jell-0 is 86% carbohydrates; but Gelatine
contains NO carbohydrate and is 91.4% protein!

(1) Battle Creek Food; (2) Borden; (3) Campbell; (4) Cellu;
(5) Knox; (6) Kraft; (7) Lister; (8) Loeb; (9) Loose-Wiles;
(10) Madison Health; (11) Mead; (12) Merck; (13) Merrel-Soule;
(14) Milwaukee Vitamin Products; (15) Nestle; (16) Post;
(17) Quaker; (18) Robinson; (19) Valentine; (20) White House.

LANDONE ACTIVATING FOODS - CHART K

SOME SPECIAL FOODS OF HIGH MINERAL CONTENT

	Calcium	Copper	Iron	Potassium
Baby Ralston (Ralston)	600	.3	24	600
Bemax (Am. Vitamins)	60	1.5	10	1160
Casec (Mead)	1780			440
Cereal (Mead)	780	1.3	30	620
Dextri-Maltrose (Mead)		2.0	8	
Embo	40		7	1080
Flax-o-lin (Jackson)**	413			1080
Food-Ferrin (Battle Creek)			Ex	
Meat Juice (Valentine)	64		9	255
Mellin's Food	15		15	225
Pablum (Mead)	780	1.3	30	620
Puffed Wheat (Quaker)	40	.7	4	420
Shredded Wheat (Natl. Bis. Co.)	40	.6	4	320
Sparkling Gelatin (Knox)*	450			230
Strained Cereal (Stokely)	210	.1		140
Vegex (Vitamin Foods)	980	.6	4	2620
Wheat Cereal (Ralston)	40		4	400
Wheat Oata (Ralston)	70		2	430

SOME SPECIAL FOODS OF EXCELLENT VITAMIN CONTENT

	A	B	C	D	E	G
Bemax (American Vitamins)	F	Ex			Ex	Ex
Bewers' Yeast Powder (Harris)		Ex			Ex	Ex
Cereal Combination (Libby)	Gd	Gd				Gd
Cerol Capsules (Milw Vit Prod)					Ex	
Embo	Gd	Ex			Ex	Gd
Fruit Combination (Libby)	Gd	Gd	Gd			F
Klim (Borden)	Ex	Gd	F	F		Ex
Maltine	F	Ex		F		Gd
Pablum (Mead)	F	Ex				Ex
Soup Combination (Libby)	F	F				F
Vegetable Combination (Libby)	Ex	Gd	F			F
Vitabose		Ex				Ex
Vitamin Powder, Catalyn (Milwaukee Vitamin Products)	Gd	Ex	Gd	Gd		Ex

Ex - Excellent; Gd - Good; and F - Fair

* Please note that Gelatines are very different from Jell-O. They look alike, but that's all. Jell-O is 86% carbo-hydrates and 11% protein. Gelatin contains NO carbohy-drates but 91.4% protein. Jell-O good carbohydrate; gelatine good protein.

** Flax-o-lin forms 25% of JACKSON MEAL; compared to entire wheat, Flax-o-lin contains 810% more calicum; 224% more magnesium; 128% more potassium; and 543% more sodium. Flax-o-lin is not sold separately. It is included in Dr. Jackson's Meal.